SEA
of
JAPAN

YELLOW
SEA

EAST
CHINA
SEA

SOUTH
CHINA

Susanna Foo

Chinese Cuisine

To Pat and Peter

Happy Cooking, Happy time.

and a great life

Susanna Foo

1/20/96

美味佳肴

To Jacob Rosenthal,
who changed
my life

SUSANNA FOO

CHINESE CUISINE

The Fabulous Flavors & Innovative Recipes
of North America's Finest
Chinese Cook

SUSANNA FOO

WITH A FOREWORD
BY AMY TAN

PHOTOGRAPHY BY LOUIS B. WALLACH

Published by
Chapters Publishing Ltd.
2031 Shelburne Road
Shelburne, Vermont 05482

Printed and bound in Canada by

Library of Congress Cataloging-in-Publication Data

Foo, Susanna.

Susanna Foo Chinese Cuisine : the fabulous flavors & innovative recipes of North America's finest Chinese cook / by Susanna Foo; photography by Louis B. Wallach.

p.   cm.

Includes index.

ISBN 1-881527-94-8

1. Cookery, Chinese. 2. Susanna Foo Chinese Cuisine (Restaurant). I. Title.

TX724.5.C5F66 1995

641.5951—dc20   95-9052

Trade distribution in Canada by
Firefly Books Ltd.
250 Sparks Avenue
Willowdale, Ontario
Canada M2H 2S4

Trade distribution in the U.S. by
Firefly Books (U.S.) Inc.
P.O. Box 1338
Ellicott Station
Buffalo, NY 14205

Metropole Litho Inc., St. Bruno de Montarville, Quebec

Designed by Susan McClellan
Food styling by Anne Disrude
Prop styling by Betty Alfenito

Cover photograph by Louis B. Wallach:
Crab Sui Mei with Red Bell Pepper Sauce (page 40)

CONTENTS

Introduction 12

Menus and Wines 21

Dim Sum and Other Small Delights 24

Soups 76

Vegetables and Salads 106

Fish and Seafood 154

Fowl 190

Veal, Pork, Lamb and Beef 222

Noodles 256

Rice 284

Breads, Pancakes and Crêpes 302

Desserts 320

Mail-Order Sources 344

Index 345

ACKNOWLEDGMENTS

A CHINESE SCHOLAR ONCE SAID THAT A CITY IS BUILT with the collective willpower of its citizenry. This work has also been a collective effort, for without the help and blessings of the following friends, I could never have written it.

I am especially grateful to Hermie Kranzdorf, who not only taught me basic French cooking techniques in 1980 but also put her heart and soul into this effort during my most difficult times, helping me write and finish this book on time.

To my editor, Rux Martin, who believed in me and made this a most beautiful book, going well beyond my wildest expectations.

To Lisa Ekus, my publicist, who encouraged me to write a cookbook four years ago, made all the necessary connections and, in so doing, made my dream come true.

To my agent, Judith Weber, always on my side, who got me through many difficult times and also brought me many wonderful surprises.

To Louis Wallach for the exceptional photographs he took. To Anne Disrude, the food stylist, for her outstanding presentations, and to Betty Alfenito, the prop stylist, for the beautiful settings in the photographs.

To Barry Estabrook, Susan McClellan, who designed the book, and the entire staff at Chapters Publishing, for their support and enthusiasm in producing it.

I also want to thank my husband, E-Hsin, for his love, patience and support. I thank my sons, Gabriel and Jimmy, who are such wonderful tasters. I am grateful to my parents, who raised me and trained me to have a good palate, and to my mother-in-law, who has always treated me as if I were her own daughter.

To my restaurant staff, whose hard work helped establish my restaurant. I particularly want to thank my kitchen staff for helping me test many of the recipes.

And last, but not least, a special thanks to my dearest friend Russell Baum, whose advice helped make my restaurant successful.

FOREWORD

BY AMY TAN

I AM A LOVER OF EXCELLENT FOOD. Unfortunately, I have never been an excellent cook.

During my childhood, my mother cooked five-course Chinese meals nearly every night. She allowed me to wash and cook the rice, which I managed to burn one out of every three times. To this day, whenever my mother comes to my house for dinner, usually two or three times a week, she cooks the meal, I prepare the rice. But now I have the advantage of an automatic rice cooker.

My mother has never been able to pass on to me her knowledge of Chinese cooking. As she explains it, "The recipes are all in my nose and tongue." I also suspect she remembers those early rice-burning days and still thinks I'm utterly hopeless. When I write my stories, however, I imagine I am an expert chef. I liberally toss in references to dancing prawns, red-cooked pork, water dumplings, all perfectly prepared from the finest ingredients, bought right in season and at a well-bargained price. This is one of the most gratifying aspects of writing fiction. In my imagination, I never buy a crab that stinks or pea sprouts that have gone to weed. Nor would my fictional self ever apply too much oil, sugar, cornstarch or soy sauce—the common blunders of so-so Chinese cooking, which, my mother says, "makes everything taste the same—only a foreigner would eat it!" I have my fictional characters eat a lot of fictional food, because I'm always hungry for the genuine article.

Naturally, I miss Chinese food when I'm on the road, which is often. Certainly there are Chinese restaurants in abundance throughout the cities and suburbs of America. But I'm not about to insult the integrity of my palate and eat just any old tofu dish or—horrors!—the ubiquitous sweet-and-sour pork platter decorated with canned carrot cubes and baby corn. To me, eating mundane or poorly prepared dishes is more disappointing than not eating them at all.

One day, during a month-long tour, I was in Philadelphia to deliver a talk at the library. A former librarian named Susanna Foo was going to introduce me later that night to the audience. But first, she offered to take me to her Chinese restaurant for an early dinner. Several non-Chinese Philadelphians whispered in my ear that the food was incredible, the best. I nodded politely. Little did they know they were talking to a born-and-bred Chinese cuisine snob, a foodaphile who lives and dines in San Francisco, who also has a mother who custom-cooks her favorite dishes at home.

Before the dinner, Susanna Foo apologized to our table of seven that we'd be able to sample only a few quick dishes, given our time limitations. This suited me fine, since I never can eat much before a talk. One runs the risk of burping into the microphone. We arrived at her restaurant at the unlikely dining hour of 5:30. The downstairs dining room would have been empty of customers had it not been for a table of five happy diners, who turned out to be Mick Jagger, Jerry Hall, one of their children and two friends.

THE APPETIZERS STARTED TO APPEAR. Crab meat dumplings, pinwheel shrimp rolls, honeyed walnuts, stuffed eggplant slices—works of edible art, delicately arranged and exquisite to taste or, rather, *devour*. More dishes arrived: oil-braised artichoke hearts. Artichoke? Is that Chinese? It certainly has all the subtlety and flavor of Chinese food. There were more innovations: sun-dried tomatoes with roasted pork loin, peanuts and bean curd. Mangos with chicken and asparagus. Soft-shell crabs with a wonderfully spicy sauce.

About an hour later, our library host appeared at the restaurant. He informed us that we had to leave in the next few minutes. Another three courses arrived. I kept eating. Our library host looked worried. Susanna wondered aloud if we had time to have dessert. Our library host gravely shook his head. I rarely eat dessert, but this time I said, "Of course! We'll eat fast."

That evening, I went on stage—on time, I should add—with the happy fullness of having eaten one of the most exquisite and exciting Chinese dinners of my life. I say "one of" because I cannot be certain my mother will not read this, and it would not bode well for the future of my palate to put Susanna Foo in a class of culinary preeminence exclusive to herself.

Now, Susanna Foo has come out with this book. It's not simply a compilation of recipes of her fabulous dishes. She provides insight into the cultural origins of various dishes, the prized flavors and textures she remembers from childhood, the cooking methods developed during an era when all was cooked over wood- or charcoal-burning stoves. She promotes a philosophy of using the freshest ingredients, homemade broths and sauces and welcoming innovation—using balsamic vinegar, caviar, Grand Marnier or Portobello mushrooms, for example. She also includes distinctive dishes not typically prepared outside of village homes in China or top restaurants in Taiwan.

Fortunately for me, Susanna also comments on the frequent mistakes that novices can make—soggy vegetables, dry meat—and how to easily avoid these cooking sins. She gives shopping advice: how to tell if vegetables or fruit are past their prime, how to check for the freshness of fish and prawns. Her remarks are straightforward, her recipes clear and simple to follow—even for a formerly hopeless case such as myself. Moreover, her book reminds me that Chinese food is a feast for all the senses, that we take sensual pleasure in the sizzle and crunch, the intense and delicate flavors, the kaleidoscope colors of many courses. To me, Chinese food is an expression of passion. It creates some of the best memories in life. I can't have enough of them.

I am looking forward to becoming an excellent cook.

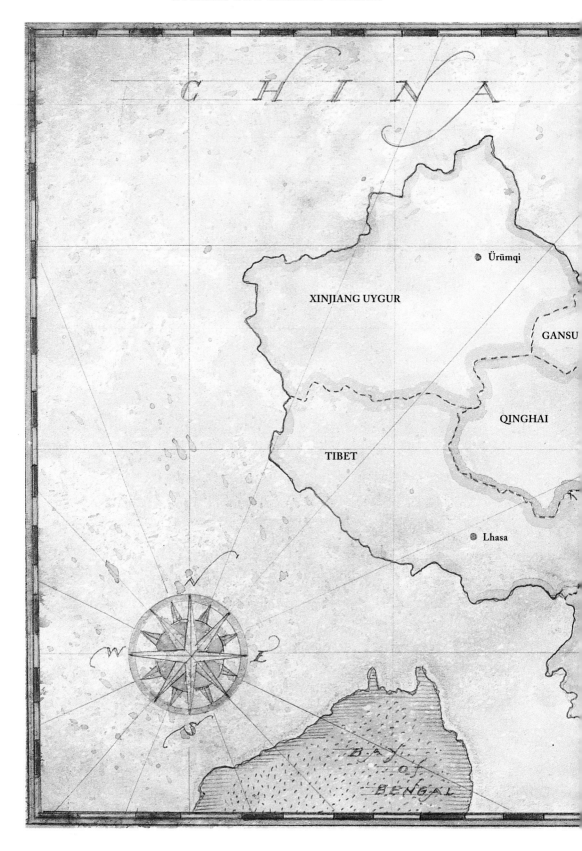

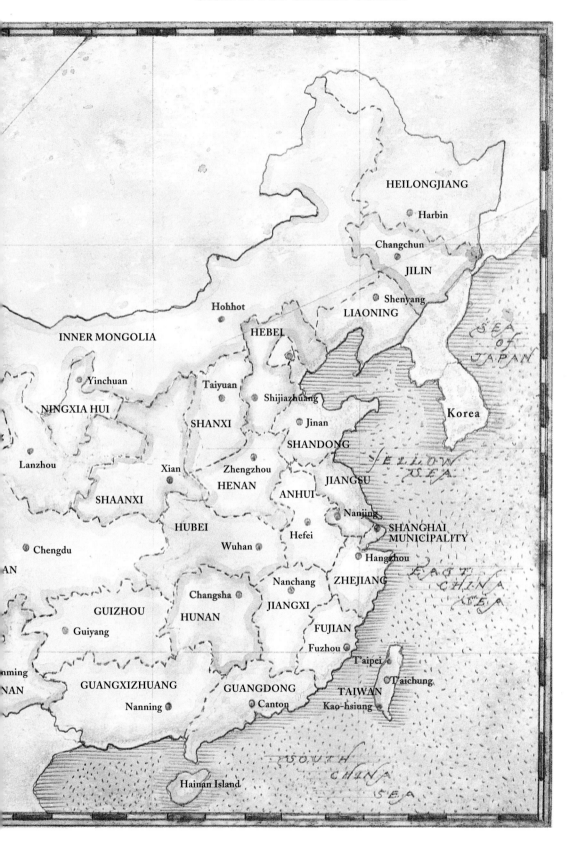

HEILONGJIANG

Harbin

Changchun

JILIN

Hohhot

Shenyang

LIAONING

INNER MONGOLIA

HEBEI

SEA OF JAPAN

Yinchuan

Taiyuan

Shijiazhuang

Korea

NINGXIA HUI

SHANXI

Jinan

SHANDONG

Lanzhou

Xian

Zhengzhou

JIANGSU

YELLOW SEA

SHAANXI

HENAN

ANHUI

Nanjing

HUBEI

Hefei

SHANGHAI MUNICIPALITY

Chengdu

Wuhan

Hangzhou

AN

ZHEJIANG

EAST CHINA SEA

Nanchang

Changsha

JIANGXI

GUIZHOU

HUNAN

FUJIAN

Guiyang

Fuzhou

T'aipei

nming

NAN

GUANGXIZHUANG

GUANGDONG

TAIWAN

T'aichung

Nanning

Canton

Kao-hsiung

SOUTH CHINA SEA

Hainan Island

INTRODUCTION

I THINK MOST PEOPLE'S TASTES ARE FORMED IN CHILDHOOD. I was born in Inner Mongolia, in the village of Wu-lan, near Hohhot, in Sui-yuan province, which no longer exists on any map. My full Chinese name is Su Sui-Lan, after my birthplace, where my mother was born as well. My father, a member of Chiang Kai-shek's armed forces, came from the Shanxi province, also in the north. His battalion was stationed in Wu-lan, and there, he met his best friend's sister—my mother. I grew up in a typical northern family, in which wheat, not rice, was the daily staple. This part of China is known for noodles and its distinctive preparations of lamb, liberally seasoned with garlic, scallions, chives and leeks.

My earliest memories center around food. When I was about 3, we moved to the neighboring northern province of Shaanxi. We lived in a courtyard-style house, with my parents occupying the main house and our relatives and the kitchen on one side and various servants' houses on the other. We had a big pomegranate tree out front, and in the fall, when the fruit ripened, the servants would pick them for me. My hands, mouth and clothes would be sticky and stained with red, making my mother angry. Often, our cook would take me with him to visit his relatives. They would give me a hard, flavorful steamed bread made with yellow cornmeal and wheat flour, which they called Wo-wo bread.

My mother did not like to cook, but she knew how food should be prepared, and she directed the servants according to her exacting standards. She loved light and delicate food, and she had a keen sense of smell and taste. Sometimes, when we were drinking tea, she would sniff the air and say, "There's an ant crawling on the floor," and sure enough, there would be one.

My grandmother lived with us, and she used to help in the kitchen. She was an amazing woman who lived to be 87. Born in another age, she had bound feet and no formal schooling. She was wonderful with all kinds of dough. I still remember her skillful hands kneading dumplings and noodles: boiled pork dumplings, cat's ear pasta, beef dumplings and steamed fish dumplings made with yellow pike and yellow chives. "Tsk, tsk, tsk," she would cluck at the servants if they made the dough too hard or too soft, and she would mutter under her breath.

As Mao's troops pushed down from the north, my father moved us to Shanghai while he was fighting in the battlefield—a fearful, uncertain time. Two years later, just before the takeover, we boarded a navy ship and left for Taiwan. We settled in T'aichung, in the middle of the country. During those years, the island was very poor. My mother had our cook raise chickens and tried in vain to teach him how to grow the potatoes she loved. After school, my brothers and I went fishing or picked tiny plums from a friend's orchard.

WHEN I WAS IN THE THIRD GRADE, we moved to Kao-hsiung, a seaport about 200 miles south of T'aipei. To me, this was paradise. The climate was warm and tropical, with an abundance of flowers and local fruits. We could buy all kinds of fresh fish and seafood: oysters, clams, squid, lobsters, live shrimp with their heads still on, ocean fish, which were cheap, and freshwater fish from surrounding lakes and streams, which were more expensive. Our garden was filled with flowering plants, vegetables and fruit trees: dragon-eyes, which are similar to lychees, mangos and papayas.

My mother and my grandmother taught the cook to make different kinds of Shanxi noodles, pancakes, steamed breads and dumplings—all their specialties. As they helped him, my brothers and I would sit and listen while they told stories of our old home in Shanxi and the relatives they had left behind.

On Sundays, my mother would take me with her to the open market. It was packed with housewives calling out their orders, greeting one another excitedly and chatting. The stalls were filled with marvelous things: sweet-smelling bouquets of jasmine and magnolias, which my mother would buy for me if I asked; cages of live chickens and ducks;

pork, freshly slaughtered at 1 A.M. and delivered to the market; counters heaped with giant tuna and swordfish steaks; big tanks of freshwater fish: grass fish, carp and eel. Outside the market, the sunny streets were lined with vendors carrying baskets of fresh bamboo shoots, baby cabbage, tender, purple basil and the delicate tendrils of snow pea shoots.

IN 1950, WHEN THE KOREAN WAR BROKE OUT, my father was sent to the United States many times for training. He would bring back exciting presents—silk stockings, a record player, records, clothes and chocolates—all of which heightened my fascination with Western culture. In 1957, when he was 47, he was promoted to Lieutenant General, the youngest of all the generals.

We moved to a bigger house in a navy compound surrounded by vegetable farms, lotus farms and mango orchards. My father made my grandmother a little garden, complete with roses, hibiscus and other flowering plants and trees. We also had a small plot in the back of the house that my grandmother and the cook used for vegetables like cucumbers and sweet, young snow peas. The cook's family had a tree-ear farm, and he brought us some of the seeds and planted them in a wet, dead log outside in back of the kitchen. I loved to pick them.

My father was not at home often, but whenever he returned, we would have his favorite foods: Shanxi noodles, scallion crêpes, dumplings or pancakes. He hated rice, so it was never served while he was home, but at other times, my mother and grandmother would make rice congee, a soup cooked with pumpkins, sweet potatoes or mung beans. All our meals were light and natural. We had lots of salads, made of root vegetables such as carrot and daikon or potatoes or steamed Chinese eggplants or napa or green cabbage. The dressings were simple, made of fried garlic, ginger, black vinegar, soy sauce and peanut oil. We ate a variety of quick vegetable, chicken or pork stir-fries. We used very little soy sauce and usually added no sugar to dishes. My mother did not like hot pepper or sesame oil, and she hated MSG. Until I met my husband, I seldom ate hot peppers.

The years in Kao-hsiung were the best and happiest of my childhood. I wandered among the farms surrounding our house, picking all the vegetables or digging sweet potatoes and peanuts—much to the consternation of the farmers. When I was a teenager, my mother finally let me ride my bicycle alone to the morning market.

In those days, Taiwan was poorly developed but rich in vegetables, seafood, fowl and meat—a paradise fast fading away in the name of progress. It was also a melting pot for people from every part of mainland China. The four major regional cuisines of China—Mandarin, Sichuan, Shanghai and Cantonese—flourished, while the local food, influenced by the island's earlier occupation by Japan, featured excellent seafood preparations. As a result, T'aipei became the world capital of Chinese cuisine, which languished in mainland China during the Cultural Revolution.

During that time, my parents often entertained American military officers at our home and learned to speak English. Their open-minded attitudes gave me an early introduction to the Western culture that has had such a profound effect on my life.

IN 1961, I ENROLLED IN NATIONAL TAIWAN UNIVERSITY IN T'AIPEI, in the north of the country. The only relative I had there was a cousin who lived close to the school—a five-minute bike ride from my dormitory. She had grown up in Shanxi. Though she had never learned to read or write—women did not in those days, at least not the ones who lived in the countryside—she was one of the smartest people I have ever met. She had three children, none of whom was interested in cooking. Knowing of my interest in food, she tried to teach me everything she knew. Perhaps because I missed home so much, I would go to her house most Sundays and help her prepare dinner.

My cousin made Shanxi specialties better than anyone I knew, and my father, who had discriminating tastes, agreed. She did everything "by feel," never measuring or using a recipe. She made chewy homemade pasta, full of body and flavor, cooking it much the way Italians do, one bowlful at a time, in a large pot of boiling water. She would proclaim with satisfaction, "Good noodles take time to make and time to cook." Sometimes, she topped them with nothing but Shanxi black vinegar and hot peppers; at other times, she served them with a variety of stir-fried vegetables, braised pork and soft bean curd with pungent fermented shrimp sauce. Her scallion pancakes were the best I have ever had.

She made another kind of pancake from a soft dough of flour, eggs and lard. She filled these pancakes with brown sugar. She cooked them over hand-picked smooth, shiny rocks, about the size of fava beans, which she had collected and used for over 20 years and kept in a biscuit box. First, she piled them on the skillet—she had no oven—and slowly heated them on the stovetop. Then she placed the pancake dough on top and cooked it until it was golden on both sides. These "rock pancakes" were a great favorite with my family. After she died, her husband gave me her rock collection so I could continue to make them.

DURING MY THIRD YEAR IN COLLEGE, I met E-Hsin Foo, whom I later married. Soon after we met, he introduced me to his mother. We had a lot in common, for she, too, loved cooking and flower arranging. When E-Hsin and I were dating, she often invited me to her home and made scrumptious dinners for me. Even though she had a cook, she would get up early each morning and prepare eight or ten dishes for her children's breakfast. When the children left for school, she would go to the market to select her own produce, meat and fish. On Sundays, when I had no classes, I would go with her.

Her preparations were unlike the simple dishes of northern China I had grown up with, and she opened a whole new world to me. Her food was much more robust than my family's: she used lots of hot peppers, black beans and smoked ham. She introduced me to the art of cooking fish; at home, we only pan-fried it.

She would let a chicken run in the backyard rather than kill it before she needed it, which would change the flavor. She would let fish swim for a day or two in a clean water bucket to cleanse their insides before cooking them. It would take her a whole day to make fish balls; they were the fluffiest and lightest I have ever eaten. And, wonder of wonders, she had a portable oven in which she could bake breads and cakes. She tried to teach me all the Hunan dishes so I would be able to make them for E-Hsin.

At the time, she was taking classes with Fu Pei-mei, a cooking teacher who was the equal of Julia Child in Taiwan. I went with her to the classes, where every week, a leading restaurant chef was invited to teach his specialty.

In 1966, after I was graduated from college, E-Hsin and I came to the United States, where he continued his studies at Carnegie-Mellon Institute in Pittsburgh, Pennsylvania, and I worked toward my master's degree in library science. The local family who was assigned to orient me gave me the name Susanna, which I kept because of its similarity to the sound of my Chinese name. After that, we moved to Tallahassee, Florida, where my husband took a job as assistant professor at the university. The climate reminded me of my years in Kao-hsiung. By this time, I had two sons and had become a full-time housewife.

GRADUALLY, I BEGAN TO USE WESTERN POTS instead of a wok. The flat-surfaced Western stove is different from the Chinese stove, which is specially designed so the wok can sit directly in the fire. On a flat surface, the wok does not cook efficiently: the heat is concentrated in the center instead of being evenly distributed around it, so the food cooks unevenly. Besides, woks were bulky and took up too much storage space. I started using heavy pots and Dutch ovens for roasting and braising and nonstick skillets for stir-frying.

In 1972, E-Hsin was offered a good job in Taiwan, and we moved back and lived there for four years. I took more classes with Fu Pei-mei and learned about local Taiwanese food and the cuisines of the various regions of China: Beijing, Shanghai, Sichuan, Hunan, Shanxi, Fujian, Canton, Hakka.

One night stands out in memory. The wife of one of my brothers invited me to her mother's home for dinner. Her mother knew the importance of using only the finest ingredients, allowing each one to stand on its own without being masked by heavy sauces. That evening, I realized that the best food does not need complicated cooking procedures or a lot of spices or expensive ingredients. Good food speaks for itself.

After the United Nations accepted the People's Republic of China rather than Taiwan as the representative of the Chinese people, my husband's parents, fearing a takeover of Taiwan, moved their family to the United States and opened a small restaurant in a former hoagie shop in

Philadelphia. Called the Hu-Nan, it featured the specialties of that province, which my mother-in-law, who was 60, cooked in the kitchen all by herself, just as if she were entertaining her own friends. The restaurant expanded, and E-Hsin's brother and wife joined them. The restaurant was so successful that they decided to open a branch in the center of Philadelphia. In 1979, my father-in-law asked E-Hsin and me to come and help with it.

THE FIRST YEAR WAS ALMOST UNBEARABLY DIFFICULT, as we had no experience in the business. But the third week after we opened, someone came to the restaurant for dinner who changed my life. He was Jacob Rosenthal, the retired president of the Culinary Institute of America. He lived in an apartment just a few blocks away and was a consultant to the nearby Monell Institute, where he was researching taste and smell. He was impressed with the freshness and variety of our dishes.

He volunteered to be our consultant at no cost. His philosophy was that to know the best, you have to taste the best. He took us to the finest Chinese restaurants in New York City, to Four Seasons and to Lutèce. He taught us about wine and helped us develop a wine list. And he suggested that I enroll in an eight-week professional training course at the Culinary Institute of America in Hyde Park, New York.

In the meantime, he sent his friend Hermie Kransdorf to the restaurant to teach me the fundamentals of French cuisine. Hermie showed me how to make basic stocks and sauces, how to brown bones for added flavor, how to use duck bones and shrimp shells to make stocks and soups. In the winter of 1981, I went to the Culinary Institute, staying there during the week and going home only on the weekends to see my husband and sons. Jacob Rosenthal watched over me, arranging for my housing and often accompanying me on the long winter commutes, so I would not have to drive alone.

Difficult as those weeks were, they were some of the most thrilling of my life. I felt as though I had become Alice in Wonderland and had passed through the looking glass. Everything was new and exciting: the vast amounts of meat, vegetables and fruits used in the small classes, the most up-to-date restaurant equipment, the excellent teachers. And the books—I had never seen so many books about food and cooking as in the Culinary Institute's library. My days began with classes at 7 A.M, with evenings spent poring over books.

WHEN I RETURNED TO PHILADELPHIA, my father-in-law gave me full authority over the kitchen and the freedom to depart from the restaurant's Hunan-based cooking. I began to prepare sauces based on classic French techniques rather than depending on the same last-minute mixtures of soy sauce, vinegar and cornstarch. Calling on my memories of taste, I expanded my repertoire so my customers could taste the simple food I grew up with. I introduced fresh vegetables made available by the normalization of relations between China and the United States: water chestnuts, lotus roots, soybeans and taro roots.

In 1987, after E-Hsin's family sold the Hu-Nan, E-Hsin and I opened our own restaurant bearing my name, and I was finally able to give full expression to my own style. Remembering the complex taste of the black vinegar of my childhood, I stopped using sharp rice vinegar and turned to balsamic vinegar, which came closer to the mellow flavor I remembered. I use balsamic vinegar in salads and stews, cider vinegar in sauces. Instead of peanut and sesame oils, which to me have much too raw a taste, I relied on lighter-flavored soybean and corn oils, which never overwhelm food. I also experimented with extra-virgin olive oil and found that I liked the way it interacted with some Chinese dishes, bringing them to a new level. I now use olive oil for salads.

In Taiwan, the locally made Shaoxing wine has a much different flavor than that which is imported into this country. Instead, I began using liquors such as vodka, brandy and whiskey, which are never used for cooking in Taiwan because of their high cost—four or five times the amount in this country. Vodka, gin and vermouth are excellent with fish, shellfish and white meat. Brandy and whiskey complement pork; Madeira goes well with red meat and game.

I almost never add sugar to a recipe, unless sweetness is specifically called for. In my family and my husband's family, sugar is rarely used. The practice of adding it may have begun in an effort to balance the sharp taste of most of the rice vinegar available here.

I seldom use commercial sauces like hoisin sauce and oyster sauce without first improving their flavor, cooking hoisin with brandy and oyster sauce with onions. For soy sauce, I prefer regular soy sauce (the Kikkoman brand), and that in moderation.

I AM STILL EXPERIMENTING WITH INGREDIENTS and changing what I do. Confucius said, "Traveling 1,000 miles is equal to reading 10,000 books." Visits to Thailand, Italy and France have inspired my cooking. I no longer limit myself to typical Chinese vegetables like napa cabbage, bok choy or Chinese broccoli but search out whatever is freshest. I have discovered that sun-dried tomatoes are similar to a dried leaf cabbage that we used to add to meat stews. Ancho chiles give a beautiful brick-red color and rich flavor to Sichuan sauces. Artichoke hearts remind me of the fresh bamboo shoots that my mother and I used to buy in the marketplace. I also use zucchini, Portobello mushrooms, French beans, fennel and baby salad greens.

Fundamentally, Chinese food is very simple. Many Americans mistakenly believe that it always involves stir-frying, which requires painstaking chopping and dicing and last-minute maneuvers at the stove. But the home cooking I grew up with included not only stir-fries but stews, braised dishes, pastas and other easy dishes. Good Chinese food is no more difficult to cook than good Italian food. The basic principles are the same: freshness, simplicity and the preservation of the uniqueness of each ingredient.

Everything I cook is based on what I remember from childhood. There is no need to "improve" the classical dishes—they have been popular for thousands of years. But a good cook should be open-minded. During the 28 years spent living and working in this country, I have developed and changed many of the Chinese dishes to suit my life and surroundings. Now I share these recipes with you.

MENUS AND WINES

WHEN I WAS A CHILD, the most exciting dinners were formal wedding banquets—lavish affairs that lasted four or five hours. These banquets, which were usually held in a large restaurant or hotel, consisted of at least 12 to 14 courses. They did not progress from light to heavy nor from fish to white or red meat but were brought out in a more or less random order, beginning with huge, beautifully arranged cold platters, followed by four stir-fried dishes. Then came whole chicken, duck, game and fish, various soups and no fewer than two desserts—one hot, one cold.

Much alcohol was consumed, for as each new dish was brought to the table, the cups were filled and quickly finished. Like the other men, my father drank Mao-tai with a high alcoholic content, over 100 proof. My mother and the other women usually drank the milder fortified Shaoxing wine that was comparable to sherry. Western-style wine was unheard of.

In this country, Chinese food has traditionally been associated with beer. (This may be because many Chinese restaurants cook with sugar and MSG, which can affect the palate and give wine an off flavor.) My husband and I, however, have found that the best companion to fine Chinese food is a good Burgundy (white or red), Bordeaux, California Chardonnay, Merlot or even an Italian wine. To highlight the marriage of Chinese food with wine at a banquet, I have adapted a progression similar to that of a French formal dinner, beginning with lighter dishes and white wines and graduating to heavier dishes and more robust wines. To simplify things for modern tastes, I have also cut back on the number of dishes traditionally served.

A BRUNCH MENU

Coho Salmon Shanghai-Style *(page 176)*
Marbled Tea Eggs *(page 62)*
Salad of New Red Potatoes *(page 136)*

Champagne "kir," made with
peach, pear or passion fruit
liqueur

Braised Spareribs *(page 259)*
Pan-Fried Noodles *(page 271)*

Merlot from California
or Washington State

Pears with Ginger *(page 330)*

A LUNCHEON MENU

Seafood Wonton Soup *(page 103)*

Chenin Blanc from California
or Sancerre

Orange Beef with Sun-Dried Tomatoes
(page 251)
Peking Thin Pancakes *(page 313)*
or good bread
Pickled Napa Cabbage, Daikon and Carrots
(page 117)

Pinot Noir from
California or Oregon

Mixed Tropical Fruit Salad with Rum Sauce
(page 337)

A FOUR-COURSE BANQUET

Curried Chicken Dumplings *(page 38)*
Pineapple Salsa *(page 121)*
Spicy Cucumbers with Sichuan
Peppercorn Vinaigrette *(page 110)*

Blanc de Noir from California

Spiced Shiitake Mushrooms *(page 66)*
"Honeyed" Pine Nuts *(page 58)*
Cold Beer Shrimp *(page 71)*

Gewürztraminer from
  California, Washington State
  or Alsace

Eight-Treasure Duck *(page 217)*
Baked Creamy Napa Cabbage *(page 143)*
Asparagus with Dried Shrimp Vinaigrette
  (page 135)

Cabernet Sauvignon from
  California or Bordeaux

Frozen Mango Soufflé *(page 326)*

A FIVE-COURSE BANQUET

Shiitake Mushrooms Stuffed with Lamb
  (page 60)
Celery Salad with Wasabi Vinaigrette
  (page 131)
Spicy Persimmon Chutney *(page 125)*

Sparkling wine or Bloody
  Mary

Baked Shrimp Toast *(page 51)*
Water Chestnut, Arugula and Endive Salad
  (page 129) or salad of baby greens
 "Honeyed" Walnuts *(page 59)*

Meritage of Sauvignon and
  Sémillon from California or
  Pouilly-Fumé

Salmon with Black Bean Sauce *(page 157)*
Broccoli Rabe with Green Peas *(page 151)*

Chardonnay from California
  or white Burgundy from
  France

Soy-Braised Cornish Hens *(page 212)*
Rice Noodles with Porcini Mushrooms
  (page 277)
Sautéed Green Beans *(page 140)*

Pinot Noir from California or
  Oregon or red Burgundy
  from France

Chilled Mango Soup *(page 329)*

CHAPTER ONE

DIM SUM
AND OTHER SMALL DELIGHTS

O NE OF THE MOST MEMORABLE DAYS of my life was when I was accepted by the National Taiwan University. To celebrate, my father decided to take the whole family to a newly opened dim-sum-style restaurant. It was 1961, and dim sum houses had just become popular there, as Hong Kong entrepreneurs opened a second or third branch of their restaurants in T'aipei. On Sundays, it was considered the height of fashion for the entire family to go to one.

When we arrived, the restaurant was packed. Waiters and waitresses pushed carts between the crowded tables, each filled with hundreds of varieties of small dishes. We stopped almost every cart that passed and feasted on hot dumplings, pastries, stuffed mushrooms, stuffed peppers, spareribs, rice noodles and sweets. This was the first time I had ever tasted Cantonese dim sum. I loved the shrimp toast, the curried pastries, the crab sui mei—delicate dumplings filled with crab and shrimp—soft, flavorful daikon rice cakes, crisp, deep-fried rice puffs, steamed buns and the many types of steamed dumplings. Since then, on Sunday afternoons, my parents often gather in a local dim sum house with family or friends for a relaxing time together.

Directly translated, dim sum means "touch your heart"—an apt reference to these little dishes that both delight the palate and capture the imagination. In China, dim sum may be served for breakfast, as an afternoon nibble or as a late-night snack, depending on the region. My family served dumplings, spring rolls and steamed stuffed buns—all mainstays of the dim sum group—as part of the meal. We never had appetizers or first courses. A typical lunch or dinner in our home usually consisted of six to eight different dishes, along with soup, pasta, steamed buns or pancakes—all served at the same time on our dining room table. This manner of serving is normal in all Chinese households.

But when my mother entertained friends, whether at an informal gathering or at a more formal occasion, she usually asked the cook to arrange a big, beautiful platter of four to six cold dishes to be served as a starter, much like an Italian antipasto. They included smoked or drunken chicken, shrimp, five-spice beef, mushrooms, honeyed nuts and various pickled vegetables.

L IKE MY MOTHER, I love to serve four varieties of cold food as the first course of a dinner, arranging them on individual plates rather than on a large platter as she did. One of the advantages is that these dishes can be prepared well before the guests arrive, often a day ahead. An ideal first course might consist of pancakes, crêpes or bread with one of each of the following: nuts, seafood, fowl or meat, salad, pickled vegetables, cold mushrooms or eggplant salsa.

Many of the dim sum in this chapter make wonderful appetizers for cocktail parties or starters before dinner. When serving dim sum as an appetizer, allow 4 to 8 per person, depending on your plans for the rest of the dinner. If they will be the entire meal—as is often done for lunch—figure on 8 to 12 per person.

Traditionally, dim sum are served with simple dipping sauces, such as gingerroot and soy or oil infused with hot peppers. But when offering them as a first course, I prefer to present them with a more flavorful sauce, much as the French would make, accompanied by a subtle salad, salsa or relish. This not only heightens the visual appearance of the dish but adds complexity and an element of surprise that never fails to "delight the hearts" of my guests.

DIM SUM AND OTHER SMALL DELIGHTS

Veal Dumplings in Ancho Chile Sauce   30

Pork Dumplings with Soy-Ginger Sauce   34

Curried Chicken Dumplings   38

Crab Sui Mei with Red Bell Pepper Sauce   40

Spring Rolls   45

One-Hundred-Corner Crab Cakes   49

Baked Shrimp Toast   51

Sizzling Rice Cakes   54

Chinese Eggplant Salsa   57

"Honeyed" Pine Nuts   58

"Honeyed" Walnuts   59

Shiitake Mushrooms Stuffed with Lamb   60

Marbled Tea Eggs   62

Taro Pancakes   64

Spiced Shiitake Mushrooms   66

Jalapeño Peppers with Pork Stuffing   67

Grilled Chinese Eggplant with Balsamic Vinaigrette   68

Cold Marinated Scallops   70

Cold Beer Shrimp   71

Squid Salad with Five-Flavor Vinaigrette   73

DUMPLINGS

Dumpling Wrappers

In my parents' house, dumpling wrappers were always made from scratch, using just two ingredients—flour and water. To this day, my mother still makes her own wrappers and never serves dumplings using ready-made skins.

There is no comparison between homemade fresh dumpling skins and the machine-made kind, but making wrappers from scratch is a big job, so ready-made fresh or frozen wrappers are becoming more popular. Today, they are carried fresh in many local stores or supermarkets (look for them in the frozen-food or produce section).

Wrappers play a very important role in the making of dumplings. If they are too thick, the dumplings will be tough. If they are too thin, the dumplings will break easily and cannot be properly cooked. There are two types of wrappers on the market: round and square. Both are 3 to 4 inches in diameter.

The round ones, usually called dumpling wrappers or *gyoza* (the Japanese name), originally came from northern China and are made from just flour and water. They have a little more body than square wrappers, are thicker and are used for pork or veal dumplings. I like to use the "Twin Dragon" brand for these dumplings.

Square-shaped wrappers, generally known as wonton skins, found most often in the south of China (Canton), have egg added, which gives the dough a yellow color and makes the skins much thinner and softer. They are used for wontons, sui mei and chicken dumplings, which need more delicate wrappers. Even for recipes calling for round-shaped wrappers, I often use the square wonton skins because of their thinness. Using a cookie cutter about 2½ to 3 inches in diameter, I cut the squares into round shapes.

The leftover pieces of wrapper from the corners can be used to make fried noodles by deep-frying them in about 4 inches of oil heated to 350 degrees until they are golden brown. Drain on paper towels, and serve at room temperature with drinks, soup or salad. Any extra wrappers can be rewrapped and refrozen for use at a later time.

Freezing Dumplings

Most of my dumpling recipes are prepared using 1-pound packages of wrappers, yielding between 60 and 90 dumplings. It is not practical to make just a few at a time: prepare the entire recipe. Uncooked filled dumplings can be frozen for up to 3 months and are handy to have around for last-minute entertaining.

The best way to freeze dumplings is to spread them out flat on a tray or baking sheet, as you would berries. Once frozen, they can be packed into plastic bags and sealed tightly. Remove as many as you need each time.

Cooking Dumplings

To Boil Dumplings: Fill a large stock pot two-thirds full of water and bring to a boil. (As for cooking pasta, the more water used, the better.) Add one-third of the prepared dumplings. Using a Chinese strainer or slotted spoon, stir the dumplings to prevent them from sticking together.

Return the water to a boil. The dumplings will rise to the top, but at this point, the filling will still be raw. Add ½ cup cold water and return to a boil again. When the dumplings float, taste one to see if it is done. If not, add another ½ cup cold water and cook until the dumplings rise again. Adding cold water slows the cooking so the dough does not break, allowing enough time for the filling to be thoroughly cooked.

Remove the dumplings from the pot using a Chinese strainer or slotted spoon, and place them on a plate, being careful to keep them separate from one another, so they will not stick together. Repeat with the remaining dumplings.

In most Chinese kitchens, one person (usually the mother) will cook the dumplings in batches while those seated eat.

If you want to cook all the dumplings in advance, they can be reheated by placing them in a single layer on top of cold blanched cabbage leaves to keep them from sticking to the steamer rack. Then the dumplings can be steamed just before they are to be served.

To Boil Frozen Dumplings: Do not thaw the dumplings first. Add the frozen dumplings directly to a pot of boiling water. Once the dumplings float to the surface, add 1 cup cold water. Bring the water back to a boil, and when the dumplings float, add cold water again. When the dumplings float to the surface again, taste one to see if it is cooked. If not, repeat this process one more time. Drain and serve as directed in the recipe.

To Pan-Fry Dumplings: Pan-fried dumplings are known as "pot stickers" because one side sticks to the bottom of the pot, becoming delightfully crisp. Heat about 1 tablespoon corn oil in a large nonstick skillet. Add as many dumplings as can fit in a single layer. Pour ½ cup cold water over the dumplings.

Cover the skillet and cook over low heat for about 10 minutes, without turning or stirring, until the water has evaporated and the dumplings are golden and crisp on the bottom. If the dumplings are not browned enough, keep cooking until they are. Remove the dumplings to a heated platter and repeat with the remaining dumplings. Defrost frozen dumplings before cooking or they will burn.

To Grind Meat Coarsely

I prefer to use coarsely ground meat for filling dumplings. The stuffing will be much juicier if the meat is left in larger pieces; if too finely ground (as is most prepackaged ground meat), it will be stiff and dry.

Traditionally, meat is hand-chopped with a cleaver to achieve the proper texture. You can approximate this by first cutting the meat into ½-inch cubes, then grinding it in small batches (⅓ to ½ pound at a time) in a food processor. To hand-chop, place the meat in the freezer for 20 minutes to firm it, then mince it with a sharp knife. Or ask your butcher to grind the meat coarsely for you. Do *not* use preground meat commonly found in supermarkets.

VEAL DUMPLINGS IN ANCHO CHILE SAUCE

MAKES 50 TO 60 DUMPLINGS

I N THE SICHUAN PROVINCE, people love hot and spicy foods. They air-dry fresh hot peppers for a couple of days. Then they simmer the peppers in oil, along with herbs and spices, until the oil turns red, then puree them. This fiery oil becomes a base for many dishes, such as the famous Sichuan dumplings in red sauce, which are sold by street vendors everywhere in the province. Traditionally, these dumplings were made with very thin wrappers, filled with ground pork and garnished with a mixture of fried chopped dried shrimp, scallions and Sichuan pickled radish.

About 10 years ago, after I had tried many times to duplicate the Sichuan pepper sauce, I discovered that ancho chiles from Mexico come closest to the taste and complexity of flavor that linger in my memory.

In my adaptation of this classical recipe, I substituted veal shoulder for the pork, because I prefer its fresher taste and lighter texture, added spinach to the stuffing and used ancho chiles for the sauce.

1	tablespoon corn or olive oil
1	pound fresh spinach, washed and stemmed
1	pound veal shoulder, coarsely ground (page 29)
2	tablespoons minced shallots
3	tablespoons soy sauce
1	tablespoon Asian sesame oil
½	cup finely chopped scallions, white part only
½	cup finely chopped fresh basil or cilantro leaves
1	tablespoon peeled, minced gingerroot
1	1-pound package round dumpling wrappers, (*gyoza*), 3 inches in diameter*
2	cups Ancho Chile Sauce (page 33)
	Julienned basil leaves for garnish (optional)
¼	cup finely chopped Sichuan preserved vegetables for garnish (optional)**
½	cup fried shallots for garnish (optional)

Heat the oil over high heat in a large saucepan. When hot, add the spinach and immediately cover the pan. Lower the heat to medium and cook for 2 minutes, or until wilted. Remove the spinach from the pan and drain off any excess liquid. When cool, chop finely and set aside.

In a large bowl, mix the veal, shallots, soy sauce, sesame oil, scallions, basil or cilantro leaves and gingerroot; add the chopped spinach.

Place about 2 teaspoons of the stuffing in the center of each wrapper (A). Moisten the edges with cold water, then fold them over the filling to form a half-moon shape (B). Pinch together the edges with your fingers. Then moisten the 2 ends with water and bring them together in a circle around the filling (C) and (D). The dumplings can be made in advance and frozen, tightly sealed, for up to 3 months (see page 27). To cook frozen dumplings, see page 28.

Cook only the dumplings you intend to serve; freeze the rest for later use. Bring a large pot of water to a boil. Add about one-third of the dumplings at a time, and cook until they rise to the surface and float. (See the directions for boiling dumplings, page 28.)

Remove the dumplings from the water with a Chinese strainer or slotted spoon, drain and place 6 dumplings on each serving plate.

Heat the Ancho Chile Sauce in a small saucepan over medium heat for 3 to 4 minutes, or until warm. Pour 3 tablespoons over each serving. Serve any remaining sauce on the side. Decorate with julienned basil leaves, Sichuan preserved vegetables and fried shallots, if desired. Serve warm.

* This size wrapper will produce the most elegant-looking dumpling.

** Sichuan preserved vegetables are available in cans in many Asian markets. Drain, rinse and soak in cold water for 5 minutes. Chop and soak again in boiling water for 5 minutes. Drain and store in a jar in the refrigerator for up to 1 week.

A   B   C   D

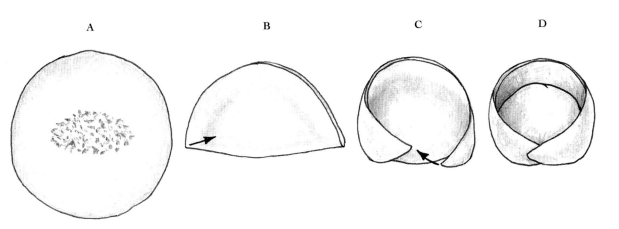

Veal Dumplings in Ancho Chile Sauce

Ancho Chile Sauce

Makes about 4 cups sauce

THIS SMOKY-FLAVORED, brick-red sauce can be used to top dumplings, sautéed fish or chicken.

3	dried ancho chile peppers
¼	cup corn oil
½	cup chopped onion
2-3	jalapeño peppers, finely chopped
1	tablespoon roasted Sichuan peppercorns (page 111)
½	cup white wine
6	cups chicken stock (page 79)
3-4	star anise
1	tablespoon coarse or kosher salt
1	teaspoon sugar
1	teaspoon freshly ground white pepper
1	tablespoon cornstarch, mixed with 2 tablespoons water

Soak the chile peppers in hot water to cover for about 30 minutes, or until soft. When soft, drain and puree; set aside.

Heat the oil in a large skillet. Add the onion and cook over high heat until soft and golden. Add the jalapeño peppers and the Sichuan peppercorns, and cook for 1 to 2 minutes.

Add the wine and the pureed chiles, and boil for about 5 minutes, or until the wine is almost evaporated. Add the remaining ingredients. Reduce the heat to low and simmer, uncovered, for about 30 minutes, or until reduced by about half. Strain the sauce and keep warm.

Any remaining sauce can be stored in the refrigerator for 1 week or frozen for up to 3 months.

PORK DUMPLINGS WITH
SOY-GINGER SAUCE

MAKES 40 TO 45 DUMPLINGS

IN NORTHERN CHINA, these dumplings were traditionally served on the first morning of the Chinese New Year, which falls in January or February. Formed in the crescent shape of ancient Chinese golden coins, dumplings are considered to be a good luck symbol. Hundreds of dumplings would be readied weeks ahead of time and left outside to freeze. They would be brought in and boiled as needed for the holiday. (For that reason, they are still called "water dumplings" in some Chinese cookbooks.)

These dumplings are the most popular appetizer in my restaurant, and even though I've been eating them forever, I'm still not bored with them.

1	pound pork butt, coarsely ground (page 29)
1	cup finely chopped scallions
3	tablespoons soy sauce
1	tablespoon Asian sesame oil
1	tablespoon peeled, grated gingerroot
½	pound Chinese napa cabbage,* finely chopped
1	1-pound package round dumpling wrappers (*gyoza*), 3 inches in diameter
	Soy-Ginger Sauce (page 36)

In a large bowl, combine the pork, scallions, soy sauce, sesame oil and gingerroot. Mix well so that the flavors will penetrate the meat. Then add the cabbage and mix until all the ingredients are thoroughly combined. The filling will not taste right if you try to combine all the ingredients at once.

Place 1 dumpling wrapper on a plate or a board. Place 1 scant tablespoon of pork mixture in the center (A). Moisten the edges of the wrapper with a little water, then fold them over the filling to form a half-moon shape (B). Pinch the center together first, then stand the dumpling up on its base and pleat one of the sides of the half-moon twice, halfway between the outer edge and the center (C). Pleat the other side in the same way and leave the dumpling standing up (D).

Stand the finished dumplings on a baking sheet lined with wax paper. Do not allow the sides of the dumplings to touch each other, or they will stick together.

Repeat, using the remaining dumpling wrappers and pork filling.

The dumplings can be made in advance and frozen for up to 3 months (see page 27), or they may be cooked immediately, either boiled or pan-fried. (See the directions for cooking dumplings, page 28.) Serve hot, with Soy-Ginger Sauce on the side.

*If you cannot get napa cabbage, substitute green cabbage. Because it is not as moist as the Chinese cabbage, add 2 tablespoons of water to the pork filling before incorporating the cabbage.

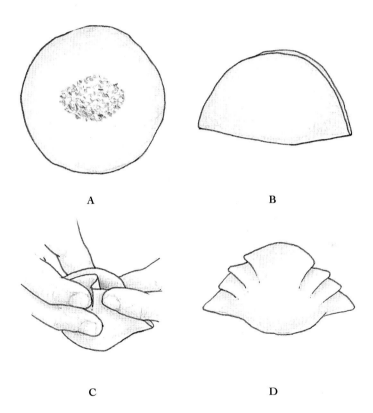

A   B

C   D

SOY-GINGER SAUCE

MAKES ABOUT ¾ CUP DIPPING SAUCE

TRADITIONALLY, my family always serves dumplings with julienned ginger-root that has been soaked in cold water, fresh hot peppers and a mixture of soy sauce, vinegar and water.

This simple gingerroot sauce is easy to prepare and is the perfect complement to Pork Dumplings and other dim sum.

¼   **cup soy sauce**

¼   **cup balsamic vinegar**

2   **tablespoons water**

1   **tablespoon peeled, julienned gingerroot,**

      soaked in ice water (page 213)

Combine all the ingredients in a small bowl. Mix thoroughly and serve.

This sauce will keep for up to 1 week in the refrigerator, without the gingerroot. Add the gingerroot when ready to serve.

DUMPLING CONTESTS

PORK DUMPLINGS have been part of my life for as long as I can remember. Twice a week during my childhood, they were served as a main course along with a cold vegetable salad, such as Pickled Napa Cabbage, Daikon and Carrots (page 117), and soup. Often, this soup was nothing more than the water in which the dumplings were cooked, along with any floating broken pieces. When the cook brought the hot pork dumplings to the table, my three brothers and I would fight with each other to see who could eat more. If there were leftovers, we would have them the next morning, pan-fried, crisp and golden.

The cook would make a dough from flour and water. First he rolled the dough into a log, then pinched off pieces by hand. These he rolled into small round wrappers, holding the dough with one hand and rolling with the other. Then my grandmother and mother would come in to help, turning out a hundred dumplings in an incredibly few minutes.

I could always tell who made which dumplings. My grandmother was the fastest: she could make 20 by the time I had finished filling and sealing one. My mother's were more elegant: she took her time and crimped the edges like a pie crust.

I stood next to my grandmother while she tried to show me her technique. "If you don't learn how to make dumplings faster, no man will ever marry you," she scolded.

CURRIED CHICKEN DUMPLINGS

MAKES 50 TO 60 DUMPLINGS

THIS IS MY ADAPTATION of the ever popular curried-beef pastries sold in Cantonese pastry shops. In early times, there were no ovens in Chinese kitchens, therefore these dumplings were always fried. Today, because of Western influences, they are often baked.

In order to keep the filling moist and juicy, I do not cook the chicken or the mushrooms before filling the dumplings. If cooked first, the chicken will be too dry and the mushrooms will get soggy.

I use thin wrappers and freeze the filled dumplings right away if they will not be cooked within 30 minutes. Otherwise, the liquid seeps out of the filling and causes the wrappers to crack.

The dumplings can be served as a first course, along with a green salad, salsa or pickled vegetable, or as an appetizer for a cocktail party. They are easy to do, since they can be made ahead of time and kept in the freezer until needed.

3	tablespoons corn oil, plus more for deep-frying
1	large onion, finely diced
1	tablespoon peeled, grated gingerroot
1	tablespoon curry powder*
4	large fresh shiitake mushrooms, finely diced (1 cup)
1	tablespoon soy sauce
1	teaspoon coarse or kosher salt
1	teaspoon freshly ground white pepper
3	scallions, finely diced
¼	cup chicken stock (page 79)
1	pound boneless, skinless chicken breast, coarsely chopped (page 29)
1	1-pound package thin, square wonton skins, cut into 3-inch rounds (page 27)
	Pineapple Salsa (page 121; optional)
	Hot mustard sauce (optional)**

Heat the 3 tablespoons oil in a medium saucepan and add the onion and the gingerroot. Cook over high heat until the onion is golden, about 3 to 4 minutes. Add the curry powder and mushrooms, and cook, stirring, for about 2 to 3 minutes.

Add the soy sauce, salt and white pepper and stir until blended. Set aside to cool.

When the mixture is cool, add the scallions and chicken stock and mix well. Mix in the chopped chicken, stirring, until all the ingredients are thoroughly blended.

Place 2 teaspoons of the chicken mixture in the center of a wonton skin. Moisten the edges of the wonton with cold water, fold the skin into a half-moon shape and seal by pressing the edges together with your fingers. Repeat, using the remaining chicken mixture and wonton skins.

Pour about 6 inches of oil into a skillet or fryer and heat to 325 degrees F. (If you do not have a thermometer, test the temperature by dropping a small piece of the wrapper into the oil; it should float to the surface immediately.) Fry the dumplings in batches, stirring until they are golden; do not crowd. Remove with a Chinese strainer or slotted spoon and drain on paper towels. Serve immediately.

The dumplings can be made in advance and frozen before frying for up to 3 months (see page 27). If frozen before frying, the dumplings will be juicier, because freezing releases the juices in the filling.

To fry frozen dumplings: Frozen dumplings must be fried in 2 stages to keep the wonton skins crisp and the filling juicy. Heat the oil to 325 degrees, and fry for about 3 minutes, or until soft and warm. Remove with a slotted spoon and set aside to drain. Fry the dumplings again until golden, 2 to 3 minutes.

Serve the dumplings with Pineapple Salsa or hot mustard sauce, if you wish.

* Madras curry powder is preferable.

** To make hot mustard sauce, thin 1 tablespoon powdered hot mustard with cold water and 1 teaspoon white vinegar; let stand for about 10 minutes.

CRAB SUI MEI WITH
RED BELL PEPPER SAUCE

MAKES 35 TO 45 SUI MEI

SUI MEI (PRONOUNCED "SHOE-MY") means "cook and sell." These Cantonese open-faced dumplings are made with thin, fragile wrappers. They are usually steamed so as to retain their light texture, but also to allow the cook to add all kinds of exotic and elaborate toppings.

My favorite sui mei are made of fresh crabmeat and have a wonderfully rich and delicate flavor. I use Maryland blue crabs—they are sweet and incredibly tender. Other fresh crabs will do as well. Pureed shrimp hold the filling together.

In the winter, when fresh crabs are not available, I make the filling using just shrimp, leaving the proportions of other ingredients the same. Pasteurized crab sold in plastic cups does not have the fresh taste I like. Under no circumstances should you use canned crab. For an extra-special touch, I sometimes top the sui mei with beluga caviar. Serve as an hors d'oeuvre or a first course with Red Bell Pepper Sauce and fresh pea shoots or spinach.

1	pound medium shrimp, peeled, deveined and cleaned with salt (page 182)
1	tablespoon vodka or gin
1	large egg white
2	ounces fresh pork fat,* at room temperature, minced by hand or in a food processor (¼ cup), or 3 tablespoons heavy cream
1	tablespoon Asian sesame oil
1	teaspoon peeled, grated gingerroot
1	teaspoon coarse or kosher salt
½	teaspoon freshly ground white pepper
½	cup finely chopped fresh water chestnuts or jicama
2	scallions, white part only, minced
2	tablespoons chopped fresh cilantro stems or parsley stems**
½	pound fresh crabmeat
1	1-pound package thin, square wonton skins, cut into 3-inch rounds (page 27)
¼	cup minced red bell pepper

¼ cup minced fresh cilantro leaves

Red Bell Pepper Sauce (page 43)

½ pound blanched pea shoots or spinach leaves (optional)

Dry the shrimp in a paper towel and finely puree them. Mix with the vodka or gin and set aside.

In a medium bowl, beat the egg white lightly. Blend in the pork fat or cream, sesame oil, gingerroot, salt and pepper.

Add the shrimp to the egg white mixture and blend well. Mix in the water chestnuts or jicama, scallions and cilantro or parsley stems. Slowly add the crabmeat, mixing carefully so as not to break up the lumps too much. Mix only until all the ingredients are combined.

Place 1 scant tablespoon of the crabmeat mixture into the center of a wonton skin. Using a knife, smooth the filling all the way to the edges but not over them (A). Place the wonton skin in the palm of your hand and cup your other hand around it to press in the sides a little, leaving the top of the wonton skin open in the center; use a knife to smooth the top of the filling (B).

Place the finished dumpling (C) on a piece of wax paper, being careful not to let the sides of the wonton skins touch each other.

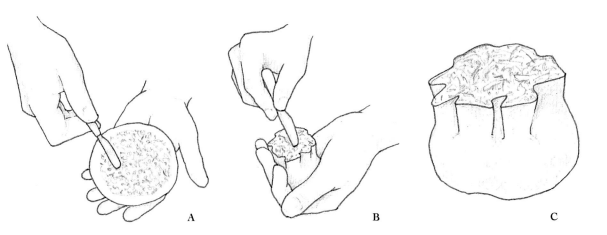

A   B   C

Repeat, using the remaining shrimp mixture and wonton skins.

Garnish each sui mei with minced red bell pepper and minced cilantro leaves.

Place the sui mei on the racks of a steamer (preferably bamboo); do not let the sui mei touch. Fill the bottom of the steamer with water close to, but not touching, the bottom rack and bring to a boil. Place the racks on top. Cover and steam over high heat for 7 to 10 minutes, or until cooked through, replenishing the water if necessary; do not overcook. Remove 1 dumpling and cut in half to check for done-

Crab Sui Mei with Red Bell Pepper Sauce

ness; if it is not fully cooked, continue to steam the dumplings for 1 to 2 minutes more.

Spoon some of the Red Bell Pepper Sauce on a plate and place 4 to 6 sui mei on top, alternating them with small mounds of blanched pea shoots or spinach leaves, if desired.

*Pork fat lends smoothness and richness to the texture of the filling.

**The stems have a more intense flavor than the leaves and retain their green color.

RED BELL PEPPER SAUCE

MAKES ABOUT 2½ CUPS SAUCE

1	**pound red bell peppers**
¼	**cup corn oil**
2	**garlic cloves, sliced**
¼	**cup chopped onion**
2	**cups chicken stock (page 79)**
	Coarse or kosher salt
	Freshly ground pepper

Core and seed the peppers, then cut into large slices.

Heat the oil in a large saucepan. Add the sliced peppers, garlic and onion and sauté over low heat, stirring often, for about ½ hour, or until the peppers are very soft.

Add the stock to the peppers and simmer over low heat for 30 minutes more.

Puree the pepper-chicken stock mixture in a food processor or a blender. Strain through a fine strainer or use a food mill fitted with a fine blade.

Return the sauce to the pan and bring to a simmer, stirring often. Season to taste with salt and pepper; serve warm.

THE SPRING ROLL MAN

WHEN I LIVED IN TAIWAN, my mother always took me with her to the open farmer's market just before the Chinese New Year. At the entranceway stood a spring roll stand, where I would stop and watch the spring roll man prepare the dough for the wrappers. He would hold a roll of soft dough in his hand and swirl it quickly over a hot skillet until he had created a wrapper so thin and translucent that one could see through it. His assistant would quickly peel off and stack the wrappers layer upon layer.

These men were so practiced and quick at their craft that they were able to make thousands of wrappers daily, enough to supply the entire market.

My mother often asked me to wait as the spring roll man prepared our order, while she did the rest of the marketing. Those freshly made wrappers were soft, with a faintly sweet flavor. At home, our cook would prepare a filling made of spring vegetables: young yellow chives, winter bamboo shoots, fresh bean sprouts, pencil-thin mountain celery, spring gingerroot and finely julienned pork. The chives had been kept under a covering of hay until they just began to sprout, so they were sweet and tender, like white asparagus. Dug from the newly unfrozen ground, the winter bamboo shoots were treasured more than any other kind, and the young gingerroot gave the filling a tangy flavor—sharp, yet with a pleasant bite. Our cook would fry the spring rolls so quickly that they were crispy and crunchy, never oily.

My mother usually served them with hot tea as a snack in the afternoon when friends and relatives came to visit us during the New Year's celebration. A favorite of my entire family, they tasted like the essence of spring.

SPRING ROLLS

MAKES 20 SPRING ROLLS

I N THIS COUNTRY, I have been unable to find the traditional filling ingredients, but I have managed to discover good substitutes for them. Instead of bamboo shoots, I use fresh green cabbage, which has a sweet flavor and a crisp texture. Fresh shiitake mushrooms replace the traditional yellow chives.

1	package frozen spring roll wrappers (20 wrappers; page 47)
1	head green cabbage (about 2 pounds), finely shredded
1	cup celery hearts (center yellow-white stalks only), cut into fine julienne
¼	pound chicken breast, coarsely chopped
1	tablespoon soy sauce
2	tablespoons vodka
1	teaspoon cornstarch
¼	pound small shrimp, peeled, deveined, cleaned with salt (page 182)
2	tablespoons corn oil, plus more for deep-frying
¼	cup chopped shallots
4	fresh shiitake mushrooms, cut into small dice
½	cup chopped chives
¼	cup finely chopped celery leaves
¼	cup chopped fresh cilantro or basil leaves
	Coarse or kosher salt
	Freshly ground pepper
3	large egg yolks, lightly beaten
	Hot mustard sauce (page 39)

Thaw the wrappers with a damp towel over them while you make the filling.

Bring a large saucepan filled with water to a boil. Blanch the cabbage and the celery hearts in the boiling water, cooking about 2 minutes; drain. When cool, place on a piece of cheesecloth or a towel and squeeze out the extra liquid. Set aside.

Combine the chicken, soy sauce, 1 tablespoon of the vodka and the cornstarch in a small bowl. Mix well and set aside to marinate.

Pat the shrimp dry with paper towels and cut into small dice. Place in a small bowl and mix in the remaining 1 tablespoon vodka; set aside.

Heat the oil in a medium skillet over high heat and add the shallots. Cook for 2 minutes, or until lightly browned Add the chicken mixture and cook over high heat, stirring, until the meat is no longer pink, about 2 minutes.

Add the shrimp mixture and cook over high heat, stirring, until the shrimp are pink, 2 to 3 minutes. Remove the shrimp-chicken mixture from the skillet and place in a medium bowl. Add the mushrooms and mix well.

When the mixture has cooled, add the chives, celery leaves and cilantro or basil to the bowl. Mix thoroughly, season to taste with salt and pepper and add the cabbage and celery. Let the filling cool thoroughly before proceeding. The wrappers will crack if the filling is used while still warm.

Remove 1 wrapper and place on a board, with a point facing you.

Place 2 tablespoons of the filling on the wrapper, slightly below the center (A). Bring the point of the wrapper up over the filling, tuck it under (B), roll once tightly, then fold in the 2 sides neatly (C). Brush the opposite point of the wrapper with some of the egg yolk. Roll up the egg roll (D) and press to seal (E). Place the filled spring roll on a platter, sealed side down, and cover with a damp towel.

Repeat, using the remainder of the wrappers and the filling. When all the wrappers are filled, cover the platter with plastic wrap.

Pour about 6 inches of oil in a large skillet or a fryer and heat to 350 degrees F.

Cook the spring rolls about 5 minutes, turning once, until they are golden brown, then drain on paper towels. Serve immediately with hot mustard sauce.

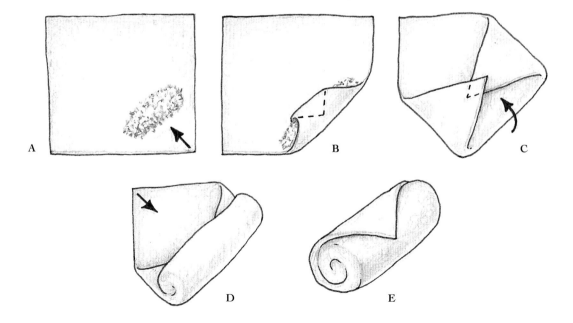

SPRING ROLL WRAPPERS

TWO KINDS OF WRAPPERS are available. The first kind, which originated in Canton, is called an "egg roll wrapper." Machine-made, it is similar to commercial pasta dough, comes in 6-inch squares and is found fresh in most Chinese grocery stores.

The second, originally from Shanghai and called a "spring roll wrapper," is paper-thin and made without eggs. It usually can be found in the freezer case of most Chinese grocery stores.

I prefer to use the spring roll wrapper because it is more tender. About 8 inches square, the egg roll wrapper is thicker and not as crisp when fried, but it can be substituted when necessary, although the rolls will have a different texture.

When using spring roll wrappers, remove the package from the freezer before you start to make the filling; the wrappers will thaw by the time you are ready to use them. Once the package is opened, cover them with a damp cloth because they dry out rapidly when exposed to the air.

Place 1 wrapper at a time on your work surface and fill, working as quickly as possible. Stack each roll as it is made in a container in a single layer. If you are not going to fry the spring rolls immediately, cover with a piece of plastic wrap to prevent the wrappers from drying out and cracking.

One-Hundred-Corner Crab Cakes and Pineapple Salsa

ONE-HUNDRED-CORNER CRAB CAKES

MAKES 20 TO 30 CRAB CAKES

WHEN I WAS A FRESHMAN at the university, I took an eight-week cooking class, thinking that when I got married, I should know something about entertaining. The class was held in the backyard of a famous teacher from Shanghai, and there she would demonstrate all manner of delicious dishes that she cooked over a small charcoal burner.

A favorite dim sum that I learned from her was crab cakes, and when I came to the United States, I tasted another version of this dish prepared by the noted Chinese cookbook author Nina Simonds. Both of these recipes have inspired my own.

These crab cakes are prepared with miniature bread cubes, with shrimp as well as crabmeat forming the base. I like to serve them with Pineapple Salsa and a salad of young, delicate lettuce leaves with Balsamic Vinaigrette (page 69).

1	1-pound loaf thinly sliced white bread, crusts removed*
¾	pound shrimp, peeled, deveined and cleaned with salt (page 182)
3	tablespoons vodka or gin
1	large egg white
1	teaspoon coarse or kosher salt
¼	teaspoon freshly ground white pepper
2	ounces fresh pork fat, minced by hand or in a food processor (¼ cup), or ¼ cup heavy cream
⅓	cup finely chopped fresh water chestnuts or jicama
2	tablespoons finely chopped cilantro stems or celery leaves
2	scallions, white part only, finely chopped
1	tablespoon peeled, grated gingerroot
¾	pound fresh crabmeat
	About 2 tablespoons olive oil for dipping
	Corn oil for deep-frying
	Pineapple Salsa (page 121)

Preheat the oven to 250 degrees F.

Cut the bread into ¼-inch dice and place on a nonstick baking sheet. Bake for about 30 minutes, without turning, or until the bread is dry; do not let the cubes brown.

Dry the shrimp well with paper towels, then place in a food processor. Add the vodka or gin and puree. Spoon the shrimp puree into a medium bowl; set aside.

Lightly beat the egg white with the salt and white pepper in a small bowl. Mix into the shrimp puree. Stir in the pork fat or cream. Add the water chestnuts or jicama, cilantro stems or celery leaves, scallions and gingerroot and mix until thoroughly combined.

Gently fold the crabmeat into the shrimp mixture (the crabmeat should remain lumpy).

Have the bread cubes ready in a large bowl on one side of the crabmeat mixture. Place the olive oil in a small bowl on the other side. Oil a tablespoon by dipping it into the olive oil, then scoop up 1 heaping tablespoon of the shrimp-crab mixture and place it on top of the bread cubes. Repeat, placing 5 or 6 spoonfuls of the crabmeat mixture on the bread cubes, spacing them so they do not touch.

Use your hand to roll each lump of crabmeat into the cubes, forming a ball as you work. Gently flatten each ball into a small cake, about 2 inches in diameter; place the crab cakes on a platter or a baking sheet.

Pour about 6 inches of oil into a skillet or fryer and heat to 325 degrees F. Fry the crab cakes in batches until they are golden, turning once, for 3 to 4 minutes on each side; do not crowd. Remove the crab cakes with a slotted spoon and drain on paper towels.

Serve with Pineapple Salsa.

*I use Pepperidge Farm thin-sliced white bread.

BAKED SHRIMP TOAST

SERVES 4 TO 6

S HRIMP TOAST is one of the most popular items served in many Chinese dim sum teahouses. Loving this combination of shrimp and bread, I have developed a simple yet wonderful way to make this delicious appetizer that eliminates a good bit of the fat.

Shrimp toast can be used for hors d'oeuvres at a cocktail party. I top it with good-quality caviar. It can be prepared well in advance and then stored before baking in plastic bags in the freezer.

8	slices thinly sliced white bread, crusts removed*
1	large egg, separated, plus 1 egg yolk
1	pound medium shrimp, peeled, deveined and cleaned with salt (page 182)
2	tablespoons heavy cream
1	tablespoon vodka
1	teaspoon coarse or kosher salt
½	cup finely chopped fresh water chestnuts or celery hearts (center yellow-white stalks only)
2	scallions, minced
3	tablespoons butter, melted
3	tablespoons water

Preheat the oven to 250 degrees F.

Cut each slice of bread into 4 triangular pieces. Place on a baking sheet and bake for about 30 minutes, without turning, or until the bread is dry but not browned; leave the oven on.

While the toast is drying, beat the egg white lightly. Dry the shrimp well with a paper towel and place in a food processor; puree. Add the egg white, cream, vodka and salt. Process until just pureed. Transfer to a bowl.

Add the water chestnuts or celery hearts and scallions to the shrimp mixture, and mix just until all the ingredients are combined.

If you are baking the shrimp toasts immediately, increase the oven temperature to 350 degrees and coat a nonstick baking sheet with the melted butter.

Spread 2 heaping teaspoons of the shrimp mixture on each piece of bread. Repeat with the remaining triangles.

At this point, the shrimp toast can be frozen for later use. Place the triangles on a baking sheet and freeze. Once frozen, they should be removed from the baking sheet, placed in a plastic bag, sealed and returned to the freezer. To bake, defrost for 1 hour and continue with the recipe.

Beat the 2 egg yolks together with the water, and brush the top of each triangle with the egg wash. Place the triangles on the greased baking sheet, making sure the bottoms are coated with the butter.

Bake the shrimp toast for about 12 minutes, or until shrimp are cooked through, all the ingredients are hot and the toast is golden brown on the bottom.

*I use Pepperidge Farm thin-sliced white bread.

STEAM HEAT

THE TECHNIQUE OF COOKING WITH STEAM was developed by the Chinese over 5,000 years ago. Chinese kitchens had no ovens, only open fires on which a wok was placed. When I was growing up, we steamed bread, whole pieces of meat, such as duck or pork shoulder, and eight-treasure rice pudding in a 2-foot-wide bamboo steamer.

Today, almost every Chinese household has at least one steamer, in which dishes are layered and a number of courses are cooked at the same time. Steaming preserves flavor, tenderizes with its moisture and uses less fat than other cooking methods. Steaming is an excellent way to cook rice, especially sweet rice, so that its flavor is maintained. It is also a good way to warm already cooked foods, such as left-over rice or dumplings, without any loss of flavor.

The best and most common type of steamer is made of bamboo. It has several layers that can be stacked on top of each other in a wok, then covered with a dome-shaped lid. The flavor of the steamed food permeates the bamboo, and a well-used steamer will impart more complex flavors to a dish.

Stainless steel or aluminum steamers can also be used. If you do not have a steamer, you can easily improvise one from the pots you have on hand. All you need is a large pot and some sort of rack, such as a metal vegetable strainer, which can hold a bowl or plate above the water, and a tight-fitting lid to keep the steam within the pot.

Bring the water to a boil before you add the food. Be sure to turn the lid away from you when lifting it; hot steam can burn.

SIZZLING RICE CAKES

MAKES ABOUT 40 RICE CAKES

THIS DISH was originally prepared from the crusts of rice that stuck to the bottom of the pot after the rice was cooked. These crusts would be air-dried overnight, then broken into pieces and deep-fried until they were puffed and crispy and used in soups or as snacks for the children.

When a boiling soup, such as Beef Broth with Pea Shoots, Tomato and Ginger-root (page 88), is poured over the hot rice cakes that have just been fried in oil and placed in a hot tureen, they sizzle, releasing a tantalizing aroma and flavoring the soup. In order for the soup to hiss dramatically, the deep-fried rice cakes must be hot, the bowl must be hot and the soup must be boiling hot.

I also like to serve the crunchy little cakes topped with cold Chinese Eggplant Salsa (page 57), Pineapple Salsa (page 121) or other cold vegetable salads. The contrast of cold and hot creates a wonderful taste sensation, reminiscent of Italian bruschetta—hot toasted bread that is often topped with fresh tomatoes and basil. The rice cakes are also good eaten plain for a snack.

The rice cakes must be deep-fried in very hot oil (about 400 degrees) to make them puff. Using oil at a lower temperature will not work.

This recipe can be doubled or tripled, since the rice cakes store well, both before and after frying.

Note: Commercial rice cakes sold in American supermarkets cannot be substituted for homemade rice cakes.

> 3 cups short-grain white sweet (glutinous) rice (page 297)
> 1 tablespoon coarse or kosher salt
> Corn oil for deep-frying

Soak the rice in a large bowl in 9 cups warm water to cover for 4 hours or overnight in the refrigerator. Drain; sprinkle it with the salt.

Prepare a steamer by placing a layer of cheesecloth in the bottom of a rack. Spread the rice in an even layer over the cheesecloth. Fill the bottom of the steamer with water close to, but not touching, the rack and bring to a boil. Place the rack on top. Cover and steam for about 20 minutes, replenishing the water if necessary, until the rice is just cooked.*

Line a 9-x-11-inch baking pan with parchment or wax paper. While the rice is still hot, spread it out in a ¼-inch layer in the prepared pan, making sure there are no holes in the layer. Cool slightly.

Sizzling Rice Cakes with Chinese Eggplant Salsa

Cut the rice into 1½-inch squares, using a sharp knife or a pizza cutter, while it is still warm. Be sure to cut all the way through, or the cakes will not separate properly once dried.

To dry the rice cakes: Preheat the oven to 250 degrees F, and bake the rice for about 1 hour, or until the cake is hard and dry. Remove from the oven. Cool completely in the pan, then separate the squares.

Or: Let the baking pan sit out in a cool, dry place until the rice cake is completely dried, overnight or longer. Once dry, separate the squares.

At this point, the cakes can be stored in a cool, dry place; do not store them in the refrigerator. After they are completely dry, they can be transferred to an airtight container or plastic bags. The rice cakes will keep for several months. The drier the cakes become, the puffier they will be when deep-fried and the more they will sizzle.

To cook the rice cakes: Pour about 6 inches of oil into a skillet or fryer and heat to 400 degrees F. Deep-fry only as many rice squares as you need at one time.

Fry in batches, 3 to 4 pieces per batch, turning once, until the rice turns white and puffs, about 1 minute per side; do not crowd. Drain on paper towels.

The fried rice cakes can be frozen. Drain well, cool, transfer to a plastic bag and freeze. The defrosted cakes can be heated in a preheated 375-degree oven for 3 to 5 minutes to crisp them before serving.

* Steaming is the best method of preparation for this recipe, since the rice grains must remain separate in order for the rice cakes to puff when fried. Cooking the rice directly in water causes it to become too sticky.

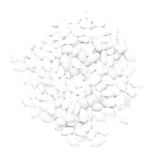

Chinese Eggplant Salsa

Makes 2 to 3 cups salsa

This popular dish is always made with garlic, vinegar and soy sauce. My mother-in-law likes to serve it cold for breakfast with rice congee. My family likes it hot for dinner as a vegetable course. It is also good cold on top of Sizzling Rice Cakes (page 54) or crisp baguettes or on a wedge of Scallion Pancakes (page 305) as an appetizer.

1	pound Chinese eggplants (about 4)*
3	tablespoons olive oil
3	garlic cloves, minced
1	jalapeño pepper or hot Italian pepper, finely chopped
2	tablespoons soy sauce
1	tablespoon balsamic vinegar
1	teaspoon sugar
1	small tomato, peeled, seeded and diced
1	tablespoon chopped fresh cilantro leaves

Remove the stem end of each eggplant. Cut each eggplant in half lengthwise. Place the halves, cut sides down, on the work surface, and slice each on the diagonal, into 1-to-2-inch-long slices, ¼ inch thick.

Heat the olive oil in a large skillet. Add the garlic and jalapeño or hot Italian pepper and cook over high heat for 2 minutes, or until golden. Add the eggplant, mix and cook over low heat, stirring occasionally, for 15 to 20 minutes, or until the eggplant is tender.

Add the soy sauce, vinegar and sugar to the skillet. Cook, stirring, until the liquid is absorbed, about 2 minutes.

Remove from the heat and add the tomato and the cilantro leaves. Stir to combine.

*Italian, white or ordinary eggplant, peeled and salted to remove bitter juices, may be substituted; see page 145.

"HONEYED" PINE NUTS

MAKES 2 CUPS NUTS

I WAS ABOUT 12 YEARS OLD when my parents took me to my first banquet in Taiwan. The occasion was the wedding of friends of the family. I still remember the banquet hall, decorated with red and gold streamers and colorful banners wishing the newlyweds good fortune and a happy and long life together.

It was a typical Chinese wedding banquet, where the guests sat at large, round tables for 12. In the center of each table was a lazy Susan, its compartments filled with an assortment of goodies, including honeyed pine nuts. I cannot remember most of the other dishes they served at that wedding, but I couldn't seem to get enough of the pine nuts. I was entranced by their sweet-buttery flavor and the contrasting texture of the nuts—crisp on the outside, meltingly soft within. I've loved honeyed nuts of all kinds since that time.

I like to serve these sprinkled over salad, "Squirrel" Sea Bass (page 162) or rice pudding.

2   cups pine nuts (pignoli nuts)

1   cup sugar

    About 1 cup water

1   tablespoon olive oil

Soak the pine nuts in warm water for 2 hours. Drain.

Preheat the oven to 300 degrees F.

Combine the sugar and the 1 cup water in a medium saucepan and bring to a boil, stirring to dissolve the sugar. Cook over medium-high heat, uncovered, without stirring, for 3 minutes, to make a syrup.

Reduce the heat to low, add the pine nuts to the syrup and stir with a wooden spoon. Simmer for 15 to 20 minutes, or until the nuts are translucent. (If nuts are too sticky and form clumps, add ¼ cup hot water to the saucepan.) Turn off the heat and let sit until the nuts are cool. Strain, discarding any excess syrup.

Toss the pine nuts with the oil and spread out on a large nonstick baking sheet. Bake for 45 minutes to 1 hour, stirring occasionally, or until the nuts are light gold in color.

If, after the nuts have cooled, they are not crisp, return them to the oven for 5 minutes more. Do not overbake. Separate the nuts with a fork or spoon.

The cooled nuts may be stored in a tightly closed container for 1 to 2 days or placed in a plastic bag and frozen for up to 3 months.

"Honeyed" Walnuts

Makes about 2 cups nuts

I<small>N</small> C<small>HINA</small>, most kinds of nuts, such as cashews, pine nuts or even walnuts, are very expensive and are reserved for special occasions. Only peanuts are affordable and are used on a daily basis. Walnuts are usually served as a starter at the beginning of a banquet or pureed in a dessert soup at the end.

In 1982, Chinese cookbook author Eileen Yin-Fei Lo shared with me her version of this classic dish. They were the best honeyed walnuts I had ever eaten. The following recipe was inspired by Eileen.

1	**pound shelled walnut halves**
1½	**cups sugar**
	About 1½ cups water
2	**tablespoons corn oil**

Wash the walnuts in lots of running water. Soak them for 10 to 15 minutes in water to cover; drain well.

Fill a large pot with water and bring to a boil. Add the nuts and cook for 10 minutes, or until the water turns dark and the nuts are beige-white in color. Drain and rinse under cool water until the water runs clear; drain.

Bring the sugar and the 1½ cups water to a boil in a medium pot over medium-high heat, stirring to dissolve the sugar. Add the walnuts, reduce the heat to low and stir well with a wooden spoon. Simmer the nuts in the syrup for about 15 minutes, stirring often, until they are well coated with the syrup. Add ¼ cup hot water if the syrup becomes too sticky. Turn off the heat and let the nuts cool in the syrup for another 10 minutes.

Preheat the oven to 350 degrees F.

Strain off the excess syrup and toss the nuts with the oil. Spread the nuts on a large nonstick baking sheet.

Bake the nuts for 30 to 35 minutes, stirring occasionally, or until they are crisp and dry. If they are not yet crisp, bake them a little longer.

The nuts can be stored in a tightly closed container at room temperature for 1 to 2 days or frozen in a sealed plastic bag for up to 3 months.

Shiitake Mushrooms Stuffed with Lamb

Serves 6 as an Appetizer

Tʜɪꜱ ᴅɪꜱʜ is traditionally made with dried shiitake mushrooms. I prefer to use fresh shiitakes, which are readily available. The lamb filling complements them especially well. Generally, they are steamed, but I like to broil them.

½	cup olive oil
1	small onion, finely chopped
1	jalapeño pepper, seeded and chopped (optional)
½	pound coarsely ground lamb (from leg or shoulder; page 29)
1	tablespoon soy sauce
1	teaspoon Asian sesame oil
½	cup finely chopped fennel or celery hearts (center yellow-white stalks only)
¼	cup pine nuts (pignoli nuts)
2	tablespoons chopped fresh cilantro leaves or basil leaves
1	teaspoon coarse or kosher salt
1	teaspoon cornstarch
1	tablespoon cold water
20	fresh medium shiitake mushroom caps or large white button mushroom caps
	Ancho Chile Sauce (page 33) or Kung Pao Sauce (page 204)

Heat 2 tablespoons of the oil in a small saucepan. Add the onion and cook over high heat, stirring, until the onion is translucent, about 2 to 3 minutes. Remove from the heat and add the jalapeño pepper, if using. Stir well and set aside to cool.

In a large bowl, combine the lamb, soy sauce, sesame oil, fennel or celery hearts, pine nuts, cilantro or basil and salt. Add the cooked onion and mix well.

Combine the cornstarch and the water and add to the lamb mixture; mix.

Toss the mushroom caps in the remaining 6 tablespoons oil. Spoon the lamb mixture into the mushroom caps, smoothing the tops with the back of a spoon.

Preheat the broiler, with the rack 4 to 6 inches from the heat source. Broil the mushrooms for 6 to 8 minutes, until the meat is cooked.

Serve with Ancho Chile Sauce or Kung Pao Sauce on the side.

SHIITAKE MUSHROOMS

OF THE MANY VARIETIES of wild and culti-vated mushrooms, I prefer shiitakes because they are meaty and long-lasting. Grown in many parts of the Orient, shiitakes are exported to this coun-try only in their dried form. Drying preserves the mushrooms for a long time and enables the cook to use them year-round.

Fresh shiitake mushrooms are now cultivated in this country and are available in almost all su-permarkets and grocery stores. Dried mushrooms still have a place in Chinese cuisine, lending a depth of flavor to many dishes, but ever since I have been able to get the fresh, I have seldom re-sorted to dried.

Fresh Shiitake Mushrooms

Choose dark brown mushrooms with thick, round caps that curl under at the edges. The gills should be tightly formed and still moist. Wipe the mushrooms clean with a damp cloth. Do not im-merse them in water, as they will absorb it and give off too much liquid when cooked, diluting their taste.

I like to cook fresh shiitakes in a good grade of olive oil over high heat. For every pound of fresh mushrooms, I use 6 to 8 tablespoons olive oil (the more oil, the better). Cook them over high heat, along with 1 tablespoon each of garlic and shallots, for 1 to 2 minutes. The flavored oil can be drained off and used to cook other vegetables or for salad dressing.

Dried Shiitake Mushrooms

There are two grades of dried shiitake mush-rooms available. The better-quality ones, known as flower mushrooms, have thick, meaty round caps, often with a marbled surface. They have a rich, intense taste. The cheaper dried ones are black, with flat, thin caps, and have less flavor. The best place to buy dried shiitake mushrooms is in Chinese grocery stores.

Flower mushrooms can cost twice as much as the cheaper shiitakes and are therefore used only for special occasions or banquets. They are often braised with chicken or vegetables or cooked in rich stock for a special soup. Cheaper shiitakes are usually relegated to stuffings or stock.

Dried mushrooms must be soaked in water for ½ to 1 hour, until the caps are soft, then rinsed. I usually discard the soaking water from the black mushrooms—it has little flavor and is often full of dirt and debris. To prepare dried shiitakes for cooking, squeeze the extra liquid out of the mush-rooms. Discard the hard, woody stems. I prepare 4 ounces of dried mushrooms at a time and keep them ready in the refrigerator. Heat 2 tablespoons olive oil in a skillet and add 1 tablespoon each gar-lic and shallots. Add the mushrooms and some chicken stock, enough to cover the mushrooms by about 3 inches, and simmer for about 20 min-utes; drain. Now the mushrooms are ready to be used for stuffings or in other recipes. Use the drained stock in soups.

MARBLED TEA EGGS

MAKES 1 DOZEN EGGS

WHEN I WAS IN ELEMENTARY SCHOOL in Kao-hsiung, in Taiwan, an old man would arrive in our neighborhood around 4 o'clock in the afternoon with his two-wheeled cart, ringing a bell. The sound would bring us running, just as American children run to the ice cream truck after school. The vendor sold braised pork and tea eggs, both cooked in the same sauce.

Marbled Tea Eggs are easily made at home. They are first hard-boiled, then their shells are carefully cracked. They are simmered in a well-seasoned combination of tea and basic brown sauce (often left over from cooking pork), until the flavor penetrates the yolks as well as the whites of the eggs. When the shells are removed, the egg white is covered with a beautiful marbled pattern.

Serve Marbled Tea Eggs as an appetizer with other cold dishes, with salad or for breakfast or lunch.

12 large eggs
3 cups Brown Sauce for Braising* (page 249)
1 tablespoon black tea leaves**

Place the eggs in a large saucepan and add cold water to cover. Slowly bring the water to a boil. Simmer the eggs over medium to low heat for 12 minutes. Plunge the eggs into ice-cold water to stop the cooking process; be careful not to overcook.

When the eggs are cool, gently tap each one with the back of a small spoon until the shells are finely cracked all over.

Combine the brown sauce and the tea in a large saucepan or Dutch oven. Stir to mix and carefully add the eggs.

Bring the liquid to a boil, then reduce the heat to a simmer. Cover the pan and cook for 1 hour.

Remove the pan from the heat. Cool the eggs in the liquid.

Remove the eggs with a slotted spoon. The liquid can be used again; strain it and store in the refrigerator for 2 weeks or in the freezer for 3 months.

Unpeeled eggs may be stored in the refrigerator for 3 days in a sealed plastic bag. Before serving, carefully peel the eggs and cut into quarters or slices.

*The eggs are best if the sauce has first been used for braising meat or fowl.
**Use loose tea leaves only; do not substitute tea bags. Chinese black tea is preferable.

Marbled Tea Eggs

TARO PANCAKES

MAKES 12 PANCAKES

P ANCAKES MADE FROM TARO ROOT are very popular in China and are often sold as a snack by small street vendors or served as dim sum in Cantonese teahouses, as we serve potato pancakes in the West.

I have taken this favorite classic dim sum recipe and added cream for texture and mushrooms for flavor to create a more sophisticated presentation for the dinner table.

If you have difficulty finding taro root, this recipe may be prepared with white potatoes or sweet potatoes. Serve warm with Cold Beer Shrimp (page 71) or other shrimp, scallop or squid dishes.

1	medium taro root (about 1 pound)
⅓	cup corn oil
2	shallots, finely chopped
¼	cup finely chopped onion
2	tablespoons minced soaked dried shrimp (page 134; optional)
2	fresh shiitake mushrooms, finely chopped (about ½ cup)*
1	tablespoon coarse or kosher salt
	Freshly ground pepper
1	large egg yolk
½	cup heavy cream
	All-purpose flour for dusting

Peel the taro root, trimming off all dry or dark spots, and coarsely chop it by hand or in a food processor in 3 batches. Place it on the rack of a steamer. Fill the bottom of the steamer with water close to, but not touching, the rack and bring to a boil. Place the rack on top, cover and steam over high heat for about 15 minutes, replenishing the water if necessary, until the taro is tender. Transfer to a bowl; set aside.

Heat 2 tablespoons of the oil in a medium skillet and sauté the shallots and the onion on medium-high heat until golden, about 3 to 4 minutes. Mix in the dried shrimp, if using, and the mushrooms and continue to cook, stirring, for about 2 minutes. Stir in the salt and pepper to taste. Remove from the heat. Add this mixture to the reserved cooked taro root and mix well.

Mix the egg yolk and the cream in a small bowl and stir into the taro mixture.

Lightly flour a clean cutting board. Flour your hand and press out the mixture on the board to a thickness of ½ inch and cut into 2-inch rounds with a cookie cutter or into 2-inch squares with a knife. Dust each round or square with flour and refrigerate until ready to cook.

Heat 1½ tablespoons of the oil in a large skillet over medium-high heat. Add half of the pancakes. Cook until brown for about 3 to 4 minutes, then turn and brown the second side for another 3 minutes. Remove the pancakes to a platter and keep warm. Repeat with the remaining pancakes, using the remaining 1½ tablespoons oil as necessary.

*If you cannot get fresh shiitakes, substitute ½ cup chopped cooked dried (from 6 whole uncooked mushrooms, prepared as directed on page 61).

TARO ROOT

Taro, a versatile root vegetable with a taste between a white potato and a sweet potato, but with a firmer texture, is popular in southern China and throughout Southeast Asia.

The larger taro, weighing from 2 to 3 pounds, is the more common variety and the one that I use. Ivory-colored with reddish tints, it has a chestnut-like flavor, and its flesh is dense and dry. It can be sliced and stir-fried along with other vegetables and meats, used as a stuffing or made into pancakes. Like other root vegetables, it is a good accompaniment to braised meats or game.

Small taro root, which is about the size of a large egg, is treated much the same way as a new potato. It has a mildly sweet flavor, hairy brown skin and grayish flesh. My mother-in-law loves to julienne small taro and cook it in soup. In Taiwan, she sometimes boiled the small taro roots whole until they were tender, and we ate them out of hand, like a banana. Small taro root is also made into sorbet and is sold by street vendors everywhere in Taiwan, all summer long.

Because of its high-starch and low-fiber content, the surface of the taro root will become sticky and slippery once it is peeled. Never mash or puree cooked taro, for its texture will become gluey and heavy. I prefer to steam taro when using it for a stuffing or in pancakes.

SPICED SHIITAKE MUSHROOMS

SERVES 4 TO 6

THESE MUSHROOMS make a fine appetizer, either alone or accompanied by "honeyed" nuts (pages 58 and 59), Cold Beer Shrimp (page 71) or Spicy Cucumbers with Sichuan Peppercorn Vinaigrette (page 110). They may also be served with meat or game.

1   **pound small fresh shiitake mushrooms, preferably 1-1½ inches in diameter**

½   **cup olive oil**

3   **garlic cloves, minced**

1   **tablespoon Asian sesame oil**

1   **tablespoon soy sauce**

1   **teaspoon fresh lemon juice**

2   **scallions, white part only, chopped**

½   **fresh jalapeño pepper, finely diced (optional)**

     Coarse or kosher salt

     Freshly ground pepper

Remove the stems from the shiitake mushrooms and wipe the caps with a damp cloth. If the mushrooms are small, leave them whole; if large, cut them into halves or quarters.

Heat the olive oil in a large skillet. Add the garlic and cook over high heat, stirring, until it is golden, 2 to 3 minutes. Add the mushrooms and the sesame oil. Stir well, cover and continue cooking over high heat for 3 to 5 minutes, or until the mushrooms are tender.

Add the soy sauce, lemon juice, scallions, jalapeño pepper, if using, and salt and pepper to taste. Cook for 1 minute, or until the mushrooms have absorbed the sauce. Remove from the heat.

Spoon the mushrooms and the sauce into a serving bowl. Serve at room temperature or cold.

Variation

You can also broil the mushrooms. In a large bowl, mix them with the olive oil, garlic, sesame oil, soy sauce, lemon juice, scallions and jalapeño pepper, if using. Place them, gill sides up, on a shallow pan, pour any leftover marinade over them and broil for 2 to 3 minutes, or until they are soft.

JALAPEÑO PEPPERS WITH PORK STUFFING

MAKES 20 PEPPERS

THIS WONDERFULLY SPICY DISH may be served as an appetizer along with other dim sum, such as dumplings, or alongside grilled meats. They are good with Black Bean Sauce (page 159).

The recipe comes from my mother-in-law, who uses long, light green Italian frying peppers, or hot red peppers. I prefer to use jalapeño peppers because they are the meatiest and the most consistent in flavor. This dish is particularly delicious at the end of the summer, when you can get red jalapeños.

1	**pound large jalapeño peppers or Italian hot peppers (about 20)**
½	**pound ground lean pork (beef may be substituted; see page 29)**
1	**tablespoon brandy**
2	**tablespoons water, or more if needed**
½	**cup minced scallions**
1	**teaspoon peeled, grated gingerroot**
1	**tablespoon minced fresh thyme, or ½ teaspoon dried**
2	**tablespoons soy sauce**
1	**tablespoon Asian sesame oil**
	About 2 tablespoons corn oil for sautéing

Remove the stem from each pepper. Slice the peppers in half lengthwise on one side, cutting almost to the tip; leave the peppers joined at both ends. With the tip of a vegetable peeler, remove the seeds; set aside.

Place the pork in a small bowl and add the brandy. Stir in the water, 1 tablespoonful at a time, until the meat mixture is soft. Mix well.

Add the scallions, gingerroot, thyme, soy sauce and sesame oil; mix until thoroughly combined. Open each pepper carefully and stuff it with some of the meat mixture, pressing it in firmly and keeping the pepper whole.

Coat a large nonstick skillet with the corn oil and heat. Without crowding the pan, add the stuffed peppers to the skillet. (Depending on the size of your skillet and the number of peppers, you may have to fry them in batches.)

Cover the peppers and cook over low heat for 5 minutes. Turn and continue cooking until the peppers are tender and the meat is thoroughly cooked, about 15 minutes. Serve at room temperature.

GRILLED CHINESE EGGPLANT WITH BALSAMIC VINAIGRETTE

SERVES 4

O NE OF MY MOTHER'S FAVORITE DISHES when she was young was a whole eggplant that was deep-fried until soft, then sliced and marinated with Shanxi black vinegar. Cooked this way, the eggplant was sweet and juicy on the inside, and its skin kept its deep purple color.

Broiling the slices of eggplant rather than deep-frying the whole vegetable produces equally good results and uses a lot less oil.

1	pound Chinese eggplant (about 4)*
¼	cup olive oil
1	tablespoon soy sauce
1	tablespoon vodka or gin
1	medium tomato, peeled, seeded and finely diced
1	tablespoon finely chopped fresh cilantro leaves, plus more for garnish
1	tablespoon peeled, finely julienned gingerroot (optional)
	Balsamic Vinaigrette (opposite page)
1	lemon, quartered

Remove the stems and cut the eggplants in half lengthwise, then cut each half crosswise into 3 pieces. Score the skin side of each piece by cutting 2 crosswise slices about ½ inch apart, cutting just halfway through the flesh. Place the eggplant in a medium bowl.

Mix the oil, soy sauce and vodka or gin in a small bowl. Pour over the eggplant and marinate for about 10 minutes.

Mix the tomato and cilantro; set aside.

Preheat the broiler, with a rack 5 inches from the heat source. Place a baking sheet large enough to hold the eggplant in a single layer under the broiler and heat until hot.

Remove the eggplant pieces from the marinade and place them on the hot baking sheet, skin sides up, and broil for about 5 minutes, without turning, or until tender.

Divide the cooked eggplant among 4 plates. Top with a little of the chopped tomato-cilantro mixture and the gingerroot, if desired. Spoon on a little of the vinaigrette and squeeze a lemon quarter over each serving.

* Small Italian or white eggplant, salted to remove bitter juices, may be substituted; see page 145. Cut the eggplants in quarters lengthwise, then cut each quarter crosswise in half. They will take longer to grill, about 10 minutes.

BALSAMIC VINAIGRETTE

MAKES ABOUT ⅓ CUP

UNLIKE MOST AMERICAN SALAD DRESSINGS, which are generally uncooked, Chinese salad dressings are usually cooked. We fry onions, garlic or other aromatic vegetables, then add soy sauce and vinegar for flavoring. These dressings are mixed with blanched vegetables or tossed with salad greens.

2 tablespoons corn or olive oil

1 teaspoon minced garlic

2 tablespoons balsamic vinegar

2 tablespoons soy sauce

1 tablespoon peeled, julienned gingerroot

Heat the oil in a small saucepan and add the garlic. Cook over high heat just until the garlic turns golden, 2 to 3 minutes. Turn off the heat and whisk in the vinegar and soy sauce.

Remove from the heat and add the gingerroot; set aside.

The vinaigrette can be prepared up to 2 days in advance and refrigerated.

COLD MARINATED SCALLOPS

SERVES 6 AS AN APPETIZER OR 4 FOR LUNCH

THE SCALLOPS ARE FIRST POACHED in warm oil to keep them moist, then topped with a refreshing, complex sauce made with Bloody Mary mix.

1	**pound medium sea scallops**
½	**cup corn oil**
1	**tablespoon fresh lemon juice**
¼	**cup diced onion**
1	**tablespoon peeled, grated gingerroot**
½	**cup scallions, white part only,**
	diced (about 3)
1	**small tomato, diced**
½	**cup bottled Bloody Mary mix***
	Coarse or kosher salt
	Freshly ground pepper
¼	**cup julienned basil or cilantro leaves**

Wash the scallops and pat dry. Place them in a single layer between sheets of paper towels until they are completely dry.

Heat the oil in a large skillet over high heat. When the oil is hot but not smoking, about 300 degrees F, add the scallops. Cook, turning, until the scallops are just cooked, about 3 minutes. Do not overcook, or they will toughen.

Using a slotted spoon, remove the scallops to a strainer and drain. Place them in a bowl, toss with the lemon juice and refrigerate.

Remove all but 1 tablespoon of oil from the skillet and lower the heat to medium. Add the onion, gingerroot and scallions. Cook, stirring, for 2 minutes. Turn off the heat, add the tomato and Bloody Mary mix and stir to combine. Let the sauce cool.

Just before serving, drain the scallops. Spoon the sauce over them and toss to combine. Season to taste with salt and pepper. Garnish with the julienned basil or cilantro leaves and serve immediately.

* Bloody Mary mix is available in most supermarkets and liquor stores.

COLD BEER SHRIMP

SERVES 6 AS AN APPETIZER, 4 FOR LUNCH OR 3 FOR DINNER

T RADITIONALLY, the Chinese cook their shrimp in Shaoxing (rice wine) to enhance the sweetness of the shrimp and help remove any unpleasant "fishy" flavor. I have found that cooking shrimp in beer, which is cheaper and more readily available, produces much the same results.

1	12-ounce bottle beer, any type
1	pound large shrimp
1	tablespoon olive oil
1	tablespoon soy sauce
1	tablespoon fresh lime juice
1	teaspoon Tabasco sauce
1	medium tomato, peeled, seeded and diced
1	teaspoon peeled, grated gingerroot
1	tablespoon chopped fresh cilantro leaves, mint or chives
	Coarse or kosher salt
	Freshly ground pepper

Bring the beer to a boil in a large saucepan. Add the shrimp, stir, and cook for 2 minutes, or until they just turn pink. Remove from the heat and let the shrimp cool in the beer, stirring or turning often; they will continue to cook in the hot liquid.

Once they are cool, remove the shrimp from the beer, using a slotted spoon. Peel and devein the shrimp; return them to the beer and stir for 1 minute to remove any remaining grit.

Transfer the shrimp to a bowl. (The beer can be strained and added to shrimp or fish stock.) The shrimp can be prepared up to 1 day in advance and refrigerated.

Heat the oil in a small saucepan. Add the soy sauce, lime juice, Tabasco, tomato and gingerroot. Cook over high heat, stirring, for 2 minutes, to heat through. Remove from the heat and let cool.

Spoon the cooled sauce over the shrimp and toss to combine. Add the cilantro, mint or chives. Season to taste with salt and pepper and toss again. Cover and refrigerate until ready to serve.

Squid Salad with Five-Flavor Vinaigrette

SQUID SALAD WITH FIVE-FLAVOR VINAIGRETTE

SERVES 4 TO 6

I N CHINESE CUISINE, squid is always cut on the diagonal so that when cooked, it will form curls. This technique not only makes for a beautiful presentation but helps the squid cook faster and remain tender. This dish is good served with Scallion Pancakes (page 305).

Squid Salad

2 pounds whole squid

2 cups chicken stock (page 79) or water

½ cup fresh shelled soybeans*

1 small jalapeño pepper, thinly sliced (optional)

1 small tomato, peeled, seeded and diced

2 scallions, finely chopped

1 tablespoon chopped fresh cilantro leaves

Five-Flavor Vinaigrette

2 tablespoons olive oil

1 tablespoon peeled, finely chopped gingerroot

1 garlic clove, finely minced

1 small jalapeño pepper, finely chopped

1 tablespoon chopped fresh cilantro leaves

1 tablespoon ketchup

1 tablespoon soy sauce

1 tablespoon white wine vinegar, cider vinegar or
   a fruit-flavored vinegar, such as peach

1 tablespoon Asian sesame oil

½ teaspoon sugar

To make the squid salad: Clean the squid by pulling apart the head and body. Cut off the head and tentacles; remove and discard the cartilage inside the mouthpiece; set aside the tentacles. Peel off the outer purplish membrane and remove and discard the cartilage inside the body sac. Rinse well. Open each squid body by cutting it in half lengthwise. Place the opened squid on a board, with the inside facing up. Score the inside of the body on the diagonal, using a crosshatch pattern, being careful not to cut through the squid.

Cut each squid body in half, and if large, cut each half into 3 or 4 horizontal pieces, each about 1 inch long. If small, cut into 2 horizontal pieces. You will have 4 to 8 pieces from each squid.

Bring the stock or water to a boil in a large saucepan and add the squid bodies and tentacles. Cook for 2 to 3 minutes, or until the squid is tender and curls. Do not overcook. Remove from the liquid with a slotted spoon; drain.

Add the soybeans to the stock in which the squid cooked, and cook the beans over high heat for 5 minutes, or until tender; drain well.

In a medium bowl, combine the squid, soybeans, jalapeño pepper (if using), tomato, scallions and cilantro.

To make the vinaigrette: Heat the oil in a small saucepan. Add the gingerroot, garlic, jalapeño and cilantro. Cook, stirring, for 2 to 3 minutes, or until the flavors are released.

Add all the remaining ingredients, stir to combine and remove from the heat.

Pour over the squid salad and toss to combine. Divide the squid among 4 to 6 salad plates and serve hot, cold or at room temperature.

*Fava beans or green peas may be substituted.

CHAPTER TWO

SOUPS

WHEN I WAS GROWING UP, every meal was accompanied by a different soup. Usually neutral-tasting and delicate, it was sipped along with the food to refresh the taste buds and cleanse the palate, much as we drink water or another beverage in this country. Both my mother and my grandmother believed that cold water was not good for us. No wine was ever served with an everyday meal, soft drinks did not exist and tea was reserved for after dinner.

When we had dumplings, the broth left over from cooking them became our soup. When we had pancakes, a big bowl of hot and sour soup or noodle soup was placed in the center of the table. My mother often simmered a whole chicken in broth seasoned with ginger and *go chi*, a dried berry that was supposed to have healthful properties. We would sip the rich stock and dip the meat in a soy-based sauce. Sometimes, we had a heavy lamb soup with steamed yeast buns, other times, a simple soup made from pork bones or liver with napa cabbage or daikon.

Winter was soup's triumphal season. One of our favorites—a specialty of the north and a meal in itself—was Mongolian hot pot. It consisted of a huge pot filled with rich stock set over a stand containing charcoal to keep it warm. Surrounding the pot were a variety of raw meats—beef, chicken and pork—shrimp and fish balls, bean curd and cellophane noodles, cooked homemade thin wheat noodles, napa cabbage, spinach and chrysanthemum leaves and sauces. Using our chopsticks, we dipped the food into the hot stock to cook it, then dipped it into whatever sauce we preferred. I liked a mixture of sesame paste, Shanxi black vinegar and soy sauce. As the cooking progressed, the stock became richer and more complex. Finally, my mother added the noodles to the pot, and the meal concluded with a steaming bowl of soup.

I N THE CHINESE LANGUAGE, "soup" and "stock" are the same word, and stock plays a crucial role in our cuisine. It is customary for a cook to place a pot of slowly simmering rich stock next to the wok to be added as needed to enhance the flavor of sauces or other dishes. My mother-in-law always said that if you don't have a good stock in your kitchen, you cannot make a wonderful meal, and the best base for a good sauce is a well-flavored stock. Good chicken stock, in particular, is a crucial ingredient in many of my dishes—an essential natural flavoring with a delicacy that never intrudes.

Whatever ingredients are added to soup, they should neither overwhelm the balance nor lose their identity to the whole. As a rule, Chinese cooks do not use pureed vegetables to thicken soups, nor is cream ever added. Root vegetables, such as daikon, are added at the beginning of the cooking time, so they become tender and release their flavor, while leafy vegetables, such as pea shoots, are held out until the end, so they maintain their integrity. Ginger plays a crucial role in all my soups, purifying the taste. In most stocks, I avoid celery, since it changes the flavor, imparting a bitter taste, unless the soup is served the day it is made. Seasonings like star anise and Sichuan peppercorns lend a marvelous aroma.

I have made one important deviation from Chinese tradition. To intensify the taste of all my stocks, I have adopted the French technique of first browning the bones and vegetables before adding them to the pot. When browned, onions and carrots give a rich color and a natural sweetness. The result: stocks and soups that possess all the traditional clarity of those I remember but with an extra dimension of flavor.

SOUPS

Rich Chicken Stock   79

Rich Pork Stock   80

Classic Hot and Sour Soup   82

Wild Mushroom Soup   85

Beef Stock   87

Beef Broth with Pea Shoots, Tomato and Gingerroot   88

Oxtail Soup with Savoy Cabbage and Tomato   90

Turkestan Lamb Soup with Mung Beans   92

Fish Stock   94

Daikon Fish Soup   95

Salmon Congee   97

Shrimp Ball Soup   100

Seafood Wonton Soup   103

Shrimp Stock   105

RICH CHICKEN STOCK

MAKES ABOUT 2 QUARTS STOCK

A GOOD CHICKEN STOCK is of the utmost importance to the Chinese cook. It is usually made by slowly simmering a whole chicken in water, with gingerroot, scallions and Sichuan peppercorns as the only added flavoring ingredients. It is similar to a French consommé—sparkling clear, with a rich, concentrated flavor. It has just the right balance to make it easily blend with other ingredients and therefore is used as the basis for many soups. My mother always served this stock with the addition of a little *go chi* (see page 126) or pea shoots.

In the following recipe, sauté the chicken parts first to develop depth and color. The wings give the soup a rich, gelatinous consistency.

2 pounds chicken necks and backs, plus 2 pounds
    chicken wings (or one 5-pound fryer, cut up)
2 tablespoons corn or olive oil
1 medium onion, quartered
1 carrot, quartered
2 garlic cloves, crushed
1 2-inch piece gingerroot, thinly sliced
½ tablespoon roasted Sichuan peppercorns (page 111)
3 star anise
4 quarts water

Wash all the chicken parts thoroughly and pat dry with paper towels.

Heat the oil in a large stock pot. Add the chicken parts to the pot and cook on high heat, stirring occasionally, until the chicken skin becomes golden brown, about 10 minutes.

Add the remaining ingredients, except the water, to the pot and cook, stirring occasionally, for 10 minutes.

Add the water and bring to a boil. Reduce to a simmer and cook, uncovered, for 2 hours, skimming any froth or scum from the stock as it cooks.

Strain through a sieve or a colander and discard the solids. Skim off the fat and strain again through a cheesecloth to rid the stock of any tiny particles.

The stock will keep in the refrigerator for up to 1 week or in the freezer for up to 3 months.

RICH PORK STOCK

MAKES ABOUT 2 QUARTS STOCK

PORK STOCK IS AS IMPORTANT to Chinese cuisine as veal stock is to French. The average home cook will take 5 or 6 hours to prepare a stock made with pork meat or pork bones. Full-flavored and subtle, this creamy off-white stock is used as a base for many dishes.

In China, when a pig is slaughtered, its blood is drained off immediately, and it is cooked the same day. In this country, pork takes several days to reach the marketplace, and its flavor is very different. Chinese pork is always fresh and sweet, and stock made from this meat is richer.

To give pork stock the same taste that I remember, I roast the bones and add browned onions, carrots and chicken bones.

4	pounds pork rib bones
2	large onions, quartered
2	carrots, quartered
1	bunch scallions (about 6)
3-4	star anise
1	1-inch piece gingerroot, sliced
1	teaspoon roasted Sichuan peppercorns (page 111)
2	pounds chicken bones*
6	quarts water

Preheat the oven to 400 degrees F. Place the pork bones in a roasting pan in a single layer. Roast, turning as necessary, until they are golden brown, about 30 minutes. Remove the bones; set aside.

Transfer 2 tablespoons of the fat from the roasting pan to a large stock pot. Heat over high heat and add the onions, carrots, scallions, star anise, gingerroot and peppercorns and sauté, stirring occasionally, for 5 to 10 minutes, or until the onions are golden. Add the chicken bones.

Meanwhile, pour off and discard the remaining fat from the roasting pan. Add 2 cups of the water to the pan and deglaze the pan by scraping up any particles sticking to the bottom. Once the onions are golden, pour the liquid from the roasting pan into the stock pot.

Add the rest of the water to cover all the bones and vegetables, and bring to a boil. Reduce to a simmer and cook, uncovered, for 6 hours. Skim off any froth or scum that form on the surface as the stock cooks.

Strain the stock through a fine sieve and discard the solids.

The stock will keep in the refrigerator for up to 1 week or in the freezer for up to 3 months.

*When you bone a chicken breast or remove a backbone or wing tips, save the bones and place them in a freezer bag and freeze until needed (for up to 6 months), or ask your butcher for extra bones.

Classic Hot and Sour Soup

Serves 4

ROM THE TIME I WAS ABOUT 3 YEARS OLD, I can clearly remember eating hot and sour soup on the coldest of winter days. Fresh vegetables were hard to get in northern China during the winter, so many dried ingredients were (and are still) used. Traditionally, hot and sour soup is made with tree-ear fungi, dried tiger lily buds, winter bamboo shoots, fresh pork blood, bean curd and eggs. It is silky, with a jellied texture, and spicy from lots of white pepper and hot peppers. Most of the time, our cook would make this soup with pork, but sometimes, he would substitute fish, seafood, duck meat or even chicken. The spiciness of the pepper made me sneeze, but it cleared my head and warmed me up immediately.

The secret of a good hot and sour soup is to use the freshest ingredients to enrich the flavor of the broth. My version is subtle—spicy yet sour at the same time. The addition of taro root gives body to the soup. Diced marinated raw chicken, beef or lamb can be substituted for the pork. You can use almost any fish or shellfish, but add them later, with the tofu and the taro root.

This soup can be served as a first course or for lunch along with Scallion Pancakes (page 305) or French bread.

Pork and Marinade

1	tablespoon soy sauce
1	tablespoon brandy
1	teaspoon cornstarch
¼	pound lean pork, cut into ¼-inch dice (page 262)

Soup

¼	cup cornstarch
¼	cup water
8	cups chicken or pork stock (page 79 or 80)
3	tablespoons soy sauce
3	tablespoons white wine vinegar
1	teaspoon freshly ground white pepper, or to taste
½	teaspoon cayenne pepper, or to taste
1	teaspoon coarse or kosher salt, or to taste
¼	cup peeled and cubed taro or potato

½   cup fresh shiitake mushrooms or white button
     mushrooms, cut into ¼-inch cubes

1   square firm tofu (bean curd), cut into ¼-inch cubes

1   large egg, lightly beaten

1   teaspoon Asian sesame oil

2   tablespoons finely chopped fresh cilantro or basil leaves

To marinate the pork: Mix the soy sauce, brandy and cornstarch; add the pork and mix well. Set aside at room temperature for 15 minutes until ready to use.

To make the soup: Combine the cornstarch and water in a small bowl.

In a large stock pot, add the stock, soy sauce, vinegar, white and cayenne pepper and salt. Blend in the cornstarch mixture. Bring to a boil. Add the pork and simmer over low heat for 30 minutes; the soup should be thick.

Add the taro or potato, mushrooms and tofu. Continue cooking until the taro is tender, about 15 minutes.

The soup may be prepared to this point up to 1 day in advance.

Using a spoon, slowly spread a fine layer of the beaten egg onto the top of the simmering soup in a smooth, thin sheet. Repeat until all the egg is used; do not stir or pour the egg into the soup, or large lumps will form.

When the strands of egg float to the surface, stir in the sesame oil.

Ladle the soup into bowls and garnish with cilantro or basil.

CORNSTARCH

CORNSTARCH IS USED IN CHINA as frequently as flour is in the West — as the preferred thickening agent for soups and sauces, as a coating for foods before they are fried or sautéed and as a tenderizer in marinades for meats and poultry.

Because cornstarch contains no gluten, it will form fewer lumps than wheat flour. As a thickener, it gives a glossy appearance to a clear sauce — much as does a last-minute addition of cold butter — but without the fat.

Most people add cornstarch to soups or sauces at the end of the cooking. I prefer to add it early so that it cooks for a while and loses its raw taste. I mix an equal portion of cornstarch and water, stir it in after adding the stock or other liquid, and cook for at least 30 minutes — sometimes even longer. When the cornstarch is treated this way, the dish never becomes pasty as it cools.

Coating foods that will be fried with cornstarch gives them a crisp texture, and the crust will not become soggy as a flour coating often does.

Wild Mushroom Soup

WILD MUSHROOM SOUP

SERVES 4

WHEN I WENT TO THAILAND IN 1986, I was influenced by the complexity of the cuisine, its fresh taste and the variety of herbs and spices. I was particularly intrigued by the use of coconut milk and have since incorporated it into some of my own recipes. Heavy cream would overwhelm the delicate mushroom essence of this soup; the coconut milk adds richness but does not dominate.

½   ounce dried shiitake mushrooms
    (about 6 medium whole)
¼   pound fresh shiitake mushrooms
¼   pound oyster or chanterelle mushrooms
¼   pound white button mushrooms
¼   cup corn or olive oil
2   shallots, minced
1   tablespoon peeled, grated gingerroot
4   cups chicken stock (page 79)
½   cup unsweetened coconut milk*
½   teaspoon freshly ground white pepper
1   teaspoon cornstarch
1   tablespoon water
1   scallion, thinly sliced, or 6 chives, chopped,
    plus more for garnish
1   tablespoon finely chopped fresh lemon grass** (page 86)
1   tablespoon white vinegar or juice of 1 lemon
    Coarse or kosher salt
    Freshly ground pepper

Place the dried mushrooms in a bowl. Add 4 cups lukewarm water and soak for 30 minutes, or until softened.

Remove the mushrooms from the water; squeeze dry. Discard the water. Remove and discard the stems. Thinly slice the mushroom caps; set aside.

Use a damp cloth to wipe clean all of the fresh mushrooms, keeping the button mushrooms separate. Remove the stems of the shiitake mushrooms only; discard. Cut all the mushrooms into thin slices.

Heat 2 tablespoons of the oil in a large stock pot. Add the shallots and cook until lightly browned, about 2 minutes. Add the gingerroot and the dried and button mushrooms and cook, stirring, over medium heat for 3 minutes.

Add the chicken stock, coconut milk and white pepper to the stock pot.

Combine the cornstarch and water in a small bowl. Mix thoroughly and stir into the soup.

Bring to a boil, then reduce to a simmer. Cover and cook for 30 minutes.

While the soup is cooking, heat the remaining 2 tablespoons oil in a small skillet. Add the sliced fresh shiitake and oyster or chanterelle mushrooms and cook over high heat until soft, about 2 minutes. Keep warm until ready to use.

Add the scallion or chives, lemon grass and vinegar or lemon juice to the soup. Taste to correct the seasonings.

Divide the reserved mushrooms among 4 soup bowls.

Ladle the soup into the bowls and garnish with additional scallions or chives.

*I prefer the Chaokoh brand, which is carried by most Asian grocery stores.

**If fresh lemon grass is not available, substitute another fresh herb, such as thyme.

LEMON GRASS

WHEN I OPENED MY RESTAURANT, many people who worked in the kitchen came from Vietnam, Cambodia and Thailand. I became fascinated with lemon grass, which they often added to stock, grilled meat, fish or chicken and curries. The long stalks of this herb contribute a delicate lemon-perfumed and refreshing taste, without the pronounced acidity that lemon juice brings.

Remove the stem and lower green parts; save for making stock. Peel off and discard the outer layers to release the flavor. Cut the creamy white heart into thin, circular slices, then chop finely. Add lemon grass at the end of the cooking time. It is available dried, but it is best when fresh and will enhance many soups, shellfish and chicken dishes.

BEEF STOCK

MAKES ABOUT 2 QUARTS STOCK

CATTLE ARE VERY SCARCE IN CHINA, so beef is much prized. This is a flavorful, clear stock. When it is brought to the table, the aroma is savored even before the first spoonful is tasted. The recipe is based on a classical Chinese recipe, but I brown the beef bones first and add brandy and lemon grass to make the stock richer.

2	tablespoons corn oil
1	large onion, sliced
4	pounds bone-in beef shank, cut into 3-inch pieces, or beef short ribs
2	scallions, cut into 2-inch lengths
¼	cup chopped fresh lemon grass* (page 86)
6	sprigs fresh cilantro
1	2-inch piece gingerroot, crushed with a cleaver
3	star anise
1	teaspoon roasted Sichuan peppercorns (page 111)
¼	cup brandy
6	quarts water

Heat the oil in a large stock pot and add the onion. Sauté over high heat until soft and lightly browned, 2 to 3 minutes. Add the beef shanks or short ribs and brown well to sear, about 5 minutes.

Add the scallions, lemon grass, cilantro, gingerroot, star anise and Sichuan peppercorns to the stock pot. Cook for about 3 minutes to release the flavors.

Add the brandy. Cover, reduce the heat to medium and cook for about 5 minutes.

Add the water. Increase the heat to high and bring the liquid to a boil. Reduce the heat until the liquid is at a simmer and cook, uncovered, for at least 2½ hours, skimming any froth or scum from the surface as the stock cooks.

Remove the beef bones from the stock. Strain the stock through a fine sieve, discard the solids and skim off the fat. The stock will keep in the refrigerator for up to 1 week or in the freezer for up to 3 months.

*The tough lower green parts may be used because the stock will be strained. Chopped leek may be substituted.

BEEF BROTH WITH PEA SHOOTS, TOMATO AND GINGERROOT

SERVES 4 AS A SOUP COURSE
OR 8 WHEN SERVED BETWEEN COURSES

THIS RECIPE CALLS FOR FRESH GINGER JUICE, made by squeezing freshly grated gingerroot through a piece of cheesecloth or a strainer. The juice has a delicate yet concentrated taste and is added to the soup at the last minute to maintain its full flavor.

2	quarts beef stock (page 87)
1	tablespoon coarse or kosher salt
	Freshly ground pepper
¼	cup peeled, grated gingerroot
2	tablespoons water
½	cup peeled, seeded and diced fresh plum tomato
1	cup fresh pea shoots, washed and dried*
1	tablespoon peeled, finely julienned gingerroot, soaked in ice water (page 213)

Heat the stock in a large stock pot and cook over high heat, uncovered, until reduced by one-third, about 20 minutes. Season with the salt and pepper to taste.

Meanwhile, mix the grated gingerroot with the water. Place a piece of cheesecloth or a fine strainer over a small bowl and pour the ginger-water mixture onto the cloth or strainer. Gather the ends of the cloth together with your hand and squeeze the liquid into the bowl or press down on the ginger with a spoon. Repeat a few times; set the ginger juice aside and save the ginger for use in sautés or discard.

After the stock has reduced, strain it through cheesecloth.

Return the stock to the pot, add the tomato and bring to a boil. Add the fresh ginger juice and the pea shoots. Remove from the heat. Ladle the soup into bowls, garnish with the julienned gingerroot and serve.

*Spinach, arugula, watercress or Swiss chard can be substituted.

PEA SHOOTS

IN TAIWAN, PEA SHOOTS—the very top leaves and tendrils of snow pea vines—are a great delicacy and often one of the most expensive vegetables in the market. They are much smaller and more delicate than the ones available in most Chinese grocery stores in this country. When we lived in Kao-hsiung, my grandmother used to grow them in our garden. It was my job to pick the tiny green shoots. My grandmother added them to soups right before serving or used them in a quick sauté of vegetables. If we didn't have as many in the garden as we needed, I would go with my mother to the market to buy more. When I was older, I was allowed to bicycle there by myself and bring them back, wrapped in an old piece of newspaper.

If you grow your own snow peas, pinch off the tender shoots from the top 2 to 3 inches of the plants and use them, along with other greens, in salad or in soups to add a fresh springlike flavor.

OXTAIL SOUP WITH SAVOY CABBAGE AND TOMATO

SERVES 4 AS A MAIN COURSE OR 8 AS PART OF A MEAL

THE CHINESE LIKE BONES and prefer to eat this soup with the oxtails left whole, served in the broth with the vegetables. Or the oxtails can be cooked in the soup and eaten separately as a second course, if you prefer.

2 pounds oxtails, cut into 1-inch pieces

2 tablespoons olive oil

1 2-inch piece gingerroot, thinly sliced

2 garlic cloves, thinly sliced

4 star anise

1 teaspoon roasted Sichuan peppercorns (page 111)

1 cup dry white wine

2 large tomatoes, peeled and diced

3 quarts water

1 large potato, peeled and diced

½ small head savoy cabbage (about 1 pound), cut into 1-inch pieces

Coarse or kosher salt

Freshly ground pepper

Wash the oxtails thoroughly and pat dry with paper towels.

Heat the oil in a large stock pot. Add the oxtails and cook over high heat, stirring occasionally, for about 10 minutes, or until browned.

Drain all but 2 tablespoons oil from the pot. Add the gingerroot, garlic, star anise and Sichuan peppercorns and cook until the garlic is lightly browned, about 2 minutes.

Add the white wine and cook for ½ hour, uncovered, skimming off any fat or scum as it rises to the surface.

Add half the tomato and the water; bring to a boil. Reduce the heat to medium-low and cook, uncovered, for 2 hours, or until the oxtails are tender.

Strain the soup through a fine sieve, discarding all solids, and return the soup to the stock pot. Reserve the oxtails for a second course, if you like.

Skim any visible fat from the soup and add the potato, the cabbage and the remaining tomato. Cook for 15 to 20 minutes, or until the vegetables are tender.

Add the salt and pepper, taste to correct the seasonings and serve.

FIRST-CLASS SOUP

WHEN I WAS IN COLLEGE in T'aipei in the 1960s, I dreamed of eating in one of the fancy Western restaurants in the first-class hotels in the city. In that dream, the silver shone, pink napkins graced the tables and crystal glasses sparkled in the flickering candlelight.

My wish was finally granted when I graduated from the university and my parents took me out to dinner. I'll never forget the waiter bringing a tureen of oxtail soup to our table and removing the lid. The savory aroma filled the dining room.

To many Chinese, oxtail soup is the quintessential Western dish, and the West, of course, means America. But when I finally came to America, I was surprised to discover that oxtail soup is not a favorite. I still love it for its complexity and richness and serve it as a two-course dinner, with oxtail consommé first, followed by the meat.

TURKESTAN LAMB SOUP
WITH MUNG BEANS

SERVES 6 TO 8

ONE OF THE RECIPES handed down from my mother's side of the family was a mutton soup that was a favorite during the cold winters in Mongolia. My grandmother would have a large pot ready when the family came home from work.

When we lived in Taiwan, my mother and our cook used lamb rather than mutton to make a more refined version. Serve it as a one-dish meal, with Pan-Fried Scallion Bread (page 316) on the side.

½ cup green mung beans*

3 cups water

2 tablespoons corn or olive oil

3 garlic cloves, thinly sliced

2 tablespoons peeled, grated gingerroot

1 pound boneless leg of lamb, cut into ½-inch cubes

2 tablespoons soy sauce

2 tablespoons brandy

3 quarts water

2 star anise

1 tablespoon coarse or kosher salt

1 teaspoon freshly ground roasted Sichuan peppercorns (page 111)

1 cup peeled, diced daikon

1 jalapeño pepper, finely chopped,
  or ½ teaspoon hot red pepper flakes

Soak the mung beans in warm water to cover for 4 hours or overnight; drain. Heat the 3 cups water in a small saucepan and add the mung beans. Bring to a boil over high heat. Cover and lower the heat, and simmer for 30 minutes. The beans should be tender, but not mushy. Skim off any loose shells that float to the top and discard. Set aside the beans and the cooking liquid until needed.

Heat the oil in a large stock pot or Dutch oven. Add the garlic and the gingerroot and cook, stirring, for 2 minutes over high heat, until the garlic is lightly browned.

Add the lamb cubes and continue to cook, stirring occasionally, until the meat is well browned, about 5 minutes.

Stir in the soy sauce and the brandy. Add the water, star anise, salt and Sichuan peppercorns. Bring to a boil, cover, reduce the heat to low and simmer for 1 hour.

Add the daikon, jalapeño pepper or red pepper flakes and the cooked mung beans, along with their liquid, and continue to cook until all is tender, about 30 minutes.

Serve hot.

*Lentils, preferably green, can be substituted for the mung beans and cooked in the same way; they do not need to be soaked.

MUNG BEANS

TINY AND HARD, dried green mung beans are widely used in Chinese cookery. The raw beans must first be soaked in warm water and then simmered until tender. They are similar to green lentils but have a more delicate flavor and are used in soups or rice congee. They are nutritious and are often eaten cold, sprinkled with sugar, in hot weather—the Chinese believe that mung beans cool down the body. When the raw beans are soaked in water, drained, covered and left in a dark place for 3 days, they will sprout and are popular in this form as well.

Raw green mung beans are ground into a flour that can be made into cellophane noodles (see page 279). When their husks have been removed, the beans, either whole or split, are yellow in color. Yellow mung beans are more tender, cook more quickly and are usually used in desserts like rice pudding (page 339).

Both green and yellow mung beans are commonly found in Asian markets. They are usually sold in 1-pound packages. Soak them in water to cover for 4 hours or overnight; drain. Cover with water and cook yellow mung beans for about 10 minutes, or until tender, or green mung beans for about 30 minutes. Store mung beans in a cool, dark place, as they sprout easily.

Fish Stock

Makes about 6 cups

Traditionally in China, a large fish head—often carp or catfish—is first browned in hot oil, then combined with napa cabbage, bean curd and seasonings, covered with water and slowly simmered in a stoneware casserole. We used to sip the rich broth while eating the tender meat from the head.

I know that many people in the United States shrink from cooking fish heads, but I recommend you try a stock made from them just once—its wonderful flavor will change your mind. Use the head from a nonoily fish, such as catfish, carp, grouper, turbot or halibut. It must be very fresh—never try to make fish stock with frozen fish heads or bones.

4	pounds fresh fish heads and bones, heads cleaned, gills removed
3	tablespoons corn oil
3	garlic cloves, crushed
1	2-inch piece gingerroot, with skin, flattened with a cleaver or a knife
1	cup dry white wine
1	celery stalk, sliced
2	scallions, sliced
1	teaspoon roasted Sichuan peppercorns (page 111)
3	quarts water

Thoroughly wash the fish heads and bones under cold running water.

Heat the oil in a large stock pot. Add the fish heads and bones and cook over high heat, stirring frequently, until the heads are white, about 10 minutes.

Add the garlic and gingerroot. Reduce the heat to medium and pour in the wine. Scrape up any bits of fish or vegetables that may have stuck to the bottom and continue to cook for 10 minutes. Add the celery, scallions, Sichuan peppercorns and water to the pot and bring to a boil. Reduce the heat to low and simmer, uncovered, for about 1 hour.

Strain the stock through a fine sieve and discard the solids. The stock will keep in the refrigerator for 2 days or in the freezer for up to 2 months.

DAIKON FISH SOUP

SERVES 4

WHEN I WAS A GUEST in her home during my college years in Taiwan, my then future mother-in-law often made this soup for dinner. She simmered a whole freshwater trout (often called grass fish because of its diet) with julienned daikon. The soup turned creamy white as the fish slowly poached, its flesh becoming tender and moist. I have simplified the recipe by adapting it to fillets.

1	tablespoon cornstarch
1	large egg white, lightly beaten
3	tablespoons vodka
½	teaspoon coarse or kosher salt
4	sea bass, striped bass or other white fish fillets, each about 3 ounces
1	recipe (6 cups) fish stock (page 94) or bottled clam juice
½	pound peeled, julienned daikon* (about 1 cup)
1	tablespoon peeled, grated gingerroot
	Coarse or kosher salt
	Freshly ground pepper
2	tablespoons chopped fresh cilantro leaves

Mix the cornstarch, egg white, vodka and salt in a bowl large enough to hold the fillets. Place the fillets in the mixture and refrigerate for 30 minutes, turning once.

Place the stock or clam juice, daikon and gingerroot in a large stock pot or Dutch oven and bring to a boil over high heat. Reduce the heat to low so the liquid is at a simmer and continue to cook for 30 minutes, or until the daikon is soft. Add the fish fillets and simmer, covered, for 5 minutes, or until the fish is tender. Season to taste with salt and pepper. Garnish with cilantro and serve.

*Napa cabbage can be substituted. Alternatively, spinach can be used; add it at the last minute.

Salmon Congee

SALMON CONGEE

SERVES 4 TO 6

THIS RECIPE combines two classical dishes: a fish soup, in which a thin slice of raw fish is placed in the bottom of a soup bowl and an aromatic broth is ladled over it, and a traditional rice soup, known as congee. Long-grain sweet rice gives a slight thickness to the soup, holds its texture and does not become mushy. Serve as a first course for dinner or as a lunch along with Scallion Pancakes (page 305) and a salad of baby greens.

½	pound salmon fillet
2	tablespoons vodka
1	tablespoon soy sauce
3	tablespoons corn or olive oil
1	celery stalk, finely chopped
3	shallots, minced
1	jalapeño pepper, seeded and finely chopped (optional)
1	tablespoon peeled, grated gingerroot
⅓	cup long-grain white sweet (glutinous) rice* (page 297), washed and drained
¼	pound shrimp, peeled, deveined, cleaned with salt (page 182) and finely chopped
8	cups shrimp, fish or chicken stock (page 105, 94 or 79)
1	tablespoon minced lemon grass (page 86; optional)
	Juice from ½ medium lemon
	Coarse or kosher salt
2	tablespoons chopped fresh thyme or basil leaves

Place the salmon fillet in a shallow dish. Mix the vodka, soy sauce and 1 tablespoon of the oil in a small bowl. Pour over the salmon. Refrigerate for at least 30 minutes, turning once to coat.

Heat the remaining 2 tablespoons oil in a large stock pot. Add the celery, shallots, jalapeño pepper and gingerroot. Sauté over high heat, stirring, for 3 minutes.

Add the rice and shrimp to the stock pot. Stir and add the stock. Bring the liquid to a boil. Reduce the heat, cover and simmer for 15 minutes, stirring occasionally to make sure that the rice does not stick to the bottom of the pot. The rice should be tender and firm, not mushy.

Meanwhile, remove the salmon from the marinade. Slice thinly, on the diagonal, into paper-thin slices 2 inches long and 1 inch wide; you will have 18 to 21 pieces.

Place 3 or 4 slices of salmon in each soup bowl, being careful to keep them in a single layer and not overlap any of the slices. Add the lemon grass, if using, and set aside until the soup is finished.

Remove the soup from the heat and stir in the lemon juice. Season with salt to taste.

Ladle the hot congee over the salmon and garnish with the thyme or basil leaves. With a fork or a knife, gently nudge the salmon to the surface of the soup.

By the time the soup is served, the thinly sliced fish will be sufficiently cooked by the hot liquid.

*Regular long-grain white rice may be substituted.

CONGEE

CONGEE, OR RICE SOUP, plays an important role in Chinese daily life. It is prepared by slowly simmering a small amount of rice in a large quantity of water or stock until it forms a soft, delicate gruel. My grandmother always said the perfect congee must be slightly glutinous and the rice grainy and soft. The liquid and solids should be well incorporated, and the mixture should not separate into layers. The technique of slowly simmering the raw rice so that it releases its starch content into the liquid gives this soup a natural thickness and a complex yet delicate flavor.

Plain rice congee may be eaten at any time of the day—for breakfast, lunch or dinner or even as a midnight snack. It can be thin or thick. Poured into individual soup bowls, it can be served plain or with additional ingredients such as chicken, seafood, beef or vegetables.

My husband's family always has plain rice congee in the morning, with fried eggs, ham, sautéed vegetables, salted peanuts and grilled or smoked fish. My family likes it cooked with sweet potatoes or pumpkin and red or green mung beans. We often ate this soup for dinner, with pancakes, steamed buns and six different entrees.

A basic rule to follow in making a good congee is to use a heavy-bottomed stock pot that will hold at least 4 quarts of liquid. For plain congee, use ½ cup rice to 6 cups water. For a more flavorful soup, the ratio should be ⅓ cup rice to 8 cups stock.

First wash the rice well. Heat the oil and add some finely chopped onion or shallots and cook over high heat, stirring, until golden. Add vegetables (cubed daikon, potato or taro) and herbs (rosemary, tarragon or thyme) and meat (cubed raw beef, pork, lamb or chicken), along with the rice, and mix well. If using wine, brandy or vodka, add it at this point. Add the water or stock and mix well. Cook over high heat until the liquid boils, then reduce the heat and continue to simmer, covered, for about 15 to 20 minutes. Test at this point to be sure that the congee has attained a proper creamy consistency. If not, cook a little longer.

If you are using seafood, fish or leafy vegetables, add them now and continue to cook for another 5 minutes, or until everything is done. Taste to correct the seasonings and serve.

SHRIMP BALL SOUP

SERVES 4 TO 6

WHEN MY FAMILY LIVED IN KAO-HSIUNG, our cook would use shrimp heads and shells to make a flavorful stock and puree the leftover meat to make shrimp balls, which were fluffy and similar to Western quenelles. Usually, he put them in soup, but sometimes, he would fry them and serve them as an appetizer with a dipping sauce. Occasionally, they were a main course, along with sautéed bok choy or baby mushrooms.

I cook the shrimp balls in water rather than in shrimp stock so that they will have a pretty light pink color; stock turns them muddy gray.

1½	pounds fresh shrimp, with heads, or 1 pound frozen shrimp
2	large egg whites
1	teaspoon coarse or kosher salt
¾	teaspoon freshly ground white pepper
1	tablespoon vodka
1	teaspoon Asian sesame oil
1	tablespoon heavy cream
1	recipe (6 cups) shrimp stock (page 105)
½	cup peeled, chopped tomato
¼	cup chopped celery hearts (center yellow-white stalks only)

Wash the shrimp carefully so as not to lose any of the fat from the heads, if they are still attached. Remove the heads, reserving them for stock, and peel the shrimp; devein them and clean with salt (page 182). Pat dry with paper towels.

Beat the egg whites until stiff; set aside.

In a food processor, puree the shrimp. Transfer to a medium bowl and mix in the salt, ¼ teaspoon of the white pepper, vodka and sesame oil. Fold in the cream, then the beaten egg whites. Refrigerate until very cold and firm, for at least 1 hour or overnight.

The shrimp mixture can be made up to 1 day in advance and stored, well covered, in the refrigerator.

Fill a 2-quart pot with water and bring to a boil over high heat, then reduce the heat so the water simmers.

Using a pastry bag or a teaspoon, drop 1-inch balls of the shrimp mixture into the water. If using a teaspoon, keep a bowl of ice water alongside. Dip the teaspoon into the water, then form a ball and place it into the boiling water. Repeat until all the shrimp mixture is used. As they cook, the shrimp balls will double in size. Cook until the shrimp balls float to the surface, about 2 minutes.

Meanwhile, bring the stock to a boil in a large saucepan and add the tomato and celery and the remaining ½ teaspoon white pepper.

Drain the shrimp balls and add to the stock. Remove from the heat, taste and correct the seasonings. Ladle into 4 soup bowls or serve from a tureen.

Seafood Wonton Soup

Seafood Wonton Soup

Makes 40 to 50 wontons; serves 10 to 12

THE VENDORS NEAR MY HIGH SCHOOL sold seafood wonton soup. The wrappers were so thin that you could see the delicate pink-shrimp filling, and the wontons were so small that you could eat them in one bite. They were served in a clear broth topped with chopped mountain celery and fried shallots.

In this recipe, I have added tender salmon and sweet bay scallops to give the filling a more complex flavor. If you halve the soup recipe, make all the wontons at once, but cook only those you need; freeze the rest.

The wontons can also be fried in oil heated to 325 degrees for 3 to 5 minutes, turned until they are golden brown and served as dim sum or a starter.

Wontons

½	pound medium shrimp, peeled, deveined and cleaned with salt (page 182)
¼	pound bay scallops, cleaned with salt
¼	pound salmon fillet, cut into small dice
2	tablespoons vodka
1	large egg white
1	ounce pork fat, finely diced (2 tablespoons), or 2 tablespoons heavy cream
¼	cup finely chopped scallions
1	tablespoon peeled, grated gingerroot
1	teaspoon coarse or kosher salt
½	teaspoon freshly ground white pepper
½	cup finely chopped fresh water chestnuts, jicama or celery heart (center yellow-white stalks only)
1	1-pound package (about 50) thin, square wonton skins (page 27)

Soup

	Double recipe (10 cups) shrimp stock (page 105)
2	plum tomatoes, peeled, seeded and diced
1	cup fresh pea shoots or young spinach leaves
¼	cup julienned fresh basil leaves

To make the wontons: Pat the shrimp and scallops dry with paper towels.

Place the shrimp in a food processor and coarsely chop. Do not puree; the pieces should be discernible. Remove and set aside. Do the same with the scallops.

Place the salmon in a medium bowl and mix in the vodka. Add the shrimp and scallops; set aside.

In a small bowl, lightly beat the egg white with the pork fat or cream, scallions, gingerroot, salt and white pepper until well mixed. Fold in the reserved shrimp mixture and mix well. Stir in the water chestnuts, jicama or celery heart.

Place 1 tablespoon of the shrimp mixture in the center of a wonton skin (A). Moisten the edges of the wonton with a little cold water. Fold one side over to enclose the filling, making a triangle (B). Bring the tips of the base of the triangle together, indenting the filling with your finger, and wrap the tips neatly around in a circle (C). Place each finished wonton (D) on a baking sheet lined with wax paper. Repeat, using the remaining filling and wonton skins.

If you will be cooking the wontons within 2 hours, cover them with damp paper towels and a layer of plastic wrap to keep the dough moist, and refrigerate. Or the wontons can be frozen (see page 27).

To cook the wontons: Fill a large pot with water and bring to a boil over high heat. Place the wontons in the water. Stir with a Chinese strainer or slotted spoon to keep the wontons from sticking together. Add ½ cup cold water to the pot. Return the water to a boil and cook until the wontons float to the top, about 5 minutes. Taste one to see if it is done, and cook for 1 to 2 minutes more if necessary. Remove with a slotted spoon, drain and set aside.

To make the soup: Meanwhile, heat the stock in a large pot. Add the tomatoes and simmer for 3 to 5 minutes.

Place 4 or 5 wontons in the bottom of each soup bowl. Place 3 or 4 pea shoots or a few spinach leaves in the bowl, along with a little of the basil. Ladle the hot stock over all and serve immediately.

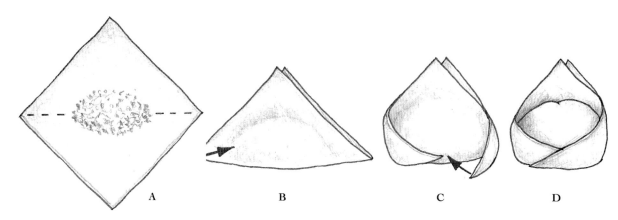

A   B   C   D

SHRIMP STOCK

MAKES ABOUT 6 CUPS STOCK

I N CHINA and throughout Southeast Asia, most of the shrimp used in cooking are fresh, with the heads still attached. Fresh shrimp have a much sweeter taste than frozen ones, and the orange fat in the heads contributes richness to the stock.

You may be able to find fresh shrimp with heads in a Chinese market. Make sure the heads are firmly attached to the body. If the shrimp feel limp or soft or have a fishy odor, they are not fresh. If fresh shrimp are not available, prepare this stock using the shells of frozen shrimp, adding 3 tablespoons dried shrimp.

Whenever you peel shrimp, do not discard the shells. Store them in a plastic bag in the freezer until you have enough to make a pot of stock. They will keep for up to 2 months.

2	tablespoons corn oil
1	small onion, chopped
	Heads and/or shells from 1½ pounds shrimp (about ½ pound shells)
3	tablespoons minced soaked dried shrimp (page 134; optional)
½	cup dry white wine
2	quarts chicken stock (page 79)
1	cup pureed fresh peeled or canned plum tomatoes
2	tablespoons chopped fresh thyme leaves or 1 teaspoon dried
1	teaspoon coarse or kosher salt
½	teaspoon freshly ground pepper

Heat the oil in a large stock pot. Add the onion and sauté over high heat until lightly browned, about 2 minutes.

Add the shrimp heads and/or the shells. Add the dried shrimp, if you have no heads. Cook, stirring, for 3 minutes.

Add the wine and bring to a boil. Add the stock, tomatoes, thyme, salt and pepper and return to a boil.

Reduce the heat to low and simmer, uncovered, for 30 minutes, or until the liquid is reduced and flavorful. Strain the stock through a fine sieve and discard the solids. The stock will keep in the refrigerator for up to 2 days or in the freezer for up to 2 months.

CHAPTER THREE

VEGETABLES AND SALADS

I N NORTHERN CHINA, where my parents came from, the winters were long and cold. Hardy vegetables like cabbage, daikon, potatoes, carrots, sweet potatoes and pumpkin, which stored well, were staples at our table and remained so even after we moved to the warmer climate of Taiwan.

Even in the depth of winter, my family had many dishes made with different kinds of vegetables at each meal. At least one of these was prepared with potatoes, which my mother and grandmother loved best of all. They were stir-fried with carrots and scallions or pan-fried until browned and crisp or lightly blanched and tossed into a crunchy salad.

Salads of all sorts were favorites of ours, though we never ate raw leafy greens, since toxic fertilizers were applied liberally to the soil. As a result, all our vegetables were either peeled, blanched in boiling water or steamed before being marinated in a simple dressing of browned garlic, gingerroot, black vinegar and soy sauce.

In contrast to the north, Taiwan, with its warm temperatures and plentiful rain, was an agricultural paradise. Year-round, the fields were full of all kinds of cabbages and different leafy greens, as well as asparagus, fresh mushrooms—not only straw, shiitake and oyster but many others—numerous varieties of melon and squash, crunchy tiny cucumbers, slender eggplant, small peas and a host of other vegetables whose English names I do not know.

I loved going to the market with my mother or, as I grew older, bicycling there alone in the early morning, wandering among the stalls and selecting produce and fresh-cut flowers. We also had a small vegetable field around our house, where we grew my grandmother's favorite leeks, and I enjoyed puttering in it each day.

WHEN I CAME TO THE UNITED STATES, I was amazed to discover many vegetables I had never before tasted—Brussels sprouts, kale, fennel and zucchini, bitter-tasting vegetables like broccoli rabe, watercress, Belgian endive and radicchio, as well as various kinds of eggplant, tomatoes and potatoes, where we had known only one variety. In addition, I encountered a wondrous multitude of leafy greens that other people seemed to take for granted.

In 1984, Chinese cookbook author Barbara Tropp cooked a dinner at my restaurant as a guest chef. "Why are you using canned bamboo shoots," she asked, "when all the other vegetables in your kitchen are fresh?" Her question freed me of feeling that I had to serve Chinese vegetables, regardless of quality, just because they were traditional. No cans ever again for me!

Now I use only the freshest produce in season: raw salads of baby greens, asparagus, fava beans and artichokes in the spring; zucchini, eggplant and tomatoes in the summer; squash, pumpkins, fennel, napa cabbage and daikon in the fall. I continue to try new vegetables with an open mind, but I still treat them as my mother and grandmother would. I never puree them, and I almost never cook them for a long time. Each vegetable retains its taste and texture, never losing its identity to the whole, and each is of the best possible quality. As they were throughout my childhood, vegetables are the star attractions of my meals.

VEGETABLES AND SALADS

Pickles, Relishes and Salsas

Spicy Cucumbers with Sichuan Peppercorn Vinaigrette   110

Green Cabbage with Sichuan Peppercorn Vinaigrette   113

Sichuan Pickled Vegetables   114

Pickled Napa Cabbage, Daikon and Carrots   117

Sun-Dried Tomatoes, Black Bean and Eggplant Salsa   118

Green Apple and Kumquat Relish   120

Pineapple Salsa   121

Four-Treasure Relish   122

Spicy Persimmon Chutney   125

Brandied Go Chi   126

Salads

Water Chestnut, Arugula and Endive Salad   129

Mango, Jicama and Cucumber Salad   130

Celery Salad with Wasabi Vinaigrette   131

Silver Sprouts with Jicama, Celery and Balsamic Vinaigrette   133

Asparagus with Dried Shrimp Vinaigrette   135

Salad of New Red Potatoes   136

Lotus Root Salad with Go Chi and Chinese Vinaigrette   139

VEGETABLES AND SALADS

Vegetable Dishes

Sautéed Green Beans   140

French Beans and Asparagus with Mushrooms   141

Baked Creamy Napa Cabbage   143

Soy-Braised Chinese Eggplant with Zucchini and Mushrooms   144

Braised Vegetables with Dried Scallops   146

Spicy Mushrooms with Garlic and Black Bean Sauce   147

Sautéed Zucchini with Sun-Dried Tomatoes   148

Oil-Braised Artichoke Hearts   149

Quick Sauté of Vegetables with Chives   150

Broccoli Rabe with Green Peas   151

Pan-Seared Tofu with Scallions and Ginger   152

SPICY CUCUMBERS WITH SICHUAN PEPPERCORN VINAIGRETTE

SERVES 6 TO 8

THIS CRUNCHY, SWEET SALAD is marinated in a garlic-sesame oil vinaigrette. We ate it with most meals when I was growing up. It can be prepared with any type of cucumber, but for the crunchiest texture, seedless are preferable. (See photograph, page 233.)

2   pounds cucumbers, preferably seedless

1   tablespoon coarse or kosher salt

1   jalapeño or Italian hot pepper, cored,
      seeded and julienned

1   tablespoon peeled, julienned gingerroot
      Sichuan Peppercorn Vinaigrette (page 112)

Wash the cucumbers and cut off the ends. Cut each cucumber lengthwise into quarters. Scrape away any seeds with the knife or a spoon. Cut the cucumbers crosswise into ½-inch-wide slices.

Place the cucumbers in a large bowl and toss with the salt. Let stand for 30 minutes. The salt will draw out much of the liquid from the cucumbers.

Transfer the cucumbers to a colander, rinse, drain and place in another bowl.

Add the jalapeño or other hot pepper and gingerroot. Toss and set aside.

Pour the vinaigrette over the cucumbers and mix well. Refrigerate for at least 2 hours. Serve cold.

SICHUAN PEPPERCORNS

SICHUAN PEPPERCORNS are as important in Chinese cookery as black peppercorns are in the Western world. Even though they originated in Sichuan province, they are widely used all over China. These small brown peppercorns have petal-like husks that give off a pleasant fragrance. Inside are tiny black seeds with a taste similar to but a little spicier than that of black peppercorns. The Chinese use these peppercorns for smoking, curing, pickling, braising and making salad dressings and soups.

Sichuan peppercorns are sold by the ounce in Chinese grocery stores as well as in bottles in the Asian section of many supermarkets. They often come packaged in 4-ounce plastic bags. They are usually quite reasonable in price and will last for a long time.

Roasting Sichuan Peppercorns

Sichuan peppercorns should always be roasted to bring out their uniquely pungent aroma before they are added to food.

Heat a heavy skillet until it is very hot, then add the Sichuan peppercorns (I usually roast a whole bag at a time). Turn the heat to medium-low and shake or stir the peppercorns until they are dark brown and their intense smell is released, 15 to 20 minutes. Turn off the heat. Store in a tightly sealed jar. Grind the cooled roasted peppercorns in a peppermill or spice mill as you need them.

SICHUAN PEPPERCORN VINAIGRETTE

MAKES ABOUT ⅓ CUP DRESSING

MANY CHEFS who specialize in the new American cuisine are currently cooking with infused oils—oils in which herbs and spices have been steeped to create a variety of flavors. It's a technique that has long been used in Chinese cooking. This vinaigrette is made with an infused oil flavored with Sichuan peppercorns.

2   tablespoons white wine vinegar
1   tablespoon Infused Sichuan Peppercorn Oil
    (see below), strained
1   tablespoon Asian sesame oil
1   tablespoon sugar
½   teaspoon coarse or kosher salt

Place all of the ingredients in a small bowl or jar and mix well.

INFUSED SICHUAN PEPPERCORN OIL

MAKES 1 CUP OIL

THIS AROMATIC AND FLAVORFUL OIL is perfect for cold marinated vegetable salads, for stir-fried vegetable dishes and in marinades for grilled fish and meat. I also like to use the oil as a base for dipping sauces for mildly flavored dishes, such as pork, steamed chicken or poached or steamed fish.

1   cup corn or olive oil
2   tablespoons roasted Sichuan peppercorns (page 111)
3   garlic cloves

Heat the oil in a small saucepan until very hot. Add the Sichuan peppercorns and the garlic, cook for 2 minutes over high heat, then turn off the heat. When cool, strain and store in a glass bottle.

GREEN CABBAGE WITH SICHUAN PEPPERCORN VINAIGRETTE

SERVES 8 AS A SIDE DISH

THE CABBAGE IN THIS COUNTRY is sweeter and juicier than the variety that I grew up with in Taiwan. Select heads that are firm to the touch, with green, moist-looking leaves. Avoid cabbage that is yellowish and dried-out looking. This recipe is for coleslaw the Chinese way. Serve it as a side dish with Grilled Pork Loin (page 230) or Mandarin Pork with Brandy-Infused Hoisin Sauce (page 232).

1   green cabbage head (about 2 pounds)

1   tablespoon coarse or kosher salt,
     plus more to taste

1   recipe Sichuan Peppercorn Vinaigrette
     (previous page)

2   tablespoons chopped fresh tarragon or parsley leaves
     Freshly ground pepper

Peel off the coarse outer leaves of the cabbage. Cut the head into quarters. Remove and discard the core. Cut the cabbage into fine shreds.

Place the cabbage in a large bowl with the salt. Mix well, cover with a plate to weight down the cabbage and let stand at room temperature for 1 hour. Rinse and drain.

Squeeze out the liquid from the cabbage. Toss the cabbage with the vinaigrette and the fresh tarragon or parsley. Season with pepper and additional salt, if needed.

Sichuan Pickled Vegetables

Makes about 10 cups vegetables

Sichuan Pickled Vegetables are the most popular of all pickled foods in Chinese cuisine. When I lived in Taiwan, almost every household made its own version. With their strong and pungent peppery flavor, they are crisp, crunchy and delightfully refreshing.

They may be served as a salad or as a side dish with grilled meat or chicken, and they are great with sandwiches.

The cold brine can be used over and over again by adding more salt and vodka or gin to restore its strength. The first batch of vegetables is usually sharper and saltier than later batches, with the vegetables becoming mellower and gaining in complexity as time passes. Allow 1 week for the vegetables to sit in the brine. You will need a sterilized 1-gallon glass jar or four 1-quart jars for pickling. (See photograph, page 208.)

Basic Brine

6	cups water
½	cup coarse or kosher salt
1	tablespoon roasted Sichuan peppercorns (page 111), wrapped in cheesecloth
¼	cup peeled, thinly sliced gingerroot
2	dried hot peppers

Pickled Vegetables

2	pounds green cabbage (1 small head)
1	small celery heart (center yellow-white stalks only)
¼	pound French beans, ends trimmed, blanched (optional)*
2	carrots, peeled and julienned
3	fresh jalapeño peppers, preferably red, stems removed, cut lengthwise into quarters
3	tablespoons vodka or gin

To make the brine: In a medium saucepan with no trace of grease, heat the water along with the salt. When the water comes to a boil, add the peppercorns and turn off the heat.

Once the water is cool, add the gingerroot and the hot peppers. The cold brine is now ready to be used for pickling.

To prepare the vegetables: Remove the outer leaves of the cabbage and cut off the base. Quarter the cabbage and remove the core. Cut the cabbage crosswise into strips ½ inch wide by 2 inches long; separate.

Cut the celery heart into slices 2 inches long, then cut each piece in half lengthwise; you should have about 1 cup.

Mix the cabbage, beans (if using), celery heart, carrots and jalapeños and pack them into the glass jar or jars. Pour the brine over all.

Use chopsticks or a spoon and mix so that the brine covers all of the vegetables. Add the vodka or gin. Screw on the lid tightly and let the pickled vegetables marinate at room temperature for ½ day, then store in the refrigerator for at least 1 week.

At the end of that time, open the jar and taste the vegetables. If they still have a raw taste, close the jar and refrigerate for 2 more days.

*To blanch the beans, cook in boiling water in a saucepan with no trace of grease for 2 minutes, or until crisp-tender; drain and rinse in cold water.

DAIKON

DAIKON, ALSO CALLED ORIENTAL RADISH, or *lo pak*, is a member of the radish family but bears little resemblance to ordinary radishes. It is crisp, juicy and sweet. It weighs between 2 and 3 pounds and looks something like a large carrot, with a long, cylindrical shape, tapered root and off-white color. Daikon that are light green at the tapered end are usually denser in texture. If cooked in soups or stews, daikon will season and sweeten the dish. I soak it in ice water before putting it in salad to crisp and mellow it.

Choose small daikon, if possible, as larger ones tend to be spongy and fibrous and have little sweetness or flavor.

Daikon is readily available year-round. However, the fall and winter roots are the most tasty and the mildest; the spring and summer daikon are somewhat sharper and can be dry in the center. Although the daikon's skin is thin, it is usually peeled before cooking.

PICKLED NAPA CABBAGE, DAIKON AND CARROTS

MAKES ABOUT 10 CUPS VEGETABLES

NAPA CABBAGE AND DAIKON, both crunchy and full of flavor, make an excellent wintertime salad. The following recipe is from my mother-in-law. She always keeps a jar of these pickled vegetables in her refrigerator to serve with meat or game or at the beginning of a meal as an accompaniment to pan-fried dumplings.

3	cups water
1	cup white vinegar
½	cup sugar
2	tablespoons coarse or kosher salt
1	napa cabbage (about 2 pounds)
1	daikon (about 1 pound), peeled
1	small carrot
2	small hot red peppers or jalapeño peppers
1	3-inch piece gingerroot, preferably spring ginger (page 213)
2	garlic cloves, minced

Combine the water, vinegar, sugar and salt in a clean, grease-free medium saucepan. Bring to a boil. Remove from the heat; cool.

Cut off the leafy upper half of the cabbage and reserve for another use. You will need only the bottom (stem) ends that have thicker ribs. Cut each ribbed leaf in half lengthwise. Cut again lengthwise into ⅛-inch strips.

Cut the daikon crosswise into thin, round slices, then cut each slice into julienne. Soak in ice water for 5 minutes; drain.

Cut the carrot into fine julienne.

Remove the stems from the peppers and slice crosswise into thin slices.

Peel the gingerroot, unless it is spring ginger, and cut into julienne slices.

Combine all the salad ingredients in a large ceramic bowl or jar and mix well. Pour the vinegar combination over all. Mix well.

Cover and refrigerate for at least 8 hours before using. The relish will keep, immersed in the brine and refrigerated, for up to 2 weeks.

SUN-DRIED TOMATOES, BLACK BEAN AND EGGPLANT SALSA

MAKES ABOUT 2 CUPS SALSA

SUN-DRIED TOMATOES remind me of the flavor of sun-dried cabbage, a popular ingredient in China. The combination of black beans and sun-dried tomatoes imparts a robust flavor to the eggplant. This unusual salsa goes well with grilled fish, such as Coho Salmon Shanghai-Style (page 176), Grilled Tuna with Jalapeño Pepper Puree (page 172) or Pan-Sautéed Pompano (page 174).

1	tablespoon fermented black beans
1	cup water
2	tablespoons vodka
6	halves sun-dried tomato (not oil-packed)
3	tablespoons corn or olive oil
1	Chinese eggplant, about 8 inches long, trimmed, cut into ½-inch dice* (about 2 cups)
½	cup diced onion
1	jalapeño pepper, finely chopped
1	large tomato, peeled and diced

Place the black beans in a small bowl. Add the water and soak for 2 minutes. Drain well and return the beans to the bowl. Add the vodka and mix to combine.

Place the sun-dried tomatoes in another small bowl and add warm water to cover. Soak for 5 to 10 minutes, or until the tomatoes are tender. Drain well and dice; set aside.

Heat 2 tablespoons of the oil in a large nonstick skillet. Add the eggplant and cook over high heat for 5 minutes, or until the eggplant is tender. Using a slotted spoon, remove the eggplant; set aside.

Heat the remaining 1 tablespoon oil in the skillet and add the onion. Cook over high heat until the onion is tender and golden, about 5 minutes.

Add the black beans, sun-dried tomatoes and jalapeño pepper to the skillet. Cook until all the ingredients are heated through, about 2 minutes.

Remove from the heat and stir in the eggplant and fresh tomato. Spoon into a serving bowl. The salsa may be prepared 1 day in advance and refrigerated.

*Italian, white or ordinary eggplant, peeled and salted to remove bitter juices, may be substituted; see page 145.

FERMENTED BLACK BEANS

When I lived with my parents in Kao-hsiung, Taiwan, our Cantonese neighbor Mrs. Young always made her own fermented black beans. She would mix black soybeans with salt, spices and gingerroot and let them sit out to ferment. She then sun-dried this concoction in her backyard for many days.

During that time, the whole neighborhood acquired a pronounced smell, and my mother would complain that the odor was offensive. It was not until I met my future mother-in-law, came to this country and married that I began to appreciate their unique taste and use them.

Fermented black beans add a robust flavor to many foods. They should be washed in plenty of water in a large bowl to remove some of the salt and take away most of the odor. Drain and squeeze any remaining water out of the beans with your hands. I then soak the beans in some vodka or gin.

Dried fermented black beans, which are often simply called "dried black beans," are usually sold in plastic bags or small jars in supermarkets or Chinese markets and keep indefinitely in a closed jar stored at room temperature.

GREEN APPLE AND KUMQUAT RELISH

MAKES ABOUT 2 CUPS RELISH

K UMQUATS ARE TINY oval-shaped members of the citrus family with smooth, yellow-orange skin. This skin is edible, and the whole fruit is often eaten raw. Kumquats are a favorite among the Chinese because of their outer sweet skin and inner tart flesh—an unusual and refreshing flavor combination.

Kumquats are readily available fresh, especially in the wintertime, and can be stored in the refrigerator for up to 4 weeks.

In this recipe, the apples retain their crunchy texture and blend with the sweet-sour flavor of the kumquats. Slicing the kumquats releases their pleasurably citrus taste. Serve with Honey-Grilled Lamb Chops with Jalapeño Pepper Puree (page 244) or Tea-Smoked Cornish Hens (page 209).

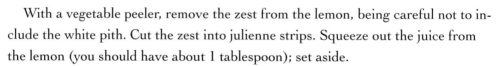

1	small lemon
3	tablespoons butter
2	tablespoons peeled, minced gingerroot
4	kumquats, thinly sliced, seeds removed
1	small jalapeño pepper, seeded and minced
4	large Granny Smith apples, peeled and cubed
¼	cup sugar

With a vegetable peeler, remove the zest from the lemon, being careful not to include the white pith. Cut the zest into julienne strips. Squeeze out the juice from the lemon (you should have about 1 tablespoon); set aside.

Heat 2 quarts of water in a saucepan. When it comes to a boil, add the lemon zest and cook over high heat for 5 minutes. Drain and rinse under cold water. Drain again; this will remove the bitter taste.

Combine the lemon zest, butter, gingerroot, kumquats and jalapeño pepper in a large saucepan. Cook over high heat, stirring, for 1 minute; do not allow the butter to brown.

Add the apples, lemon juice and sugar. Bring this mixture to a boil.

Reduce the heat to a simmer, then cook for 2 more minutes, or until the sugar is melted.

Remove from the heat and serve at room temperature. The relish will keep in the refrigerator, covered, for about 3 days.

PINEAPPLE SALSA

MAKES ABOUT 3 CUPS SALSA

THIS EASY-TO-PREPARE SALSA is delicious served with seafood dim sum, such as One-Hundred-Corner Crab Cakes (page 49). It adds a spicy touch to hot or cold roast pork. Or serve on top of Scallion Pancakes (page 305). See photograph, page 48.

1	cup coarsely chopped fresh pineapple, preferably very ripe
2	large tomatoes, peeled, seeded and coarsely chopped
¼	cup coarsely chopped red onion
1	jalapeño pepper, cored, seeded and finely chopped
½	cup finely chopped fresh cilantro leaves
½	cup bottled Bloody Mary mix*
1	teaspoon coarse or kosher salt
	Freshly ground pepper
	Juice of 1 lime

Combine all the ingredients in a bowl. Mix well and allow to stand for 1 hour before serving. This salsa can be refrigerated, covered, for up to 1 week.

*Bloody Mary mix is available in most supermarkets and liquor stores.

Four-Treasure Relish

Makes about 2 cups relish

I N THE SUMMERTIME, my mother often made a dish with fresh soybeans, fresh peanuts, mushrooms and diced bean curd, which she held in reserve in the refrigerator for lunch or dinner. I was crazy about the relish and usually ate most of it myself. I have modified this dish somewhat and added fresh corn because of its excellent quality and flavor in this country.

This relish is best when prepared in the summer from fresh, young vegetables. Serve it with grilled fish or meat.

½ cup fresh soybeans,* shelled

3 tablespoons corn oil

1 cup diced white button mushrooms

4 scallions, white part only, diced

1 cup fresh corn kernels

1 tablespoon soy sauce

1 teaspoon coarse or kosher salt

¼ cup chicken stock (page 79)

1 large, ripe tomato, peeled, seeded and diced

Freshly ground pepper

Place the soybeans in a small saucepan. Add water to cover and cook over high heat for 3 minutes, or until just tender. Drain and set aside.

Heat the oil in a medium skillet. Add the mushrooms and scallions and cook over high heat, stirring occasionally, until the mushrooms are tender, about 3 minutes.

Add the corn, soybeans, soy sauce, salt and stock to the skillet. Cook for about 3 minutes, or until the corn is tender and the stock has been absorbed. Add the tomato and cook for 1 minute, just until hot.

Remove from the heat and spoon into a serving bowl. Season to taste with lots of freshly ground pepper. This relish is best at room temperature.

*If you can't find fresh soybeans, use fresh green peas.

FRESH SOYBEANS

WHEN MY HUSBAND AND I moved to Valparaiso, Indiana, in 1976, my father-in-law came to visit us. The nearby farmland reminded him of Hunan province, where he had spent his childhood, and he decided to buy a 60-acre piece of land, which he rented to a local farmer to grow a crop of soybeans each year. At the end of July, for the four years we lived in Indiana, my mother- and father-in-law visited us, and we picked soybeans when the pods were plump. We boiled the young and tender beans to eat as an evening snack. My mother-in-law would wrap and freeze the whole soybean pods and take them back to Philadelphia to give to her friends.

The farmers who were our neighbors were amazed at what we regarded as a commonplace yet delicious food. They had never seen soybeans eaten fresh but waited until late in October to harvest them, when they were dried and hard, and used them for animal fodder or exported them to Asia for making into soybean oil.

The outer green shells of fresh soybeans have a fuzzy coating, earning them a Chinese name that translates as "hairy bean." When soybeans are peeled, the inside is green, smooth and sweet. They resemble baby lima beans but are only about one-third the size, and they have a slightly sweet taste, less sweet than fresh peas but sweeter than fava beans.

I often surprise guests by offering this treat when entertaining. Cook the whole bean pods in boiling water for about 5 minutes. Drain and cool the beans and serve them plain, while still in the pod, and squeeze out the fresh-flavored beans with your teeth to eat as a snack.

You can find fresh soybeans in Chinese grocery stores in the late summer. Although not as good as fresh, frozen packaged soybeans, both shelled and in the pod, are sold all year long.

FUYU PERSIMMONS
(SHARON FRUIT)

PERSIMMONS HAVE BEEN CULTIVATED for centuries in many parts of the world. In Taiwan, we enjoyed two kinds. The first, Hachiya persimmons, are most familiar to Westerners. Dome-shaped, they look something like a tomato and turn a deep reddish orange color when ripe. We peeled them and ate them out of hand: they were juicy, sticky and delicious. Unless fully ripe and soft, these persimmons are bitter and unpleasant to eat. I like to use them in sorbet (page 328).

The second type of persimmon was my favorite. Called the Fuyu persimmon, it is apricot-colored and shaped like a plum, with a crisp texture and a mild, sweet taste. These persimmons need no embellishment: just peel, core and eat them raw. I use Fuyu persimmons in chutney, and in the wintertime, when fresh mangos are not available, I cut them into 1-inch cubes and use them in Chicken with Mango, Asparagus and Ginger (page 199). Like apples, they are also excellent braised with pork.

Fuyu persimmons are grown in California. In Israel, where they are also common, they are called Sharon Fruit. Choose Fuyu persimmons with smooth but shiny orange skins. The fruit should be firm, with no visible black spots. If the skin is more yellow than orange, the fruit has been picked before it is ripe; it will have little flavor and an unpleasant raw taste. Store in a cool, dry place—Fuyu persimmons develop black spots if left in the refrigerator for very long.

Both varieties of persimmons are harvested in the fall and are available from late summer until January.

SPICY PERSIMMON CHUTNEY

MAKES ABOUT 1½ CUPS CHUTNEY

M Y MOTHER OFTEN SERVED FUYU PERSIMMONS this way as a dessert during the Chinese New Year Festival; she said the round shape and orange-red color signified good fortune as long as the whole family was together.

The following recipe uses very firm, crisp persimmons. Serve this chutney with a rack of lamb, Tea-Smoked Pompano (page 169) or Roast Chicken with Black Bean Sauce (page 196).

4	Fuyu persimmons, ripe but still firm
¼	cup honey
2	tablespoons fresh lemon juice
1	tablespoon peeled, minced gingerroot
¼	teaspoon almond extract
¼	cup sliced almonds

Peel and dice the persimmons. Place them in a medium bowl and immerse in ice water to prevent them from browning; drain.

Combine the persimmons, honey, lemon juice and gingerroot in a medium saucepan.

Bring to a boil over medium heat. Continue to cook, stirring frequently, for 5 minutes, or until the persimmons are slightly softened. Remove from the heat and stir in the almond extract and the sliced almonds.

Cool to room temperature. This chutney can be refrigerated in a sealed container for up to 1 week.

Brandied Go Chi

Makes 1 cup

G O CHI CONTRIBUTE A HINT OF SWEETNESS to chicken, game or soups. This recipe is my own creation; cooking the *go chi* in orange juice and adding brandy heightens their flavor. I sprinkle brandied *go chi* over salads or add them to chicken soups or braised fowl, especially chicken, just before serving.

1   cup *go chi*

2   cups water

½   cup orange juice

1   tablespoon fresh lemon juice

2   tablespoons brandy

Soak the *go chi* in the water for 2 minutes. They will swell. Drain and rinse well in cold water to remove any dirt; drain well.

Place the orange juice and lemon juice in a medium saucepan. Bring to a boil and add the *go chi*. Mix well, turn off the heat and add the brandy. Cool.

When cool, use immediately or store in a jar in the refrigerator. The *go chi* will keep for up to 1 month.

Go Chi

G O CHI are members of the berry family. Usually sold dried, they are about the size of raisins, oval-shaped with few wrinkles and a beautiful bright red color. They are moderately sweet, with just a tinge of bitter and sour overtones and a flavor reminiscent of dried cherries.

My mother would often steam a whole chicken, ginger and *go chi* berries together. The broth would take on a reddish gold color with a hint of sweetness from the *go chi*. Because of their beautiful color, *go chi* lend a decorative appeal to many dishes. They are also used in Chinese households for medicinal purposes, since they are considered good for the blood.

Go chi have been imported from eastern China since the early 1980s and can be found in most Chinese grocery stores. They come packed in 1-pound boxes, usually with cellophane windows so that you can see the condition of the berries. Buy them only if they are bright red. If they have turned brown and are very wrinkled, they are too old. The larger they are, the more expensive.

WATER CHESTNUTS

WHEN I WAS A LITTLE GIRL, I always volunteered to help peel fresh water chestnuts alongside my grandmother and the cook. I wasn't much help, for I would eat them as fast as they were peeled.

While water chestnuts are generally used in cooked dishes, I like them best raw and often use them in salads. Their fresh, crispy-sweet taste is incomparable—canned ones taste like potatoes by comparison.

Water chestnuts are grown in man-made water-storage ponds among the rice paddies in southern China. The aquatic bulbs of an Asian marsh plant, they grow in ponds with muddy bottoms, and their leaves float on the surface of the water. The outer skin of the water chestnut is a dark reddish mahogany brown; the inside flesh is white, crisp and slightly sweet. It resembles a daffodil bulb.

Since the early 1980s, fresh water chestnuts have been flown in from China and are available in Chinese grocery stores and even in some specialty food markets. They come packed in large wooden crates and are often still covered with mud. Select water chestnuts with hard, large, unwrinkled shells that have no soft spots. Every outside defect means a bruised inside with a bitter taste. Before buying, rub off some of the mud to check the shell—it should shine with a lacquer-like luster.

I wash the water chestnuts as soon as I get them home from the market to remove the mud. They will keep for much longer if they have no bruises and can be refrigerated for up to 2 weeks. Wash, dry and store, wrapped in paper towels, in the refrigerator.

But a more reliable way to keep them fresh is to cut off both ends immediately and peel the chestnuts with a small paring knife or a vegetable peeler, wash and immerse them in a bowl of ice water. (Like peeled apples, water chestnuts turn brown once their flesh is exposed to the air.) Prepared this way, they will last for 1 to 2 weeks in the refrigerator. This method keeps the water chestnuts crisp and prevents any bad nuts from spoiling the rest of the batch.

Water Chestnut, Arugula and Endive Salad with "Honeyed" Walnuts

WATER CHESTNUT, ARUGULA AND ENDIVE SALAD

SERVES 6

THE CRUNCH OF THE FRESH WATER CHESTNUTS, the tang of the balsamic vinegar, the nutty taste of the arugula—all contribute to this salad. There is no substitute for fresh water chestnuts.

Balsamic Vinaigrette

3   tablespoons extra-virgin olive oil

2   tablespoons balsamic vinegar

1   teaspoon peeled, minced gingerroot

1   teaspoon coarse or kosher salt

Freshly ground pepper

1   pound fresh water chestnuts, peeled and washed

2   Belgian endives

¼   pound arugula,* stems removed; washed and dried

½   cup "Honeyed" Walnuts (page 59; optional)

1   tablespoon minced fresh chervil leaves, for garnish (optional)

To make the vinaigrette: Combine all the ingredients and stir well to blend. Set aside.

Cut each water chestnut into thin slices and set aside in a bowl of cold water until needed, to keep them from turning brown.

Cut off the stem end of the Belgian endives. Remove the large outer leaves (you will need 12 of them). Cut each leaf in half lengthwise and place in a large bowl filled with ice water to crisp the leaves. Julienne the remaining smaller inner leaves and immerse them in another bowl of ice water.

Just before serving, drain and dry the water chestnuts and the julienned endive. Place them in a bowl, add the vinaigrette and mix well.

Place 4 of the halved endive leaves around the perimeter of each of 6 salad plates. Mound some of the arugula in the center of each plate. Spoon the water chestnut mixture over the top and garnish with the walnuts, if using. Decorate with the chervil leaves, if using.

*I prefer tender baby arugula.

JICAMA

IN TAIWAN, we always ate jicama raw, never cooked, peeling it and eating it much like an apple, savoring its crunch and juicy sweetness. Called "mud melon" for its brown skin, huge size and rounded shape, the jicama can range in size from ½ pound to as much as 4 pounds. Choose only those that are smooth, unbruised and free from moldy spots. Jicama will keep in the refrigerator for 2 to 3 weeks. Cut, peeled and washed, it can be stored in ice water to keep it white and crisp. Raw jicama lends a delightful crunch and a refreshing sweetness to salads.

MANGO, JICAMA AND CUCUMBER SALAD

MAKES ABOUT 3 CUPS SALAD; SERVES 6 TO 8

THE CRUNCH OF THE CUCUMBER, the crispness of the jicama and the soft sweetness of the mango combine to make this a beautifully refreshing salad. Be sure to select tender, slim cucumbers with deep green skins. The long variety is best, if available, because it has fewer seeds.

1	cup peeled, seedless cucumber, cut into ½-inch dice
1	tablespoon coarse or kosher salt, plus more to taste
1	cup jicama, cut into ½-inch cubes
¼	cup minced red onion
2	cups ice water
1	medium mango (ripe but still firm), peeled and diced
1	jalapeño pepper, seeded and minced
3	tablespoons fresh lemon juice
2	tablespoons extra-virgin olive oil
1-2	tablespoons chopped fresh mint leaves (optional)

Mix the cucumber with the 1 tablespoon salt and let stand for 10 minutes. Rinse and drain.

Soak the jicama and the onion in the ice water for 2 minutes; drain.

In a medium bowl, mix the cucumber, jicama, onion, mango, jalapeño pepper, lemon juice and oil. Taste and season with more salt, if desired.

Refrigerate. This salad can be prepared up to 4 hours in advance.

Serve cold as a relish, garnished with the mint leaves, if using.

CELERY SALAD WITH WASABI VINAIGRETTE

SERVES 6 TO 8 AS A SALAD COURSE

ABOUT 15 YEARS AGO, American celery was exported to Taiwan and became an immediate hit. Now, whenever I visit, one of my mother's friends makes me a celery salad like this one. It is a good starter course.

2	pounds celery hearts
	(center yellow-white stalks only)
1	teaspoon coarse or kosher salt
½	teaspoon sugar
2	tablespoons white wine vinegar or
	fruit-flavored vinegar
2	tablespoons Infused Sichuan Peppercorn Oil (page 112)
1	tablespoon wasabi powder, mixed with 1 tablespoon water*

With a vegetable peeler, remove and discard the outer stringy stalks of the celery. Trim and cut the stalks into 2-inch lengths, then lengthwise in half. Cook the celery pieces in a large pot of boiling salted water for about 3 minutes, or until they are just tender. Drain and refresh under cold water; drain again.

Place the celery in a large bowl. Stir in the salt, sugar and vinegar. Refrigerate until ready to serve.

Right before serving, drain the celery well and discard the vinegar mixture. Add the Sichuan peppercorn oil and the wasabi and mix well. Refrigerate and serve cold.

*Wasabi has a very strong and spicy flavor, somewhere between mustard and horseradish. The amount used can be increased or decreased according to your taste. Powdered wasabi can be found in Asian grocery stores and in some supermarkets. Mix it with the water and let sit for 10 minutes to develop its flavor. Store this mixture in the refrigerator until ready to use. Wasabi is also available in paste form and comes in 1-ounce tubes. The paste does not have the same bite as the freshly mixed powder; it does not need to be mixed with water.

If you have trouble finding wasabi powder, mix 1 tablespoon hot mustard powder with 1 tablespoon water and 1 teaspoon white wine vinegar; let sit for 10 minutes.

BEAN SPROUTS

ONE OF THE MOST MEMORABLE MEALS in my life took place when I was invited to my sister-in-law's mother's house in T'aipei. She prepared dinner using only simple ingredients of the finest quality—every dish was light and bursting with flavor. She made a dish from bean sprouts that was the best I have ever eaten. Every single snowy white sprout was beautifully trimmed—she used only the middles—and barely cooked, served with some finely julienned spring gingerroot and just a touch of vinegar.

In China, it is unthinkable for most people to use bean sprouts without first removing the root. Whole bean sprouts with the roots still attached have an unclean look and an unpleasant flavor. For banquet dishes, both the root and head ends are removed; when prepared this way, they are often called "silver sprouts."

Both green and yellow bean sprouts are commonly used in Chinese cooking. Green bean sprouts, grown from green mung beans, are much preferred. They are more delicate, easier to grow and readily available in most supermarkets. Yellow bean sprouts, grown from soybeans, are bigger and more fibrous than the green. The best bean sprouts are 2½ to 3 inches long and pure white in color, have no bruises and are heavy for their size. Smaller sprouts have little flavor.

Bean sprouts are usually blanched for a moment in boiling water. Rinse immediately in cold water to stop the cooking, then drain well and use in salad. Or add to a sautéed dish just before removing from the heat and cook for 1 to 2 minutes.

SILVER SPROUTS WITH JICAMA, CELERY AND BALSAMIC VINAIGRETTE

SERVES 8 AS A SIDE DISH

MY MOTHER often serves this salad as one of several dishes along with Scallion Pancakes (page 305) or bread. It is especially good in the summer, with grilled fish or meat. Or serve on top of cooked rice noodles as a light vegetarian course for lunch. (See photograph, page 245.)

1	pound bean sprouts, tops and roots pinched off
1	carrot, peeled and julienned
½	cup julienned celery hearts (center yellow-white stalks only)
1	small jicama (about ½ pound), peeled and julienned
3	tablespoons olive oil
2	shallots, thinly sliced
2	tablespoons balsamic vinegar
	Coarse or kosher salt
	Freshly ground pepper
2	tablespoons chopped fresh chervil or tarragon leaves

Fill a medium saucepan with water and bring to a boil. Add the bean sprouts and remove after 30 seconds with a slotted spoon or Chinese strainer. Rinse under cold water. The sprouts should still be very crunchy, but the raw taste will be gone. Drain and place in a large bowl.

Add the carrot and the celery to the boiling water and cook over high heat for 2 minutes, or until tender but still crunchy. Rinse under cold water and drain well. Add to the sprouts along with the jicama.

Heat the oil in a small saucepan. Add the shallots and cook until they are lightly browned, about 3 minutes. Turn off the heat.

Add the vinegar to the saucepan; pour this dressing over the vegetables. Season with salt and pepper to taste. Add the chervil or tarragon and toss.

Mix well and serve.

DRIED SHRIMP AND DRIED SCALLOPS

IN ANCIENT TIMES IN CHINA, there was no refrigeration for the long-term storage of food and no well-developed transportation system for moving perishables from one place to another. The Chinese developed the technique of drying foods in order to preserve them better, and they applied it to all types of edibles—meats, seafood, vegetables and fruits. People living along the coast of China sun-dried shrimp, scallops, mussels, squid, clams and fish. Today, the Chinese still use dried seafood to enhance the flavor of vegetables, soups and stuffings. Prepared correctly, dried seafood imparts a mysterious depth of flavor that is not at all "fishy." People are always surprised to hear that the delicious taste of many of my vinaigrettes and vegetable dishes comes from dried shrimp.

Dried Shrimp

Dried shrimp are the most commonly used of all dried seafood. Traditionally, they are added whole, but I find their flavor too strong. Instead, I soak them in hot water to cover for 10 to 15 minutes to soften them, drain well, then mince in a food processor or by hand. Prepared in this manner, they do not overwhelm the finished dish, producing a much more delicate effect. The minced soaked dried shrimp can be refrigerated in a tightly sealed jar for up to 2 weeks or frozen for up to 3 months.

Dried shrimp come in different sizes, the larger being more expensive. Be sure to buy shrimp with a golden reddish color; they are usually fresher.

Dried Scallops

Dried scallops are an even greater delicacy, for their flavor is much more subtle than that of dried shrimp. They are often served at formal banquets in such dishes as Braised Vegetables with Dried Scallops (page 146).

Dried scallops have to soak in warm water for about 1 hour, or until they are soft, before they can be added to soups or vegetables. Unlike dried shrimp, the scallops, when soaked and cooked, soften into delicate, tender shreds, blending into the finished dish.

Dried scallops come in different sizes. The larger the scallops, the higher the price. They are commonly sold by the ounce.

ASPARAGUS WITH DRIED SHRIMP VINAIGRETTE

SERVES 4 AS A SALAD OR 8 AS A SIDE DISH

THIS SWEET, TENDER VEGETABLE is one of my favorites. I prefer to use the mid-sized stalks—they seem to have more flavor than those with either very thick or very thin stems. Select asparagus that is green and firm, with tightly closed heads. The addition of dried shrimp to the vinaigrette dressing lends a special touch to this salad.

¼ cup Infused Sichuan Peppercorn Oil (page 112)

1 tablespoon minced soaked dried shrimp

½ teaspoon peeled, grated gingerroot

2 tablespoons balsamic vinegar

1 teaspoon soy sauce

1 teaspoon sugar

1 teaspoon coarse or kosher salt

2 pounds asparagus, washed and trimmed

Heat the oil in a small saucepan. When the oil is hot, add the dried shrimp and immediately remove the pan from the heat. Stir in the gingerroot, vinegar, soy sauce, sugar and salt and mix until thoroughly combined.

The vinaigrette may be prepared 1 day in advance. The flavor of the shrimp will be stronger and richer if the vinaigrette is refrigerated overnight.

Cut the asparagus on the diagonal into 2-inch pieces.

Bring a large pot of lightly salted water to a boil. Add the asparagus and cook until just tender, about 3 minutes. Do not overcook, or the asparagus will be limp. Rinse under cold running water to stop the cooking, and drain well; set aside.

Just before serving, combine the asparagus and vinaigrette in a large bowl, toss gently, taste and correct the seasonings and serve.

SALAD OF NEW RED POTATOES

SERVES 4 TO 6

THE CRISP TEXTURE of my mother's salad makes it unlike the typical American version. New potatoes have a natural sweetness that undercooking brings out. I usually serve the salad with Braised Spareribs (page 239) or Crispy Duck with Star Anise Sauce (page 214), but it goes equally well with fish dishes or cold sliced meats. (See photograph, page 238.)

1 pound new red potatoes

2 tablespoons fresh lemon juice

2 tablespoons corn oil

2 garlic cloves, finely minced

1 teaspoon coarse or kosher salt

1 jalapeño pepper, seeded and julienned,
   or ½ teaspoon hot red pepper flakes

1 tablespoon chopped fresh peppermint
   or other mint leaves

1 tablespoon balsamic vinegar (optional)

Scrub the potatoes and cut into julienne. As you cut, immediately place the potatoes in a bowl filled with cold water and wash under cold running water to remove any excess starch.

Bring 2 quarts of water to a boil over high heat and blanch the potatoes for 2 minutes, just until they become transparent and lose their raw taste.

Drain the potatoes and place them in a colander. Rinse under cold running water to stop the cooking.

Place the potatoes in a medium bowl and toss with the lemon juice; they should be crisp and white. Set aside.

Heat the oil in a small skillet. Add the garlic and cook over high heat, stirring, for 1 minute. Remove from the heat. Add the salt and the jalapeño pepper or hot pepper flakes. Stir to mix.

Spoon the garlic mixture over the potatoes and toss gently to combine. Add the chopped mint, toss again, and refrigerate for at least 1 hour, or until ready to serve.

Sprinkle the balsamic vinegar, if using, over the potato salad just before serving.

SWEET MEMORIES

IT IS NOT POSSIBLE for me to think of the years when I was growing up in the southern Taiwan countryside without remembering those carefree summer days spent picking lotus flowers by the water fields in which they grew.

As a child, I used to press the petals between the pages of my textbooks, and I enjoyed nibbling the tender, sweet lotus seeds. By the time fall came, the various dishes prepared from its crunchy roots were my passion.

Lotus grows throughout China and is considered by the Buddhists to be a symbol of purity. The plant has its roots in the mud, yet it is able to produce a beautiful flower. Leaves, seeds and roots—almost all parts of the lotus plant are edible and are much favored by the southern Chinese.

When my husband and I lived in Tallahassee, Florida, we found fresh lotus plants growing in the swamplands. We would often cut the leaves and pick some of the seeds to eat. They brought back poignant memories of my childhood.

LOTUS

Lotus Roots

Whenever I work with lotus roots, I never cease to be amazed at God's creation of such an exquisite vegetable. When sliced, its hidden beauty is made evident—a flower pattern formed by the holes becomes visible.

The roots are yellow-brown, and the tuberous stems grow to about 2 inches in diameter and 8 inches in length. Lotus roots grow underwater and can reach up to 3 feet in length. They grow in segments resembling the arms of a chubby baby. The root is starchy, much like a potato, and when peeled and lightly poached in boiling water, it has a crisp texture and a pure white color, with a delicate, faintly sweet taste.

Lotus roots can be stir-fried so they retain their crunchiness. They can be sautéed with a mixture of other vegetables, such as Shanghai bok choy, mushrooms and fresh bamboo shoots. They are often cooked with pork ribs in a soup, where they add body and flavor.

Since 1980, I have been lucky enough to get fresh lotus roots from a local Chinese market. They come packed in wooden crates, flown here directly from mainland China. They are available from the end of September until March.

Choose lotus roots that have smooth skin, with no blemishes or black spots. The whole root will keep in the refrigerator for no more than 1 week.

When I bring lotus roots home from the market, I usually peel them immediately with a vegetable peeler, then slice them and immerse in cold water. Covered and refrigerated, they will last that way for up to 2 weeks. Or they can be blanched in boiling water, drained and, when cool, stored in a container of olive oil until needed; they will keep for 1 week, and the olive oil can be reused.

Lotus Seeds

After the lotus flower fades, the pod gradually grows 3 to 4 inches in diameter. Tiny holes form in the center, in which seeds grow. The lotus seeds in Chinese grocery stores in this country are usually dried and come in ½- or 1-pound packages. They are white, with a nut-like flavor similar to that of chestnuts. Since they are more delicate than chestnuts, they need less time for cooking and so are easier to handle. They are most often used for soups and stuffings. They can also be candied, and, in this sweet form, are used as pastry fillings.

Soak dried lotus seeds in warm water for 1 hour before cooking, until they swell to almost double in size. Bring ½ cup seeds, 2 cups water and 1 tablespoon sugar to a boil and simmer, uncovered, for 15 minutes, to partially cook them; drain. Add the cooked seeds to soups, or stew them along with meat, or use them in stuffing, as in Eight-Treasure Duck (page 217).

LOTUS ROOT SALAD WITH GO CHI AND CHINESE VINAIGRETTE

SERVES 4

BLANCHED LOTUS ROOTS remain crisp and have a slight sweetness. In this dish, they are served over salad greens. The *go chi* add a note of color. (See photograph, page 250.)

Chinese Vinaigrette

¼ cup extra-virgin olive oil

2 tablespoons peach or other fruit vinegar

1 tablespoon minced soaked dried shrimp (page 134)

1 teaspoon peeled, grated gingerroot

1 teaspoon coarse or kosher salt

1 tablespoon minced fresh cilantro leaves

Freshly ground pepper

Lotus Root

1 pound fresh lotus roots

1 tablespoon fresh lemon juice

2 tablespoons Brandied Go Chi (page 126)

1 small Belgian endive or radicchio

4 ounces baby greens, such as mâche or arugula (about 2 cups)

To make the vinaigrette: Mix all the ingredients in a jar until well blended. This dressing will taste best if made 1 day ahead and refrigerated. Mix again just before serving.

To prepare the lotus roots: Bring a small pot of water to a boil. Peel the lotus roots with a vegetable peeler and cut crosswise into very thin slices. Blanch in the boiling water until transparent, about 1 minute. Rinse under cold water and drain well. Place in a medium bowl and mix with the lemon juice to keep them from turning brown. Refrigerate until needed.

Mix the *go chi* with 1 tablespoon of the Chinese vinaigrette; set aside.

To assemble: At serving time, toss the lotus root with the remaining vinaigrette. Arrange 4 Belgian endive or radicchio leaves on each of 4 plates. Place a mound of the greens in the center of the plates. Divide the lotus root among the plates, arranging them on top of the greens, and decorate with the *go chi.*

SAUTÉED GREEN BEANS

SERVES 6 TO 8

A FAVORITE CLASSICAL DISH is twice-cooked green beans, in which the beans are first deep-fried, then stir-fried. Boiling them just until they are tender and briefly sautéing them produces a less oily, much fresher result. Use the freshest and most tender green beans you can find.

1½	pounds green beans (preferably thin French beans)
3	tablespoons corn or olive oil
2	scallions, chopped
2	garlic cloves, minced
2	tablespoons minced soaked dried shrimp (page 134)
2	tablespoons water
1	tablespoon soy sauce
1	teaspoon sugar
	Hot red pepper flakes
	Coarse or kosher salt
	Freshly ground pepper

Cook the green beans in boiling salted water, testing them frequently, until they are crisp-tender, about 5 minutes. Drain and rinse under cold running water to stop the cooking. Drain and set aside.

Heat the oil in a large skillet. Add the scallions and garlic and cook over high heat for 1 to 2 minutes, until softened.

Add the shrimp and the green beans and mix well to coat the beans.

Stir in the water, soy sauce, sugar and pepper flakes to taste and continue to cook for 1 to 2 minutes, until all is hot. Season to taste with salt and pepper.

PORTOBELLO MUSHROOMS

I LOVE PORTOBELLO MUSHROOMS because they are big and thick and have a marvelous flavor. When fresh, the gills will be a grayish color; they turn black when old. Scoop out any blackened gills with a spoon and discard them, as they will not taste good and will turn any food they are cooked with black. Halve Portobellos, slice, and cook them with chicken, meat or by themselves.

FRENCH BEANS AND ASPARAGUS WITH MUSHROOMS

SERVES 4 TO 6

I N THIS SALAD, the French beans and the asparagus are quickly blanched to preserve their bright green colors. Do not destroy their texture by overcooking them. French beans are always tender and have more flavor than regular string beans. If they are not available, try to find the youngest, smallest green beans possible—those that will snap when broken. Chinese long green beans also make a good substitute for French beans.

Plain white mushrooms will work in place of Portobellos or shiitakes, though a certain richness will be missing from the finished dish. (See photograph, page 216.)

½	pound French green beans
½	pound thin asparagus, washed and trimmed
1	medium Portobello mushroom, halved, or 4 fresh shiitake mushrooms or 4 large white button mushrooms
3	tablespoons corn or olive oil
3	garlic cloves, minced
1	tablespoon soy sauce
1	teaspoon coarse or kosher salt
1	teaspoon hot red pepper flakes
¼	cup chicken stock (page 79)

Snip off both ends of the beans, then blanch in boiling water for 4 minutes, just until barely tender. Drain and rinse under cold running water to stop the cooking; drain and set aside.

Cut the asparagus on the diagonal into 2-inch pieces. Blanch in boiling water for 1 minute. Drain and rinse under cold running water to stop the cooking. Drain and set aside.

Remove the mushroom stems and set aside for another use. Slice the caps.

Heat the oil in a large skillet. Add the garlic and cook over high heat, stirring, for 1 minute, or until lightly browned. Add the mushrooms and cook for 1 minute.

Add the green beans and asparagus. Cook, stirring, for 1 minute.

Add the remaining ingredients and cook over high heat until the vegetables are well coated with the sauce. Taste and correct the seasonings and serve.

NAPA CABBAGE

NAPA CABBAGE IS THE MOST POPULAR leafy vegetable in northern China. Of the many kinds of cabbage available, it is my favorite. Weighing from 1 to 3 pounds, it has a delicately sweet flavor and is good in many kinds of dishes.

Washed and shredded, it can be mixed with a little salt, pepper, vinegar and olive oil and eaten raw as a slaw. It can be pickled with salt and fresh chiles and served as a relish. Slowly sautéed in good olive oil, it is a wonderful side dish. Cooked in stock, it makes an excellent soup.

Napa cabbage is easily obtained in most supermarkets, especially in the wintertime. Select those with heavy heads and in which the white or cream-colored leaves are tightly packed. If the leaves are very loose and green in color, the cabbage is old and will have little taste.

BAKED CREAMY NAPA CABBAGE

SERVES 4 TO 6

I LIKE THE COMBINATION of sweet napa cabbage and cream; the cream makes the cabbage smooth and rich-tasting. This dish goes well with grilled fish, game and meat.

2	pounds napa cabbage
¼	cup (½ stick) butter
1	tablespoon all-purpose flour
¼	cup diced onion
2	tablespoons minced soaked dried shrimp (page 134; optional)
½	cup chicken stock (page 79)
½	cup heavy cream
2	teaspoons coarse or kosher salt
	Freshly ground pepper
2	tablespoons freshly grated Parmesan cheese

Cut off the stem end of the cabbage and separate the leaves. Wash well and pat dry.

Cut the leaves in half lengthwise, through the stem, then slice crosswise into 1-inch pieces; set aside.

Heat 2 tablespoons of the butter in a small saucepan over low heat. Add the flour, mix well and cook for 1 to 2 minutes, just until the flour is lightly golden. Remove from the heat; set aside.

Heat the remaining 2 tablespoons butter over high heat in a large skillet. Add the onion and cook for 2 to 3 minutes, until softened. Add the cabbage and the dried shrimp, if using. Mix in the stock. Cover, reduce the heat to medium and cook until the cabbage is tender, about 5 minutes.

Stir in the butter-flour mixture, mixing well to dissolve. Add the cream to the skillet. Add the salt and pepper. Place the mixture in a baking dish and sprinkle with the cheese.

The recipe can be made up to 1 day in advance to this point. Cover and refrigerate the casserole if not baking within 1 hour.

Preheat the oven to 375 degrees F.

Bake for 15 to 20 minutes, or until the mixture is bubbling and the cheese is lightly browned.

SOY-BRAISED CHINESE EGGPLANT WITH ZUCCHINI AND MUSHROOMS

SERVES 4 TO 8

THIS IS A VERY HOMEY VEGETABLE DISH —tender and full of flavor. In Taiwan, my mother usually made this with fresh straw mushrooms and silk squash, a type of zucchini with a rough green skin and sweet, tender flesh. I like to serve this vegetable combination on top of pan-fried noodles or plain steamed white rice.

½   pound Chinese eggplants (about 2 eggplants),* trimmed

½   pound large white button mushrooms

½   pound small zucchini (5-6 inches in length)

2   plum tomatoes

3   tablespoons olive oil, or more if needed

3   garlic cloves, crushed

1   fresh jalapeño pepper or Italian hot pepper,
    seeded and diced

¼   cup chicken stock (page 79)

2   tablespoons soy sauce

    Coarse or kosher salt

    Freshly ground pepper

Remove the stems and cut the eggplants in half lengthwise, then crosswise into ⅛-inch-thick slices. Set aside.

Wipe the mushrooms clean with a damp cloth, then trim off and discard the bottom part of the stems; cut the caps into ¼-inch-thick slices and set aside.

Cut the zucchini in half lengthwise, then thinly slice on the diagonal into ⅛-inch slices. Set aside.

Cook the tomatoes in boiling water for 1 minute, just to loosen the skins. Peel, slice and set aside.

Heat the oil in a large skillet. Add the garlic and sauté over high heat for 1 minute, or until lightly browned. Add the eggplants and reduce the heat to low. Cover and slowly cook for 10 minutes, stirring occasionally.

Add the mushrooms and cook, stirring, for 1 minute. Add the zucchini, tomato, jalapeño or Italian pepper, stock and soy sauce. Stir-fry for about 3 minutes, or until the stock has evaporated and the vegetables are heated through. Season to taste with salt and pepper.

Remove from the heat and serve hot.

*You can substitute white or Italian eggplant or use regular eggplant, peeled and salted to remove bitter juices; see below.

CHINESE EGGPLANT

THERE ARE MORE THAN 50 VARIETIES of eggplant on the market, but my favorite is the Chinese eggplant. It is about 6 to 10 inches in length, slim (1 to 1½ inches in diameter) and more lavender than purple in color. The flesh is sweet and creamy white and contains few seeds. There is no need to salt this eggplant to remove any bitter flavor, for it is naturally sweet. The delicate-tasting skin does not need to be peeled.

When choosing Chinese eggplant in your local market, select those that are long and thin, with a shiny lavender skin. They should give a little when pressed gently. If the eggplants are too big or too light in color, they are old and have many seeds inside.

Do not confuse Chinese eggplants with the Japanese variety, which are much shorter, about 4 to 5 inches in length, with dark purple skin and greenish flesh. Because of their bitter taste, Japanese eggplant cannot be substituted for Chinese.

When you can't get Chinese eggplant, you can use any small Italian variety, white eggplant or ordinary eggplant. Whatever variety you choose, a good eggplant should be small to medium and firm, but not rock-hard. The skin should be glossy and taut. A white eggplant should be snowy white, not green. The seeds in the flesh should be barely visible.

If substituting ordinary eggplant, first draw out its bitter juices by slicing it and sprinkling with 1 to 2 tablespoons coarse or kosher salt. Let stand for 30 minutes to 1 hour, then rinse well and pat dry.

BRAISED VEGETABLES WITH DRIED SCALLOPS

SERVES 6 TO 8

T HIS MAKES A FINE SIDE DISH, but if you want to serve it as a main course, omit the dried scallops and stir in ½ pound of fresh bay scallops once the vegetables are tender. Cook for an additional 3 minutes. As a main course, this will serve 4.

4	small soaked dried scallops (page 134; optional)
½	pound small Brussels sprouts
½	pound baby carrots, peeled
3	tablespoons olive oil
¼	cup chopped onion
½	pound daikon, peeled and cut into ½-inch cubes
1	cup chicken stock (page 79)
	Coarse or kosher salt
	Freshly ground pepper

Place the dried scallops, if using, in a small bowl. Cover with warm water and soak for about 1 hour, or until tender. Drain and set aside.

If the Brussels sprouts are large, cut them in half. Trim off and discard the lower stems and outer leaves.

Cut the carrots in half lengthwise if they are 2 inches long or longer. Otherwise, cut them on the diagonal into 1-inch slices; set aside.

Cook the Brussels sprouts in boiling water for 4 to 5 minutes, or until tender but still crisp. Drain and set aside.

Heat the oil in a large skillet. Add the dried scallops, if using, and the onion and cook over high heat, stirring, for 1 minute.

Add the carrots, daikon and stock, and cook over medium heat for about 10 minutes, stirring occasionally, until the vegetables are tender. Stir in the Brussels sprouts and continue to cook for 5 minutes, until they are crisp-tender. Season to taste with salt and pepper and serve.

Spicy Mushrooms with Garlic and Black Bean Sauce

Serves 8 as a side dish

THIS IS ONE of my mother-in-law's favorite recipes. She serves it at room temperature as one of many first courses. It will keep in the refrigerator for 2 days. The mushrooms must be completely dry before cooking, or they will produce too much liquid, diluting the flavor of the finished dish. Try to use uniformly sized ones. Choose those with pure white caps that are tightly closed. If the gills are open and dark, the mushrooms will be too soft after cooking.

2	pounds small white button mushrooms, rinsed and dried
1	tablespoon fermented black beans
1	cup water
1	tablespoon vodka
½	cup corn or olive oil
3	garlic cloves, chopped
3	scallions, white part only, diced
2	fresh jalapeño peppers, minced, or 1 teaspoon hot red pepper flakes
2	tablespoons balsamic vinegar
1	teaspoon coarse or kosher salt
	Freshly ground pepper

Trim off and discard the bottom parts of the mushroom stems. (If using larger mushrooms, cut into ¼-inch slices.)

Soak the black beans in the water for 2 minutes. Strain, squeeze dry and discard the water. Place the beans in a small bowl and add the vodka; set aside.

Heat the oil in a small saucepan. Add the garlic and the black bean mixture and cook over high heat for 1 to 2 minutes, until the garlic is golden.

Reduce the heat to low, stir in the mushrooms and cook until they are well coated with the oil, about 3 minutes.

Add the scallions, jalapeño peppers or pepper flakes, vinegar, salt and pepper to taste. Mix well and remove from the heat. Serve hot, at room temperature or cold.

SAUTÉED ZUCCHINI WITH
SUN-DRIED TOMATOES

SERVES 4 AS A SIDE DISH OR 8 AS A RELISH

I PREFER TO USE YOUNG, TENDER ZUCCHINI, no more than 5 to 6 inches in length, with dark green skins. When zucchini become too big, the insides are full of seeds, and they have very little flavor. If you must use larger zucchini, cut them into quarters lengthwise, then remove and discard most of the seeds. I lightly blanch them to keep their color and shorten the stir-frying time.

Sun-dried tomatoes lend a bright intensity to vegetables or meats, as in this dish. Use them only when they are bright red. If their color has darkened, they have already been stored too long.

2	pounds small, young zucchini
8	halves sun-dried tomatoes (not oil-packed)
1	cup water
2	tablespoons vodka
3	tablespoons olive oil
4	garlic cloves, thinly sliced
1	jalapeño pepper, stemmed and seeded, thinly sliced (optional)
1	teaspoon coarse or kosher salt
	Freshly ground pepper

Trim the ends from the zucchini and cut them in half lengthwise. Cut them, on the diagonal, into ¼-inch-thick slices and place in a bowl of ice water.

Fill a medium saucepan with water and bring it to a boil. Drain the zucchini and add them to the pan. Cook only until the water returns to a boil, about 1 minute, drain and set aside.

Soak the sun-dried tomatoes in the 1 cup water until they are softened, about 10 minutes. Drain, squeeze dry, cut into thin slices and place in a small bowl. Add the vodka.

Heat the oil in a large skillet. Add the garlic and the jalapeño pepper, if using, and cook over high heat until lightly golden, 1 to 2 minutes. Add the sun-dried tomato mixture and cook for 2 minutes.

Add the zucchini and mix well. Sprinkle with the salt and pepper to taste and cook to blend the flavors, about 3 minutes. Remove from the heat. Serve at room temperature or refrigerate and serve cold as a relish.

OIL-BRAISED ARTICHOKE HEARTS

SERVES 6 TO 8 AS A SALAD OR A FIRST COURSE

WHEN VISITING FRANCE, I was served a first course that I thought was fresh bamboo shoots. The dish turned out to be made with thinly sliced fresh artichoke hearts. I've since realized that the two vegetables are similar in both taste and texture. Artichoke hearts replace fresh bamboo shoots in this classic Shanghai dish. The dish makes a great side dish or a starter, along with "Honeyed" Walnuts (page 59) or Cold Marinated Scallops (page 70).

4	large artichokes
	Juice of 1 lemon
¼	cup olive oil
6	garlic cloves, thinly sliced
¼	cup very thinly sliced red bell pepper
2	tablespoons chopped cilantro stems*
1	tablespoon finely chopped lemon grass (page 86; optional)
1	tablespoon balsamic vinegar
½-1	teaspoon coarse or kosher salt
	Freshly ground pepper

Remove the stems of the artichokes and peel off the tough outer leaves. Using a sharp knife, cut off the tops about one-third of the way down. Remove the remaining leaves and trim off any outer hard green portion left on the bottoms.

Cut each artichoke heart in half and remove and discard the fuzzy choke. Cut each artichoke half into 4 sections and immediately immerse in a bowl of ice water; stir in the lemon juice.

Drain the water from the artichokes into a large pot. Bring to a boil and add the artichokes. Simmer for about 5 minutes, or just until the artichokes are tender; drain well.

Heat 1 tablespoon of the oil in a large skillet. Add the garlic and bell pepper and cook over high heat until the garlic is lightly browned, about 2 minutes.

Add the artichokes and stir in the remaining 3 tablespoons oil. Stir in the cilantro stems, lemon grass, if using, and vinegar; season with salt and pepper to taste. Remove from the heat.

This dish can be served hot, at room temperature or chilled.

*Chopped scallions or celery can be substituted.

QUICK SAUTÉ OF VEGETABLES
WITH CHIVES

SERVES 4

THIS SAUTÉ OF POTATOES, carrots and bean sprouts was one of my favorite dishes when I was a child. Sometimes I wrap this vegetable mixture with Peking Thin Pancakes (page 313) or serve it with Scallion Crêpes (page 315). It is good with grilled fish.

3	tablespoons corn or olive oil
1	garlic clove, thinly sliced
1	carrot, peeled and cut into julienne
1	large red potato, peeled and cut into julienne
¼	cup chicken stock (page 79)
10	Chinese chive buds, cut into 2-inch pieces (about 1 cup), or 1 cup garlic chives*
¼	pound (about 1 cup) bean sprouts, root ends snipped
1	teaspoon hot red pepper flakes
1	teaspoon coarse or kosher salt
1	teaspoon red wine vinegar or balsamic vinegar
	Freshly ground pepper

Heat the oil in a large skillet. Add the garlic and cook over high heat, stirring, for about 2 minutes, or until lightly browned.

Add the carrot, potato and stock to the skillet. Continue to cook, stirring often, until the vegetables are tender, about 10 minutes.

Add the chives, bean sprouts and red pepper flakes. Stir to combine.

Stir in the salt and vinegar and continue to cook until all the ingredients are heated through, about 2 minutes. Season to taste with pepper.

*Regular chives or green scallion tops may be substituted.

BROCCOLI RABE WITH GREEN PEAS

SERVES 4

THIS WAS A POPULAR DISH in Taiwan when I was growing up, served both at home and in many restaurants. There, it consisted of pickled mustard greens and fava beans. I have substituted broccoli rabe for the mustard greens and peas for the fava beans.

When cooked for just a few minutes, the broccoli rabe tastes similar to mustard greens. (See photograph, page 158.)

1	pound broccoli rabe or mustard greens
1	teaspoon coarse or kosher salt
3	tablespoons olive oil
2	garlic cloves, thinly sliced
1	jalapeño pepper, chopped
½	cup chicken stock (page 79)
½	pound baby green peas, shelled (frozen may be substituted)
	Freshly ground pepper

Prepare the broccoli rabe or mustard greens by removing and discarding any large, tough leaves. Peel the stalks and discard the tough ends. Rinse well and shake off the excess water. Chop the broccoli rabe or mustard greens into ¼-inch pieces and place in a bowl. Add the salt and toss.

Heat the oil in a large skillet. Add the garlic and the jalapeño pepper and cook over high heat, stirring, until the garlic is lightly browned, 1 to 2 minutes.

Add the stock and bring to a boil over high heat. Add the peas, reduce the heat to low and cook for 5 minutes, or until the peas are tender.

Add the broccoli rabe or mustard greens, mix well and cook for 2 minutes, or until the greens are tender; do not overcook. Season to taste with pepper. Remove from the heat and serve hot or cold.

Pan-Seared Tofu with Scallions and Ginger

Serves 4 as a side dish or 2 as a main dish

My mother-in-law and I serve this dish all the time. My mother-in-law prepares it for dinner or for breakfast. My family likes it with Scallion Pancakes (page 305). The jalapeño pepper and the pan-frying give it a pleasing flavor and texture—soft inside and crunchy outside. Serve as a side dish or as a vegetarian main course with rice.

1	pound firm tofu (bean curd)
1	leek, white part only, well washed
¼	cup corn or olive oil
3	garlic cloves, thinly sliced
1	tablespoon peeled, julienned gingerroot
3	scallions, trimmed, cut on the diagonal into 2-inch lengths
2	jalapeño peppers, thinly sliced (optional)
3	tablespoons soy sauce
1	tablespoon balsamic vinegar
	Coarse or kosher salt
	Freshly ground pepper

If using supermarket tofu (the kind sold in a plastic-topped tub), cut the tofu in half, lengthwise. Cut each half crosswise into ½-inch-wide pieces. Drain the tofu pieces on a paper towel.

Remove the tough outer skin of the leek and cut the leek in half lengthwise, then into 2-inch crosswise slices. Wash again to remove any remaining grit; drain.

Heat the oil in a large skillet and add the garlic and gingerroot. Cook over high heat, stirring, until the garlic is lightly browned, 1 to 2 minutes.

Add the tofu pieces and cook for about 3 minutes per side, turning once, until browned on both sides. Add the leek, scallions and jalapeño, if using, and cook for 2 minutes, stirring. Add the soy sauce and vinegar. Bring to a boil, reduce the heat, cover and simmer, turning occasionally, until the leek is softened, about 10 minutes. Season to taste with salt and pepper and serve hot.

TOFU
(BEAN CURD)

Tofu IS ALMOST AS MUCH A STAPLE in Chinese cooking as is rice, and we had it nearly every day. Our cook diced it small and cooked it with coarsely chopped pork and scallions. He pan-fried it with black vinegar, ginger, leeks and garlic. He mashed it with pork to make meatballs, and he put it in stuffing for duck.

No wonder tofu is so popular: it is nutritious, has a high protein content and is low in cost. Although tofu is nearly tasteless and has little smell when fresh, it readily absorbs the flavors of whatever it is cooked with, making it an ideal staple.

Fresh Tofu

Tofu is sold in plastic-topped containers in most supermarkets. In Chinese markets, firm, larger squares are stored loose in buckets filled with water. I prefer the fresh tofu in buckets because its flavor is better, but supermarket tofu is fine. If you buy the loose tofu, cover it with cold water and change the water every other day; it will keep for up to 1 week.

Japanese tofu, which is sold in supermarkets in cardboard cartons, keeps for a longer time, but its custard-like texture is too soft for my recipes.

CHAPTER FOUR

FISH AND SEAFOOD

E
VEN AS A SMALL CHILD, I loved fish. Whenever a whole yellow fish or pomfrey was served at our dinner table, I would devour it greedily, while my brothers, who hated having to pick around the small bones, turned up their noses. My grandmother was horrified at what she regarded as my astonishing lack of table manners. Seeing my plate heaped with an untidy pile of fins, tails and bones, she would scold, "Who would ever marry anyone who makes such a mess?"

Growing up in a landlocked northern region, my mother and grandmother were unfamiliar with seafood until we moved to the Taiwanese seaport town of Kao-hsiung. Surrounded by ocean and with many internal lakes and streams, the country had an abundance of not only seafood but many varieties of freshwater and saltwater fish that were new to us. When she went to the market, my mother would return home with squid, grass carp, shad or fresh shrimp with their heads still attached. Inevitably, she would pan-fry them all, for that was the only method of preparation she knew.

But my mother-in-law, who had grown up in a different region, was a master of fish cookery in all its variety. She steamed fresh fish with fermented black beans, garlic and hot peppers. When shad was in season — it was expensive and a special treat — she would steam it with the scales left on so that it would be extra-moist. Occasionally, she pan-fried whole fish like pompano, first coating them with cornstarch so they would be crisp. At other times, she browned small freshwater grass fish, then slowly simmered them with black vinegar and lots of scallions. She pan-grilled steak fish like swordfish or tuna with just a sprinkling of salt. Or she poached whole fish in rich stock with julienned daikon, whose delicate taste complemented it perfectly. Often, she refrigerated cooked fish and served it cold the next day, along with the juices that had gelled into a natural consommé.

For their part, my parents took me and my brothers to Taiwan's sophisticated Shanghai-style restaurants, famous for their preparations of fish and shellfish of all kinds, liberally seasoned with soy sauce, ginger, sugar and spices — ranging from slippery braised fish tails to deep-fried eels to Shanghai-style smoked fish.

M Y FISH AND SEAFOOD DISHES APPLY traditional Chinese methods to the gloriously abundant seafood in this country. I take advantage of blue crabs from Maryland; soft-shell crabs, which I had never tasted before coming to the United States; salmon; sea bass; and southern varieties like pompano. To this day, I prefer whole fish, cooked with its head, skeleton and skin intact — just the way my mother always prepared it. Fillets, however, are undeniably convenient — and often more affordable — so I have adapted some recipes accordingly.

My fish dishes have also been subtly influenced by a trip to France that I took in 1983. While dining in three-star restaurants, I tasted some of the best fish and shellfish I have ever eaten outside of China.

Although I prefer the more robust flavor of the Chinese way, I have learned from and adopted some of the French sauce techniques and, especially, their beautiful presentations. Following the traditions of my own country, I treat each fish differently so that its characteristics are not lost. In all fish and shellfish cookery, one rule is paramount: it must be very, very fresh.

155

FISH AND SEAFOOD

Salmon with Black Bean Sauce   157

Auntie Wu's Braised Red Snapper with Garlic and Ginger   160

"Squirrel" Sea Bass with Caramelized Sweet-and-Sour Ginger Sauce   162

Mahimahi with Pineapple-Coconut Sauce   166

Tea-Smoked Pompano   169

Red-Braised Monkfish Fillets   171

Grilled Tuna with Jalapeño Pepper Puree   172

Pan-Sautéed Pompano with Sun-Dried Tomatoes,

Black Bean and Eggplant Salsa   174

Coho Salmon Shanghai-Style   176

Prawns with Poached Pears and Curry Sauce   179

Sautéed Shrimp with Corn in Spicy Wine Sauce   183

Spicy Soft-Shell Crabs   185

Steamed Crabmeat Soufflé   186

SALMON WITH BLACK BEAN SAUCE

SERVES 4

THIS SUBTLE MARINADE OF OLIVE OIL, soy sauce and vodka keeps the salmon tender and moist. I like to undercook the fish slightly, for when it is placed on warm dinner plates and topped with the hot black bean sauce, it will continue to cook for another minute or two. Julienne the vegetables for the garnish ahead of time and store them in a bowl of ice water in the refrigerator.

4	salmon fillets, each about 6 ounces
¼	cup plus 3 tablespoons olive oil
¼	cup vodka
1	tablespoon soy sauce
	Freshly ground pepper
	Black Bean Sauce (page 159)
1	tablespoon peeled, finely julienned gingerroot
1	tablespoon peeled, finely julienned carrots
	or red radishes (optional)

Slash each salmon fillet diagonally in 2 or 3 places, being careful not to cut all the way through, so the marinade will penetrate the fish. Place the fillets in a shallow dish.

Mix ¼ cup of the oil, the vodka, soy sauce and some pepper; spoon over the salmon. Refrigerate for 1 hour, turning once.

Meanwhile, prepare the Black Bean Sauce and place in a medium saucepan.

Preheat the broiler, with a rack 4 to 6 inches from the heat source.

Remove the fish from the marinade and add the marinade to the sauce. Bring the sauce to a boil, reduce the heat to low and keep warm while you cook the fish.

Heat the remaining 3 tablespoons oil in a large ovenproof skillet. When it is hot, add the fillets and cook over high heat, turning once, until the salmon is browned on both sides, about 1½ minutes per side.

Place the fish on a broiler pan and broil, without turning, just until the fillets are done, about 5 minutes.

Divide the fillets among the 4 dinner plates, spoon over the sauce and garnish with a little of the gingerroot and carrots or red radishes, if using, and serve.

Salmon with Black Bean Sauce and Broccoli Rabe with Green Peas

BLACK BEAN SAUCE

MAKES ABOUT 1¼ CUPS SAUCE

FERMENTED BLACK BEANS have a strong, earthy flavor. The Cantonese love to sauté them with garlic, pile them on top of a whole fish or chicken and steam the dish. I find that the black beans are too dominant when the fish is prepared in this way. I have changed and adapted this sauce so that the black beans add just enough flavor without overpowering.

The sauce is also great over chicken or Jalapeño Peppers with Pork Stuffing (page 67).

1	tablespoon fermented black beans (page 119)
1	tablespoon vodka
1	tablespoon corn oil
2	shallots, finely chopped
2	garlic cloves, finely chopped
1	tablespoon peeled, grated gingerroot
2	teaspoons white wine vinegar
1	teaspoon cornstarch
1½	cups fish or chicken stock (page 94 or 79)
1	tablespoon chopped red bell pepper
1	tablespoon chopped fresh cilantro leaves

Wash the black beans and place in a small bowl. Cover with warm water and soak for 2 minutes; drain well and squeeze out any remaining liquid. Mix with the vodka.

Heat the oil in a medium saucepan and add the black beans, shallots, garlic and gingerroot. Cook over high heat, stirring, for 5 minutes, or until the garlic is lightly browned. Add the vinegar.

Mix the cornstarch with the stock in a small bowl and add to the saucepan. Mix well and bring to a boil. Reduce the heat to low and cook for 20 minutes more, or until the cornstarch has lost its raw taste. Mix in the bell pepper and the cilantro and remove from the heat.

The sauce can be prepared 3 to 4 days in advance, covered and refrigerated, or frozen for up to 1 month.

Auntie Wu's Braised Red Snapper with Garlic and Ginger

Serves 4

MY MOTHER'S BEST FRIEND, Auntie Wu, who lived in T'aipei, always prepared this dish with red snapper when we came to visit. I loved it so much that I could have eaten the whole fish all by myself. In the Sichuan province, where Auntie Wu came from, one of the most popular methods of cooking whole fish is to sear it in hot oil. It is then slowly braised with ginger, garlic and scallions, as well as with hot peppers, vinegar, wine and soy sauce. This double-cooking process does two things: it makes the skin crisp and flavorful, and it keeps the flesh juicy, infused with the essence of the braising ingredients.

I often prepare this dish with yellow-tail snapper, an ocean fish with a beautiful yellow stripe and a golden tail. Found in Florida, it is even better-tasting than the fish I grew up with in Taiwan. Sea bass, striped bass or porgy can be used as well.

Serve with rice.

1	whole red snapper, about 2 pounds, cleaned*
1	teaspoon coarse or kosher salt
	Freshly ground pepper
½	cup corn oil
½	cup finely chopped onion
¼	cup minced scallion
4	garlic cloves, minced
2	tablespoons peeled, grated gingerroot
2	jalapeño peppers, seeded and chopped
¼	cup gin
2	tablespoons soy sauce
2	tablespoons white wine vinegar
1	teaspoon sugar
½	teaspoon freshly ground white pepper
1	cup fish or chicken stock (page 94 or 79)

Wash the fish well and pat dry. Score the fish 3 or 4 times on each side, cutting ¼ inch into the flesh.

Sprinkle with the salt and pepper.

Heat the oil in a large skillet until very hot. Place the fish in the skillet, cover and brown over high heat for about 3 minutes, or until well browned; turn and brown on the second side for 3 minutes more. Remove all but 1 tablespoon of the oil; discard.

Add the onion, scallion, garlic, gingerroot and jalapeño peppers. Cook for 2 minutes more, or until the onion is lightly browned.

Pour in the gin, soy sauce, vinegar, sugar and white pepper. Cover, reduce the heat to low and cook the fish for 2 minutes, turning once, to coat with the sauce. Add the stock, cover again and cook over low heat for 5 minutes. Turn the fish, cover and cook for 2 minutes more, or until the flesh is tender. If the fish can easily be separated from the bone, it is cooked through.

Carefully remove the fish to a platter. Serve immediately.

*If you prefer to use fillets, substitute 4 red snapper fillets, each approximately 7 ounces. Do not score the flesh. Sprinkle with salt and pepper and brown the fillets in hot oil, skin side down, until golden, about 2 to 3 minutes. Add the onion, scallion, garlic, gingerroot and jalapeños and cook for 1 minutes. Turn the fillets skin side up, then add the gin, soy sauce, vinegar, sugar and white pepper and cook for about 3 minutes. Add the stock, cover the fish and cook for about 10 minutes. Insert the tip of a small knife into the thickest part of the fish to make sure it is completely cooked. Serve immediately.

"Squirrel" Sea Bass with Caramelized Sweet-and-Sour Ginger Sauce

Serves 4

The most popular fish in China is the yellow fish, found along the seacoast from as far north as Beijing to as far south as Shanghai. One of the classic fish preparations of Beijing is called "squirrel yellow fish," which got its unusual name because of the way the body of the fish curls up when it is deep-fried. The whole fish is filleted in such a way as to keep both fillets attached at the tail, so that it resembles a puffy-tailed squirrel.

The complexity of this dish—the crunch of the crusty skin and the tender moistness of the flesh when combined with the caramelized sweet and tangy sauce and the delicate pine nuts—makes this my favorite of all fish preparations.

The best substitute for yellow fish, which I have not yet found in this country, is sea bass, usually in season from November until April. If sea bass is unavailable, you can substitute grouper, striped bass, snapper, porgy or catfish. Sea bass is best, for its skin is thin and will be crisp after it is fried, whereas the skin of grouper is much tougher. If you use grouper, you may want to remove the skin before serving. Instead of the whole fish, you can use 4 fillets, with skin attached. Serve with Vegetable Rice (page 292).

1	2-2½-pound sea bass, cleaned and scaled, preferably with head
	Coarse or kosher salt
	Freshly ground pepper
1½	cups Caramelized Sweet-and-Sour Ginger Sauce (page 165)
	Corn oil for frying
¼	cup all-purpose flour
¾	cup cornstarch
2	large egg yolks, mixed with 1 teaspoon water
¼	cup diced onion
1	garlic clove, minced
1	tablespoon peeled, minced gingerroot
¼	cup diced red bell pepper

¼   cup coarsely chopped scallions

¼   cup fresh corn kernels, preferably white
      (or frozen, thawed)

½   cup "Honeyed" Pine Nuts (page 58)

Wash the fish and dry it, inside and out, with paper towels. Using kitchen shears, remove the back fins, but leave on the tail.

With a sharp knife, remove the head; set aside. Place the fish on its side and cut along the backbone on each side to loosen the fillets, leaving them attached at the tail. Cut off and remove the backbone and any small bones remaining in the flesh.

Score the flesh side of the fish crosswise about 1 inch apart, cutting down to, but not through, the skin. Sprinkle with the salt and pepper.

Prepare the sweet-and-sour sauce; set aside.

Pour about 6 inches of oil into a large wok or fryer and heat over high heat to 350 degrees F.

Meanwhile, mix the flour and cornstarch in a small bowl until thoroughly combined. Pour the mixture onto a flat plate. Place the egg yolk mixture in a large shallow plate. Hold the fish by the tail and shake it hard so that the scored flesh opens. Dip the fish fillets, then the reserved fish head, if using, into the egg yolk mixture to coat, and use your hand or a spoon to coat the flesh completely. Roll the fish in the flour-cornstarch mixture, making sure all the pieces are well coated; shake off the excess.

When the oil is hot, hold the fish by the tail and carefully lower it into the pan, skin side up. If you are using the head, add it to the oil at the same time and fry for 3 to 4 minutes, then turn the fish and cook for 3 to 4 minutes more, or until the fish is golden and crispy. Drain well and keep warm.

Transfer 1 tablespoon of the oil to a small skillet. Add the onion, garlic and gingerroot and cook, stirring, for 2 minutes.

Add the bell pepper, scallions, corn and the sweet-and-sour sauce. Stir well and bring to a boil. Remove the pan from the heat.

Place the fish on a platter, with the head on top. Spoon the sauce over the fish and garnish with the "Honeyed" Pine Nuts. Serve immediately.

"Squirrel" Sea Bass with Caramelized Sweet-and-Sour Ginger Sauce

CARAMELIZED SWEET-AND-SOUR GINGER SAUCE

MAKES ABOUT 2 CUPS SAUCE

A T THE CULINARY INSTITUTE OF AMERICA in Hyde Park, New York, I was taught a recipe for orange duck. The duck was roasted and boned, and the bones were used to make a rich stock. Sugar and vinegar were caramelized, then the strained duck stock and some orange zest were added to make a classic orange sauce. I applied this technique to rework a typical Chinese sweet-and-sour sauce.

2	tablespoons corn oil
¼	cup chopped onion
4	garlic cloves, minced
3	thin slices gingerroot
3	star anise
1	teaspoon roasted Sichuan peppercorns (page 111)
½	cup chicken or fish stock (page 79 or 94)
1	cup sugar
½	cup white vinegar
½	cup white wine
½	cup soy sauce*
½	cup ketchup
1	teaspoon cornstarch
1	tablespoon water
1	teaspoon coarse or kosher salt

Heat the oil in a small skillet. Add the onion, garlic, gingerroot, anise and peppercorns. Cook over high heat, stirring, until the onion is soft and translucent, about 5 minutes. Set aside until needed.

In a medium saucepan, place 2 tablespoons of the stock and the sugar and cook, stirring constantly, over medium-high heat, until the mixture is caramelized, about 5 minutes.

Add the vinegar and the wine to the sugar mixture and continue to cook, stirring, for about 4 minutes, until the sugar completely dissolves.

Stir in the onion mixture, soy sauce, ketchup and the remaining 6 tablespoons stock, and cook over high heat for about 5 minutes, until the flavors are blended.

Combine the cornstarch and water in a small bowl. Mix thoroughly and add to the sauce. Mix in the salt.

Cook over low heat, stirring occasionally, until the sauce is reduced by half, approximately 30 minutes.

Strain the sauce and discard the solids. The sauce can be made up to 1 week ahead and refrigerated, covered.

*Preferably Kikkoman soy sauce.

MAHIMAHI WITH
PINEAPPLE-COCONUT SAUCE

SERVES 4 AS A MAIN COURSE

MAHIMAHI TASTES A LITTLE LIKE SWORDFISH, with a moist, sweet flavor and a firm texture. It blends well with tropical fruits and is especially delicious when prepared with fresh pineapple and coconut milk. This recipe was inspired by similar preparations in Thai and Vietnamese cuisines.

The best way to tell if a fish fillet is very fresh is to touch it—it should feel firm and smooth. The flesh should be shiny, with no sticky film present. Smell also plays an important part in judging freshness. There should be none—a fresh piece of fish should not smell "fishy." If it does, it is probably several days old. Don't buy old fish, for no matter how you cook it, it will not be good.

Serve with Sautéed Zucchini with Sun-Dried Tomatoes (page 148), Four-Treasure Relish (page 122) or Chinese Risotto with Wild Mushrooms (page 295).

Fish

½	cup sliced almonds
4	8-ounce mahimahi fillets
2	tablespoons vodka
6	tablespoons corn oil, or more if needed
1	teaspoon crushed gingerroot
1	teaspoon coarse or kosher salt
	Freshly ground pepper
¼	cup cornstarch

Sauce

¼ cup diced onion

2 garlic cloves, thinly sliced

1 cup fish stock (page 94), clam juice or chicken stock (page 79)

¼ cup unsweetened coconut milk*

¼ cup finely chopped fresh pineapple

1 teaspoon hot oil or 1 tablespoon chopped fresh jalapeño pepper

1 teaspoon cornstarch, mixed with 2 teaspoons water

2 teaspoons chopped fresh lemon grass (page 86)

Coarse or kosher salt to taste

To prepare the fish: Preheat the oven to 400 degrees F. Place the almonds on a dry baking sheet and toast, stirring occasionally, for about 4 to 5 minutes, until they have turned light brown and smell fragrant; set aside.

Wash and dry the fish fillets and place them in a shallow pan or dish.

Combine the vodka, 2 tablespoons of the oil, gingerroot, salt and some pepper. Mix thoroughly and pour over the fish. Marinate for 30 minutes in the refrigerator, turning a few times.

Preheat the broiler, with a rack 4 to 6 inches from the heat source. Remove the fillets from the marinade and pat dry. Place the cornstarch on a large plate and sprinkle the fillets lightly with it; keep the coating as thin as possible.

Heat the remaining ¼ cup oil in a large skillet. Add 2 of the fish fillets and sauté over high heat, turning once, until browned on both sides, about 2 minutes per side. Remove the fish from the skillet and place in a baking dish. Repeat with the remaining 2 fillets, adding a little more oil if necessary.

To make the sauce: Add the onion and garlic to the same skillet and sauté over high heat until the onion is softened, about 5 minutes. Add the stock or clam juice, coconut milk, pineapple and hot oil or jalapeño. Stir in the cornstarch mixture. Bring to a boil on high heat, then reduce heat to low and simmer for 10 minutes to remove the raw taste of the cornstarch; keep warm. Add the lemon grass and season with salt.

To cook the fish and assemble: Place the fish under the broiler and cook for 4 to 5 minutes. Part the flesh with a sharp knife; if it meets with no resistance, the fish is done.

Divide the cooked fish among 4 plates. Spoon some of the sauce over each fillet. Sprinkle with the toasted almonds.

*I prefer the Chaokoh brand, which is carried by most Asian grocery stores.

THE CHINESE TECHNIQUE OF SMOKING

THE CHINESE METHOD of smoking differs from that practiced in the West. In China, the food is cooked first, either by steaming or frying. It is then smoked over high heat for a shorter period of time, indoors rather than outdoors, as in the West, not so much to cook it but to add flavor.

A mixture of sugar, flour, rice and tea leaves is placed in the bottom of a wok or heavy pot. For flavoring, dried orange peel, Sichuan peppercorns, star anise or chips of camphor, an aromatic wood native to China, may be added. The food is then put on a rack just above the mixture, and the pot is tightly covered. When the sugar and starch in the flour are heated in the enclosed chamber, they produce smoke and steam, while the tea leaves and rice aerate the mixture, enabling it to burn more evenly. The tea leaves also contribute a subtle aroma to the food. What happens is really a combination of techniques: smoking, baking and dry-steaming, all taking place at the same time. Smoking also reduces the fat layer under the skin, since much of it oozes out during the process.

I reverse the traditional order of cooking, smoking the food first and then finishing it off under the broiler. That way, I can better control the cooking and crisp the outside skin. Essentially, my technique combines Chinese smoking, American barbecuing and French timing, producing fish or poultry cooked to the perfect state of doneness with a hint of smoke.

For a Gas Stove

❋ Use a heavy Dutch oven or cast-iron pot with a tight-fitting lid. Line the bottom with a large piece of heavy-duty aluminum foil.

❋ Mix equal portions of the smoking mix—sugar, rice, flour and tea leaves. Pour it on the foil.

❋ Use high heat at first to create the smoke.

❋ Place the rack so that it is 3 inches above the smoking mixture and lay the food on the rack.

❋ Cover tightly and smoke the food for a very short time only, depending on the size of the portion. This will usually take 5 to 15 minutes. It is a good idea to take the pot outside before opening it so the smoke can escape.

For an Electric Stove

If you don't own a gas stove, you may want to do your smoking out-of-doors on a barbecue grill. Smoking is trickier on an electric stove, since it heats slowly, making it difficult to generate the right amount of smoke.

❋ Heat the burner until it is very hot.

❋ Use a heavy Dutch oven or cast-iron pot with a tight-fitting lid. Line it generously with aluminum foil and place on the hot burner. Heat until the bottom of the pot is very hot, about 5 minutes.

❋ Add the smoking mixture to the bottom.

❋ Place a rack about 3 inches above the smoking mixture and place the food on the rack. Cover tightly and smoke for 5 to 15 minutes.

Smoked food can be stored in the refrigerator for up to 1 week before it is cooked.

TEA-SMOKED POMPANO

SERVES 4 AS A MAIN COURSE OR 8 AS A FIRST COURSE

AMONG THE CLASSICAL CHINESE FISH DISHES is tea-smoked pompano or yellow fish. The fish is first smoked on top of the stove for a short time, then deep-fried. The smoking can be done a few days in advance and the fish refrigerated until needed. Instead of deep-frying, I broil the fish after smoking it for a healthier preparation.

The buttery flavor of the pompano is beautifully enhanced by this technique. The smoking process helps retain the natural moisture of the fish. The thin skin remains crisp and takes on a golden color when browned, while the flesh stays moist and tender.

Accompany with Sichuan Pickled Vegetables (page 114) or serve with Rice Noodles with Porcini Mushrooms (page 277).

Fish and Marinade

1 2-2½-pound pompano (with head on),
   scaled and cleaned*

2 tablespoons olive oil

1 tablespoon peeled, crushed gingerroot

1 tablespoon vodka

1 tablespoon Roasted Sichuan Peppercorns
   and Salt (page 211)

Smoking Mixture

½ cup all-purpose flour

½ cup sugar

½ cup rice (any kind)

½ cup tea leaves**

1 tablespoon Asian sesame oil

To marinate the fish: Clean the fish well and dry thoroughly. Score 3 diagonal slits, about 1 inch deep, on each side of the fish.

Mix the marinade ingredients in a shallow dish and marinate the fish at room temperature for 30 minutes, turning to coat both sides, or refrigerate, covered, overnight. Reserve the leftover marinade.

Preheat the oven to 350 degrees F.

To smoke the fish: Mix the smoking ingredients. Line a heavy Dutch oven or cast-iron pot with heavy-duty aluminum foil. Pour the smoking mixture on the foil. (See page 168 for more details about smoking, particularly if you are using an electric stove.)

Drain the fish well, reserving the marinade.

If you are using a gas stove, turn the heat under the Dutch oven or pot to high and place a rack about 3 inches above the smoking mixture so the fish does not touch it.

Place the fish on the rack. Cover with a heavy lid or a tent made of a double layer of heavy-duty foil.

Smoke the fish over high heat for about 5 minutes, or until it is flavored with the smoke.

Remove the pot from the heat and let stand, covered, for 5 minutes. To avoid smoking up your house, take the pot outside before uncovering it. Uncover. Transfer the fish to a nonstick broiler pan.

The recipe can be prepared to this point up to 1 day in advance and refrigerated, covered.

Mix the leftover marinade with the sesame oil and brush on both sides of the fish.

Preheat the broiler, with a rack 4 to 6 inches from the heat source. Broil for 3 minutes per side, turning once, until the flesh parts easily when pierced with a knife. Serve hot or at room temperature.

*Butterfish, red snapper or even flounder can be substituted.

**Jasmine tea is preferred, but green or black tea leaves can also be used.

RED-BRAISED MONKFISH FILLETS

SERVES 4 AS A MAIN COURSE OR 8 AS ONE OF MANY COURSES

SHANGHAI CUISINE IS NOTED FOR ITS HEARTY FISH and seafood dishes, which are often served with a sauce based on soy, vinegar and sugar. One of the region's most popular preparations is called "red-braised slippery fish fillet." It is usually made from a small or medium-sized freshwater fish with very few bones that is slowly braised with soy sauce, rice wine, brown sugar and black vinegar. By the time it has finished cooking, the fish has caramelized, and its flavor is intense. Monkfish fillets make a great substitute for slippery fish.

2	pounds monkfish fillets
¼	cup corn oil
½	cup finely chopped onion
2	tablespoons soy sauce
2	tablespoons oyster sauce
2	tablespoons black vinegar or balsamic vinegar
1	cup fish or chicken stock (page 94 or 79),
	mixed with 1 teaspoon cornstarch
1	whole garlic head, cloves separated and peeled (10-12 cloves)
1	tablespoon peeled, finely chopped gingerroot
¼	cup gin or sake
	Freshly ground pepper

Remove all the dark skin and veins from the monkfish — use only the white flesh. Wash well in cold water and pat dry with paper towels. Cut into 1-inch cubes; set aside.

Heat 1 tablespoon of the oil in a heavy medium saucepan. Add the onion and cook over high heat until browned, about 5 minutes. Add the soy sauce, oyster sauce and vinegar. Bring to a boil, add the stock mixture and simmer for about 15 minutes to blend the flavors. Remove from the heat and strain; set aside.

Heat the remaining 3 tablespoons oil in a heavy large skillet or saucepan. When it is hot, add the garlic cloves and sauté over high heat for 2 to 3 minutes, or just until they turn golden. Add the fish cubes and the gingerroot and sauté, stirring, until the fish turns white, 3 minutes. Add the gin or sake and continue to cook over high heat for 2 minutes more.

Add the reserved sauce, reduce the heat to low and cook for about 10 minutes, or until the fish is completely coated. Add the pepper to taste and serve.

Grilled Tuna with Jalapeño Pepper Puree

Serves 4 as a main dish

TAIWAN WAS OCCUPIED BY JAPAN from 1895 to 1945, and Taiwanese cuisine still shows the influence of Japanese cooking. One of my favorite Taiwanese specialties was made with sushi-quality tuna, brushed with teriyaki sauce and quickly grilled on a table-side stove, then thinly sliced. The fish was nicely browned, but its center was still raw. The contrast of tastes and textures was extraordinary. As much as I loved this dish, I wanted to create something with a more stand-up flavor, so I added lemon grass, pureed jalapeño peppers and yellow soybean paste.

Be sure to use the best-quality tuna available; it will have a bright red color, be firm to the touch and have no fishy smell.

Serve the tuna with Silver Sprouts with Jicama, Celery and Balsamic Vinaigrette (page 133). It is also wonderful with Green Cabbage with Sichuan Peppercorn Vinaigrette (page 113) or Sweet Rice, Taro and Pineapple Compote (page 298).

3	tablespoons olive oil
1	tablespoon vodka
1	teaspoon freshly ground pepper
4	8-ounce tuna steaks, about 1 inch thick
2	tablespoons yellow soybean paste*
1	tablespoon Jalapeño Pepper Puree (page 243)
1	tablespoon finely chopped fresh lemon grass (page 86)**
1	tablespoon fresh lime juice
2	tablespoons corn oil

Mix the olive oil, vodka and pepper in a shallow dish. Add the tuna and turn to coat both sides. Marinate for 10 minutes at room temperature.

Meanwhile, mix the soybean paste, jalapeño puree, lemon grass and lime juice in a small bowl. Preheat the broiler, with a rack 4 to 6 inches from the heat source. Brush a broiler pan with the corn oil and place under the broiler until it is hot.

Brush the tuna on both sides with the jalapeño pepper mixture and place on the hot broiler pan. Broil for 3 minutes per side, turning once, or until the fish is nicely browned on the outside but still pink inside. Serve immediately.

*You can substitute 3 tablespoons of soy sauce.
**Washed, finely chopped cilantro root may be substituted.

Variation

Instead of broiling the tuna, you can pan-sear it in the corn oil in a large skillet over high heat for 3 minutes on each side. Or cook outdoors on a lightly oiled grill.

YELLOW SOYBEAN PASTE

I GREW UP LOVING yellow soybean paste, for my family regularly used it. Also called brown bean sauce, it is made from fermented yellow soybeans, to which flour, salt and water have been added. Two varieties are marketed: one containing whole pieces of fermented beans and the other a smooth puree. Both types are brown, thick and salty and are common flavoring ingredients in the northern and western provinces of China.

My mother used the whole bean paste for stir-frying red meat, chicken or fish. She put the pureed version in marinades or rubbed it over pork or chicken before braising them. She also added it to pasta sauces.

In the western provinces of Sichuan and Hunan, chili peppers and even garlic and spices are added to the whole bean sauce. My mother-in-law seasoned tofu with this highly flavored sauce or gave meat extra zing with it. One of her favorite dishes was a whole fish braised with this spicy bean sauce.

PAN-SAUTÉED POMPANO WITH SUN-DRIED TOMATOES, BLACK BEAN AND EGGPLANT SALSA

SERVES 4

M Y MOTHER BOUGHT POMFRET whenever she could find them fresh in the market. Our cook would sprinkle them with salt and pepper and sear them in hot oil. Then he would quickly glaze the fish, which were usually no more than 1 pound each, with a mixture of ginger, soy sauce and vinegar. The skin was golden and crispy, the hot buttery flesh was rich and moist.

Even though it is different from pomfret, I love the delicately flavored pompano found along the east coast of this country and prepare it similarly.

3	tablespoons olive oil
3	tablespoons vodka
2	tablespoons soy sauce
1	teaspoon peeled, grated gingerroot
4	7-ounce pompano fillets, with skin*
½	cup cornstarch
½	cup corn oil
2	cups Sun-Dried Tomatoes, Black Bean and Eggplant Salsa (page 118)
1	lemon, cut into 4 wedges
½	cup peeled, julienned daikon or carrots, soaked in ice water (opposite page; optional)

Mix the olive oil, vodka, soy sauce and gingerroot in a small bowl.

Place the fish fillets, skin side down, in a shallow pan. Pour the marinade over the fish, turning once or twice to make sure that it coats the fish.

Place the cornstarch on a large plate. Remove the fillets from the marinade. Dust the skin side only with the cornstarch, making sure the skin is well covered; do not dust the flesh side.

Heat ¼ cup of the corn oil in a large, heavy nonstick skillet over medium-high heat. When oil is very hot, add half the fish fillets, skin side down; do not crowd the pan.

Cook, turning once, until the fish is firm, cooked through and nicely browned, about 7 minutes total. Repeat, using the remaining ¼ cup oil to cook the rest of the fillets.

Divide the salsa among 4 dinner plates and top with the fish, skin side up. Squeeze a wedge of lemon over each fillet and garnish with the julienned daikon or carrots, if using.

*Flounder, red snapper or Dover sole fillets may be substituted.

VEGETABLE GARNISHES

IN CHINESE CUISINE, chefs often top meat or fish with a decoration of finely julienned raw scallions, ginger and leeks. Root vegetables, such as carrots, daikon, kohlrabi or red radishes, also make beautiful, crisp garnishes.

To make a garnish, first peel the vegetable, then cut it into paper-thin slices. Stack the slices together and cut them into a fine julienne.

Soak the prepared vegetables in a bowl of ice-cold water, along with some ice cubes. They will remain crisp. The vegetables can be readied a day in advance, drained and stored in the refrigerator in a bowl covered with a wet paper towel or plastic wrap.

Coho Salmon Shanghai-Style

Serves 4 as a main course or 8 as a starter or with salad for lunch

THE ORIGINAL METHOD of preparing this Shanghai specialty is to deep-fry river trout or grass bass and then smoke it. Today, few modern Chinese households use this technique to smoke fish at home. They simplify the preparation by deep-frying the fish fillets, then dipping them into a mixture of soy sauce, sugar and five-spice powder so that the fillets look smoked.

I have adapted this preparation and make it with Coho salmon, when it is available. It tastes like the fish I remember enjoying with my father. It is great as a lunch dish or as a starter when served with a salad made with baby greens. It also makes an excellent sandwich. Rainbow trout, rockfish or ordinary salmon can be substituted.

4   whole 10-12-ounce Coho salmon, cleaned*
⅓   cup vodka, sake or gin
¼   cup soy sauce
2   scallions, flattened with a cleaver, cut into 2-inch lengths
1   tablespoon peeled, grated gingerroot
1   cup chicken or fish stock (page 79 or 94)
1   teaspoon roasted Sichuan peppercorns (page 111)
2   tablespoons sugar
¼   teaspoon five-spice powder (optional)
    Corn oil for deep-frying

Remove the heads and split the fish in half lengthwise.

Wash the fish, pat dry, and place on a shallow platter.

In a small bowl, mix the vodka, sake or gin, soy sauce, scallions and gingerroot; pour over the fish. Refrigerate for 30 minutes, turning the fish often to coat them completely with the marinade.

Remove the fish from the marinade, draining them well. Reserve the marinade. Place the stock and peppercorns in a large, wide saucepan. Over high heat, bring to a boil, cover and cook for 5 minutes. Add the sugar, the reserved marinade and the five-spice powder, if using, reduce the heat and simmer the sauce while you cook the fish.

Heat the oil to 375 degrees F in a fryer or large skillet. Place the fish, one at a time, into the fryer. Cook for 5 to 10 minutes, turning, until the fish is crisp and well browned.

Using tongs, dip the fish, one at a time, into the simmering sauce. After each fish is thoroughly coated with the sauce, place it on a serving platter.

Cool the fish and serve at room temperature or refrigerate, covered, and serve cold.

The fish may be prepared up to 1 day in advance. If you want to serve it hot, re-heat in a preheated broiler, 4 to 6 inches from the heat source, for 3 minutes, or until heated through.

*Farm-raised Coho salmon, which are about the size of trout, are usually sold boned and butterflied. You can use sea trout or 8 regular salmon fillets instead. The salmon fillets should be about 3 to 3½ ounces each and ½ inch thick.

PICNICS WITH FATHER

Picnics HAVE BEEN FASHIONABLE among Chinese aristocrats since ancient times. Multi-layered picnic baskets made of bamboo and lacquer can still be found in many antique markets. Favorite dishes included tea eggs, red-braised beef shanks, smoked fish, soy-braised whole chickens, sesame noodles and scallion pancakes. Most of these were served cold, with dipping sauces on the side. Portable stoves were brought along just to boil water for tea and to warm the rice wine.

After my father spent time in the United States as a Lieutenant General in the Chinese armed forces, which were attached to the American forces, he returned to Taiwan, bringing with him a taste for American-style picnics. On many warm and sunny weekends, he would take my three brothers and me on an outing, telling the cook to prepare a meal that could be eaten out-of-doors without too much fuss. He would then pile us into the car and drive to a nearby lake for the afternoon.

One of his favorite foods to take along was Shanghai-style smoked fish, a popular dish in Taiwan that is made with either river trout or river bass.

Prawns with Poached Pears and Curry Sauce

PRAWNS WITH POACHED PEARS AND CURRY SAUCE

SERVES 6

MARINATING SHRIMP IN A LITTLE VODKA adds sweetness to the shrimp and improves their flavor. The following recipe has been influenced by the cuisines of Southeast Asia, where curry powder is often mixed with coconut milk to give richness to a finished dish. Serve with white rice or Pan-Fried Scallion Bread (page 316).

2	pounds prawns or large shrimp (about 36 shrimp), peeled, deveined and cleaned with salt (page 182)
2	tablespoons vodka
1	large egg white, lightly beaten
2	large, firm, ripe pears (any kind)
2	cups water
½	cup fresh lemon juice
⅓	cup corn oil
3	shallots, minced
1	tablespoon peeled, julienned gingerroot
1	tablespoon julienned lemon zest
1	cup Curry Sauce (page 181)
	Coarse or kosher salt
	Freshly ground pepper
½	cup toasted almond slices*

Pat the shrimp dry. Mix the vodka and the beaten egg white in a large bowl, add the shrimp and toss to combine. Marinate for 20 minutes at room temperature, turning occasionally; drain. Set aside.

Peel the pears, cut in half lengthwise and remove the cores. Cut each pear half into 6 to 8 thin slices and place in a small bowl.

Mix the water and lemon juice and pour over the pears; let steep for 5 minutes. Transfer the pears and all the liquid to a large saucepan. Bring the liquid to a boil. Cover and poach the pears for about 3 minutes, or until they are just tender. Remove from the heat, drain and set aside.

Heat the oil in a large skillet until it is hot but not smoking. Add the shrimp and cook in 2 batches, stirring occasionally, until they just turn pink, about 3 minutes.

Remove from the skillet with a slotted spoon and set aside. Repeat with the remaining shrimp.

Remove and discard all but 2 tablespoons of oil from the pan.

Add the shallots, gingerroot and lemon zest to the skillet. Cook for 2 minutes, stirring, until the shallots are golden.

Add the curry sauce and the poached pear slices. Bring the sauce to a boil over high heat. Add the shrimp and cook for 2 minutes, tossing in the sauce until they are hot and well coated. Remove from the heat and add salt and pepper to taste.

Remove the shrimp and pears with a slotted spoon and divide among 6 plates. Top with any sauce remaining in the skillet. Sprinkle with the toasted almonds and serve.

*To toast the almonds: Preheat the oven to 400 degrees F. Place the almonds on a dry baking sheet and toast, stirring occasionally, for about 4 to 5 minutes, until they have turned light brown and smell fragrant.

COCONUT MILK

COCONUT MILK is made from fresh coconut meat that has been removed from the shell, peeled, grated and soaked in water. It is then squeezed through a towel or a piece of cheesecloth to extract its flavor.

The soaking liquid, along with the squeezings, is a staple in Southeast Asian cooking. Added to soups, stews, roasts and desserts, coconut milk imparts richness.

I like the Chaokoh brand, which can be found in most Asian grocery stores. It is thick, rich and natural, with no added sugar. It usually comes in 14-ounce cans. When I open a can, I pour all of the coconut milk into a large bowl; the liquid has usually risen to the top and solids have sunk to the bottom. I whisk it until smooth and thick and store any leftovers in a sealed glass jar in the refrigerator. It will keep for up to 1 week.

CURRY SAUCE

MAKES ABOUT 1¼ CUPS SAUCE

THIS EXCELLENT CURRY-FLAVORED coconut sauce can be simmered with cooked, cubed chicken or poured over cooked fish fillets, such as salmon or bass.

1	tablespoon cornstarch
⅓	cup unsweetened coconut milk*
2	tablespoons corn oil
1	small onion, finely chopped
1	garlic clove, minced
1	teaspoon peeled, grated gingerroot
1	tablespoon curry powder (preferably Madras)
½	teaspoon freshly ground white pepper
	Dash of Tabasco sauce
2	cups chicken stock (page 79)
	About 1 teaspoon coarse or kosher salt (optional)

Mix the cornstarch and coconut milk in a small bowl; set aside.

Heat the oil in a medium saucepan. Add the onion, garlic and gingerroot. Cook over high heat until the onion is golden, about 4 minutes. Add the curry powder, white pepper and Tabasco. Cook over high heat, stirring, for 1 minute.

Add the stock and the coconut milk mixture. Mix well and cook over low heat for 20 minutes, or until the cornstarch no longer has a raw taste and the sauce is lightly thickened.

Remove from the heat and cool. When cool, puree the sauce in a blender or a food processor. Taste to correct the seasonings, adding the salt if needed.

The sauce can be prepared 3 to 4 days in advance, covered and refrigerated.

*I prefer the Chaokoh brand, which is carried by most Asian grocery stores.

ABOUT SHRIMP

Frozen Shrimp

In general, most of the shrimp available in this country has been previously frozen, though it is often thawed before being sold. Shrimp comes in many different grades and is priced accordingly. Those with pink shells are the best quality; they usually come from South America and are firmer, contain less iodine and last longer than the other varieties. White-shelled shrimp are also good quality. Whenever possible, avoid brown shrimp, which have a strong iodine flavor.

Choose shrimp that are firm and plump. Press the body with your fingertip; it should feel firm to the touch and bounce back when released. If the shrimp is flabby, it has been frozen for too long. Once cooked, it will shrink in size and become mushy.

Cleaning Shrimp

In order to make frozen shrimp taste better, I refresh them by cleaning them with salt and washing them in lots of water before cooking. Peel and devein the raw shrimp. Place them in a bowl and sprinkle generously with salt. Toss them well in the salt and quickly rub it in with your fingers so that it coats the shrimp. Place the bowl under a faucet and immediately rinse them well, running cold water over them until the water becomes clear and all the salt has been washed away.

Fresh Shrimp

In Taiwan, we were always able to get both freshwater and saltwater shrimp with the heads still attached. They were never frozen. Fresh shrimp are sweet, firm yet tender, with no unpleasant iodine taste. In recent years, farm-raised shrimp have become available in some parts of this country.

If you are lucky enough to be able to get fresh shrimp, buy those whose shells are shiny, with no fishy smell. When you press your finger onto the body of the shrimp, it should feel firm. When properly cooked, fresh shrimp will retain their firmness, while frozen shrimp will be more flaccid.

Clean, peel and devein the shrimp and wash with lots of cold water; no salt is needed. Save the shrimp heads and shells for making stock.

SAUTÉED SHRIMP WITH CORN IN SPICY WINE SAUCE

SERVES 4 AS A MAIN COURSE OR 8 AS PART OF A MULTI-COURSE DINNER

T HIS RECIPE IS BASED on two classical shrimp dishes: a Cantonese preparation cooked in a wine made from fermented sticky or sweet rice and a Sichuan specialty in which the shrimp is cooked with many spices. I add fresh plum tomatoes and white corn; it is sensational.

1	pound large shrimp, peeled, deveined and cleaned with salt (previous page), shells reserved
2	tablespoons vodka
1	large egg white, lightly beaten
3	tablespoons corn oil
5	garlic cloves, minced
1	tablespoon minced soaked dried shrimp (page 134; optional)
¼	cup sake
3	large plum tomatoes, peeled and finely chopped
1½	cups chicken or shrimp stock (page 79 or 105)
1	teaspoon coarse or kosher salt
½	teaspoon freshly ground white pepper
1	teaspoon cornstarch, mixed with 1 tablespoon water
½	cup fresh corn kernels, preferably white (or frozen, thawed)
¼	cup finely chopped red bell pepper
1	large jalapeño pepper, minced
1	tablespoon peeled, grated gingerroot
3	scallions, finely chopped

Combine the shrimp, vodka and egg white in a medium bowl. Mix well and refrigerate for 30 minutes, turning occasionally.

Heat 1 tablespoon of the oil in a small saucepan. Add the garlic and dried shrimp, if using, and cook over high heat until the ingredients release their flavor, about 1 minute. Add the reserved shrimp shells, sake and half the chopped tomatoes. Reduce the heat to medium and cook, stirring, for 3 minutes.

Add the stock, salt, white pepper and cornstarch mixture, bring to a boil, reduce the heat to low and cook for 20 minutes, or until the liquid is reduced by half, stirring occasionally. Strain through a fine sieve; set aside the liquid.

Heat the remaining 2 tablespoons oil in a large skillet until hot but not smoking. Add the shrimp and stir-fry until half-cooked, 1 to 2 minutes. Remove the shrimp with a slotted spoon; set aside.

Add the remaining tomatoes, corn, bell pepper, jalapeño pepper and gingerroot to the skillet. Cook, stirring occasionally, for 2 minutes. Return the shrimp and the reserved liquid to the skillet. Stir-fry over medium heat until the ingredients are heated through and the shrimp are cooked, about 3 minutes. Add the scallions, toss and serve immediately.

SPICY SOFT-SHELL CRABS

SERVES 2 AS A MAIN COURSE OR 4 AS A FIRST COURSE

THE FIRST TIME I ATE SOFT-SHELL CRAB was here in Philadelphia. I quickly gobbled up the whole thing! I had never before eaten a crab with an edible shell.

Soft-shell crabs are in season from May until late August. I prefer to use the "whale"-sized ones; they are the largest available and very meaty. I pan-fry them in hot oil so that the outsides get crunchy.

4	whale-sized or jumbo soft-shell crabs
2	large egg whites
1	tablespoon pureed jalapeño pepper
1	tablespoon finely chopped fresh lemon grass (page 86)*
1	teaspoon peeled, grated gingerroot
	Cornstarch for dusting
½	cup olive oil

Clean the soft-shell crabs by cutting off the face of each crab, just behind the eyes, with kitchen shears. Remove and discard the bile sac from the exposed cavity. Lift up the loose piece of shell on either side and snip off and discard the spongy gills. Remove and discard the tail (apron flap) from under the body.

Rinse the crabs well under cold running water and pat them dry with paper towels.

Beat the egg whites in a shallow bowl with a fork or a whisk until they are white and fluffy but not stiff. Add the jalapeño pepper, lemon grass and gingerroot; mix well to combine. Place the cornstarch on a plate.

Dip the crabs in the egg white mixture, making sure they are well coated on all sides. Then dust with cornstarch, shaking off the excess.

Heat ¼ cup of the oil over high heat in a large skillet. Place 2 of the crabs in the skillet, being careful not to crowd them. Cover and fry until golden brown, about 3 minutes. Turn the crabs, cover and fry on the second side. Remove from the skillet and drain on paper towels. Repeat with the remaining crabs, using the remaining ¼ cup oil. Serve immediately.

*Washed, finely chopped cilantro root may be substituted.

Steamed Crabmeat Soufflé

Serves 6 to 8

NOT EATEN AS A DESSERT, as custards often are in the West, Chinese custards contain ingredients like clams, seafood, ground meat or chicken. In China, custards are never made with milk or cream; stock is used instead. This stock must be completely fat-free, clear and highly concentrated to produce a light yet silky, full-flavored result, for its proportion is high in relation to the amount of egg.

Served piping hot, this steamed crabmeat custard soufflé is an elegant beginning for a formal dinner. Although not necessary, the caviar makes an extraordinary addition.

2	cups shrimp or chicken stock (page 105 or 79), all fat removed*
3	large eggs, lightly beaten
1½	teaspoons coarse or kosher salt
½	teaspoon freshly ground white pepper
½	pound jumbo lump crabmeat, picked over, cartilage removed
1	tablespoon olive oil
2	fresh medium shiitake mushroom caps, wiped clean and finely chopped
1	tablespoon vodka
1	tablespoon chopped fresh chives
1	ounce Beluga or other caviar of your choice (optional)

Pour the stock into a small bowl.

Gradually add the eggs to the stock, stirring until all the ingredients are well blended. Add 1 teaspoon of the salt and the pepper. Mix well, then strain.

Divide the crabmeat evenly among 6 to 8 espresso, custard or demitasse cups, or Chinese tea cups with lids.** Divide the stock mixture among the cups. Cover each cup tightly with plastic wrap or foil (I prefer the tighter seal that plastic wrap provides), and if you are using Chinese tea cups, place the lid on top. The cups must be tightly covered to prevent moisture from dripping into the custards. If your cups do not have lids, cover them with a second layer of plastic wrap or foil.

Fill the bottom of a steamer with water close to, but not touching, the rack and bring to a boil. Place the cups on the rack. Cover and steam over high heat for 5

Steamed Crabmeat Soufflé

minutes. Reduce the heat to medium-low, and continue steaming for about 20 more minutes; the surface of the soufflés should be moist and slick when done.

Meanwhile, heat the oil in a small saucepan. Add the mushrooms and vodka and cook over high heat until the mushrooms are tender, about 5 minutes. Add the remaining ½ teaspoon salt and remove from the heat.

To serve, unwrap and uncover each custard cup. Spoon some of the mushrooms onto each soufflé. Sprinkle with the chives and top with the caviar, if using. Serve at once.

Variation

The custard can also be baked in a preheated 325-degree oven. Place the covered cups in a large, shallow baking dish. Fill with hot water to come halfway up the sides of the custard dishes. Place a sheet of foil over all, tightly sealing the edges. Bake for 30 minutes, or until the custards set.

*If you don't have any shrimp stock on hand, you can make a quick version as follows: Place 2 tablespoons of minced soaked dried shrimp (page 134) in a medium saucepan. Stir in 3 cups of chicken stock (page 79) or clam juice. Bring to a boil over high heat; reduce the heat to low. Cook, uncovered, until the stock is reduced to 2 cups, about 20 minutes.

**Chinese tea cups are about the same size as demitasse cups but have no handles. They often come with matching lids for keeping the tea warm.

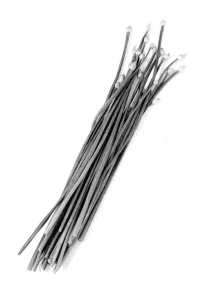

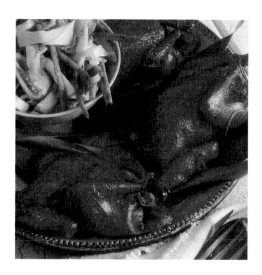

CHAPTER FIVE

FOWL

WHEN MY FAMILY MOVED TO T'AICHUNG, a small town in the middle of Taiwan, the country was so poor that every household had to raise its own fowl. My brothers and I amused ourselves by feeding rice to the chickens running around our backyard and were thrilled when their eggs hatched into tiny chicks.

It was always a treat to have chicken for dinner. When they grew big enough, the cook would kill them by slitting their necks with a sharp knife. No part of the bird was ever wasted: even the blood was drained into a bowl to be used. The head and the feet flavored a soup that my grandmother loved. Even as a child, though, I never liked the taste of that soup. The remainder of the bird was plucked, cleaned and prepared for cooking.

Our cook saved the prettiest feathers for me. Often, my mother fashioned them into a beautiful toy by attaching the feathers to two old coins with holes in the middle. We kicked this "bird" around with our feet, seeing who could keep it in the air the longest. I had a large collection of feathers that I stored in a cookie box, and sometimes I brought them to school to trade with my classmates.

When we moved to Kao-hsiung, which was more prosperous, my mother and I were able to go to the market to buy live chickens, ducks, squab and quail. There were many different species of free-range chicken to choose from—all called simply "local chicken." One kind had white feathers and black skin—even its bones were black. It was the most expensive, for it was believed to be highly nutritious, especially for pregnant women. My mother always returned to the same butcher, for she trusted him to select good breeding hens that had been properly raised and had not yet laid eggs, so they would be tender.

Sometimes our cook slowly braised the fresh chicken with soy sauce, Shaoxing rice wine and spices. Or he would stuff it with sweet rice and chestnuts and steam it. Often, he just cut it into small pieces and stir-fried it with fresh bamboo shoots and mushrooms. No matter how it was prepared, the chicken always had a natural sweetness and a rich flavor, since it was allowed to run loose until the day it was killed.

BY THE TIME I REACHED COLLEGE, the fast-growing, commercially raised chickens familiar in the West had become available for the first time in the marketplace. My mother called them "Western chicken." These processed, packaged birds were four to five times cheaper than the live local chickens, yet most Chinese I knew would not buy them because they had little flavor.

Duck was also popular in our home. My mother used to buy whole fresh ducks and braise them with soy sauce or marinate them with roasted Sichuan peppercorns, then steam them. My mother-in-law, too, loved duck. Her famous eight-treasure duck stuffed with sweet rice, studded with "treasures" like fresh shrimp, ham and fresh water chestnuts, took a whole day to prepare. That and her duck breast sautéed with bitter squash, hot pepper and spring ginger were my favorites.

On special occasions, my father would take our family to a restaurant specializing in Peking duck, which no family I knew ever made at home because it was so time-consuming. These restaurants raised their own ducks, force-feeding them, much as is done in France, so they were plump and meaty. Weighing 12 to 14 pounds, one was more than enough to feed the whole family. My father always ordered the three-course dinner that consisted of Peking duck served with thin pancakes, followed by vegetables that had been sautéed in duck fat, concluding with a soup made from the leftover duck bones.

WHEN I FIRST CAME TO THE UNITED STATES, I discovered that the great variety of poultry I had taken for granted in Taiwan was nowhere to be found. I could get only supermarket chicken, which tasted musty and had a mushy texture. Then, during my second year, when my husband and I lived in Pittsburgh, I went to a farmer's market and found a stall that sold free-range chickens. I was so excited! But when I cooked one, it was tough as a boot—an ancient stewing hen and not the delicate young bird I was expecting.

Recently, however, many supermarkets have begun to carry tender organically grown "natural" chickens, as well as fresh-killed kosher chickens, which are firm-textured and fresh-tasting. The range of other birds available in this country has also expanded considerably. Some specialty markets sell poussin, very young chickens that weigh about 1 pound each, farm-raised squab and pheasants. As a result, I can now make the favorite dishes of my childhood without disappointment.

PREPARING POULTRY FOR COOKING

Cutting up a Whole Bird

Holding the chicken on its side, cut through the backbone along one side of the neck, from neck to tail, with a sharp boning knife or cleaver.

Pull the chicken open, breast side down. Remove the backbone by cutting along the other side of the neck, from neck to tail. Reserve the backbone for making stock.

With the chicken breast facing down, push down on the center breastbone with your hand to loosen it. Then break out the breastbone with your fingers, removing it along with any attached cartilage.

Cut though the center of the breast with your knife, separating the chicken into 2 halves. Turn skin side up and cut to separate the breast and leg sections on each half of the chicken; you will have 4 pieces.

Remove the wings from the breast sections by cutting around the ball and socket of the first joint to separate them so you have 6 pieces. Cut off the wing tips and reserve them for making stock.

Cut the drumsticks from the thigh sections at the joint connecting them so that you have 8 pieces.

Boning a Breast

Place the breast skin side up, and using a sharp boning knife, cut as close to the rib bones as possible, starting at the thicker edge (center) of the breast. Use your hand to pull the meat away from the bone as you cut, until it is completely freed. Reserve the bones for making stock.

FOWL

Breast of Chicken Sautéed with Mushrooms   194

Roast Chicken with Black Bean Sauce   196

Chicken with Mango, Asparagus and Ginger   199

Kung Pao Chicken   202

Roasted Chicken with Dried Chestnut Stuffing   206

Tea-Smoked Cornish Hens   209

Soy-Braised Cornish Hens   212

Crispy Duck with Star Anise Sauce   214

Eight-Treasure Duck   217

Tsing Tao Duck   220

BREAST OF CHICKEN SAUTÉED WITH MUSHROOMS

SERVES 2 AS A MAIN COURSE OR 4 AS ONE OF SEVERAL COURSES

THIS IS EASY TO PREPARE and one of my sons' favorites. The chicken is first marinated in soy sauce to tenderize the meat and give it flavor, then dipped into egg yolk and dusted with cornstarch for a crispy coating. Most Chinese prepare this dish by deep-frying the meat, but I think the natural juices of the chicken are lost that way. I prefer to pan-fry the chicken breast.

4	boneless, skinless chicken breast halves (about 1 pound)
2	tablespoons soy sauce
2	large egg yolks, lightly beaten
½	cup cornstarch
5	tablespoons olive oil
3	tablespoons vodka
2	garlic cloves, sliced
1	pound white button mushrooms, stems removed, sliced
2	plum tomatoes, diced
2	scallions, chopped
	Coarse or kosher salt
	Freshly ground pepper
1	tablespoon chopped fresh tarragon leaves

Place the chicken breasts between 2 sheets of plastic wrap and pound them lightly with a flat mallet or the back of a cleaver until they are about ½ inch thick. Place the breasts in a shallow pan or bowl. Add the soy sauce and turn the chicken to coat it well.

Place the beaten egg yolk in a shallow pan and the cornstarch on a plate.

Remove the chicken breasts from the marinade and dip them into the egg yolk, coating on all sides. Dredge them very lightly in the cornstarch.

Heat 3 tablespoons of the oil in a large nonstick skillet. When the oil is hot but not smoking, add 2 of the chicken breast halves and brown on high heat on both sides for 3 to 4 minutes per side.

Remove from the skillet and keep warm. Add 1 tablespoon oil and repeat with the remaining 2 halves.

Add the vodka and the garlic to the skillet and cook over medium heat, stirring to scrape up any particles clinging to the bottom or sides of the pan. Boil for about 1 minute to reduce and concentrate the flavor.

Add the remaining 1 tablespoon oil to the skillet. Add the mushrooms, tomatoes and scallions and cook over high heat, stirring, for about 3 minutes, or until the mushrooms are tender. Season to taste with salt and pepper.

Remove the pan from the heat and stir in the tarragon.

Place the chicken pieces on a serving platter and spoon the sauce and vegetables over all.

Roast Chicken
with Black Bean Sauce

Serves 4

THIS IS A POPULAR CANTONESE DISH, but traditionally, the chicken is steamed after it is browned. The Chinese prefer their chicken to have a velvety texture, but most Americans like a crispy skin. Roasting is much simpler than steaming and produces a better-flavored bird.

Fresh kosher chicken is best for this dish. It is now available in many local supermarkets. I serve this dish with Green Apple and Kumquat Relish (page 120) or Baked Creamy Napa Cabbage (page 143).

2	tablespoons fermented black beans (page 119)
1	cup water
3	tablespoons vodka
1	3-3½-pound chicken
3	tablespoons corn oil
3	garlic cloves, minced
2	scallions, chopped
1	tablespoon peeled, minced gingerroot
2	tablespoons soy sauce
2	tablespoons balsamic vinegar
1	teaspoon sugar
½	cup chicken stock (page 79), plus up to ½ cup more, if needed

Place the beans in a bowl and soak them in the water for 2 minutes. Drain and discard the water. Add the vodka. Set aside.

Wash the chicken well and pat dry. Cut into 8 pieces (see page 192).

Heat the oil in a large skillet. Add the chicken pieces and cook over high heat, turning, until chicken has browned on all sides. Add the garlic, scallions and gingerroot to the skillet and cook for 1 to 2 minutes, until the garlic turns light brown.

Add the black beans and turn the chicken pieces so that they are well coated. Add the soy sauce, vinegar and sugar and mix well.

Turn the heat to low, cover and cook for about 10 minutes. Add ½ cup of the stock to the pan, bring it to a boil, then turn off the heat.

The recipe can be completed to this point up to 1 day in advance and refrigerated.

Preheat the oven to 375 degrees F. Place the chicken, skin side up, in a shallow roasting pan. Spoon any extra pan liquids over the chicken.

Roast the chicken, adding ¼ to ½ cup more stock to the pan if the liquid has evaporated, until it is golden brown and cooked through, about 30 minutes.

Variation

To cook the chicken whole, wash, pat dry and place in a large bowl. Cook the soaked black beans, garlic, scallions and ginger in the oil over high heat for 2 minutes, until the garlic turns brown. Add the soy sauce, vodka, vinegar and sugar. Pour this mixture over the chicken, rubbing it in well, both inside and out. Marinate, covered, in the refrigerator, overnight, turning occasionally to make sure the bird is well coated.

Roast in a preheated 350-degree oven for 1 hour, or until the outside skin is crisp and juices run clear when the thigh is pierced with a fork.

Chicken with Mango, Asparagus and Ginger

CHICKEN WITH MANGO, ASPARAGUS AND GINGER

THIS DISH IS BEST IN LATE APRIL and early May, when young spring gingerroot can be found and first-of-the-season mangos and firm baby asparagus are readily available. When mangos and asparagus can't be had, I use peeled and sliced Fuyu persimmons and snap peas instead. I serve this with Chinese Risotto with Wild Mushrooms (page 295), Curried Brown Rice with Broccoli Rabe (page 294) or Sweet Rice, Taro and Pineapple Compote (page 298).

Chicken and Marinade

1	pound boneless, skinless chicken breast, cubed (page 200)
1	tablespoon vodka or dry vermouth
1	large egg white, lightly beaten
1	tablespoon cornstarch
½	teaspoon coarse or kosher salt
1	tablespoon corn oil

Sauce

1	tablespoon corn oil
½	cup finely chopped onion
1	garlic clove, minced
½	cup dry white wine
2	tablespoons oyster sauce
1	tablespoon soy sauce
1	cup chicken stock (page 79)
1	teaspoon cornstarch
1	tablespoon water

1	cup plus 1 tablespoon corn oil
1	2-inch piece gingerroot, peeled and thinly sliced
¼	cup julienned red bell pepper
6	thin asparagus spears, sliced diagonally into 1-inch pieces (1 cup)
1	ripe mango, peeled and cut into chunks
½	cup "Honeyed" Walnuts (page 59)

To marinate the chicken: Place the chicken in a shallow pan. Add the vodka or vermouth and mix well. Add the egg white, cornstarch and salt and mix into the chicken. Add the oil. Toss the chicken in the marinade and refrigerate for 30 minutes.

To make the sauce: Heat the oil in a medium saucepan. Add the onion and cook over high heat, stirring, until it is golden, about 3 minutes.

Add the garlic and cook for another minute. Pour in the wine, oyster sauce and soy sauce. Cook, stirring, for 2 minutes. Add the stock.

Combine the cornstarch and water and add to the saucepan. Stir to combine.

Cook the sauce over low heat for 20 minutes, until the cornstarch has lost its raw taste. Strain and set aside.

To cook the chicken: Heat 1 cup of the oil in a large skillet over low heat. Add all of the marinated chicken and cook, stirring constantly, until the chicken cubes turn white and are half cooked, about 2 to 3 minutes. Drain in a strainer set over a bowl to catch the oil; set aside. Once cold, the oil can be strained through a fine sieve and reserved for another use.

Heat the remaining 1 tablespoon of the oil in the skillet, add the gingerroot and cook over high heat for 1 minute. Add the bell pepper and asparagus.

Pour in the reserved sauce. Add the chicken and cook over high heat, stirring, for 2 minutes, or until the chicken is completely cooked. Add the mango and cook just long enough to heat through, about ½ minute.

Add the walnuts and mix well. Spoon the chicken mixture onto a platter and serve immediately.

CUBING A CHICKEN BREAST

In CHINESE COOKING, a variety of flavorful dishes are made by cutting chicken breasts or legs into small pieces, with or without the bones, marinating them and quickly stir-frying the meat. I prefer to use the breast meat.

To cube the breast, skin it and cut into 2 halves. Trim off and discard any visible fat and veins. Cut each half into four 1-inch strips on the diagonal, then cut diagonally in the other direction, making 1-inch squares. I usually cut off the tip of the breast and save it for another use.

THE EMPEROR'S NEW CHICKEN

LEGEND HAS IT that Governor Ding of Sichuan, who had the title of Kung Pao (which means "governor" in Chinese), was to entertain a special delegation sent by the Emperor himself. Just before the banquet scheduled in their honor was about to begin, an ashen-faced kitchen helper ran to the chef and tearfully confessed that the dried hot pepper that was supposed to be infusing in the peanut oil had burned because the flame had been turned up high by mistake.

Time was too short to change the menu or to remake the infusion. Fearfully, the decision was made to use the oil as it was, with the burnt pepper flavor, in the hope that no one would notice. Peanuts were added to cover up the taste. Much to the chef's surprise, everyone loved it. The Emperor's delegation spread the fame of the newly created dish far and wide as they traveled from place to place.

KUNG PAO CHICKEN

SERVES 4 AS A MAIN COURSE OR 8 AS PART OF A LARGE DINNER OR BANQUET

KUNG PAO CHICKEN is one of the best known and most widely prepared of all classic Sichuan foods. Usually, whole dried small red peppers are purposely burned in order to flavor the oil in which the chicken is then cooked.

When I was small, my father often took us to a Sichuan restaurant in T'aipei, where I always ordered this dish. I loved the tender chicken, sweet young bamboo shoots and crunchy peanuts coated with the piquant sauce, but I never liked the burnt flavor of the dried hot peppers. I have changed this recipe by using Western sauce techniques and Chinese seasonings, without the burned peppers.

This chicken is tender and bursts with garlic, gingerroot and fiery fragrant peppers. Serve with plain rice, Pan-Fried Noodles (page 271) or Rice Noodles with Porcini Mushrooms (page 277).

1	pound boneless, skinless chicken breast, cut into 1-inch cubes (page 200)
1	tablespoon gin or vodka
1	large egg white, lightly beaten
1	tablespoon cornstarch
½	teaspoon coarse or kosher salt or 1 teaspoon soy sauce
1	cup plus 2 tablespoons corn oil
⅓	cup blanched raw peanuts*
2	garlic cloves, thinly sliced
2	tablespoons peeled, julienned gingerroot
⅓	cup red bell pepper, cut into ¼-inch dice
½	cup small white button mushroom caps, whole, or quartered, if large, stems removed**
3	scallions, white part only, cut into ½-inch pieces
1	cup Kung Pao Sauce (page 204)

Place the chicken cubes and the gin or vodka in a large bowl and mix well. Add the egg white and the cornstarch, and sprinkle with the salt or soy sauce, mixing well. Add 2 tablespoons of the oil to the chicken and toss. (Adding some of the oil at this stage will make the chicken pieces easier to separate when cooked.) Place the marinated chicken in the refrigerator for at least 30 minutes or up to 2 hours.

Heat the remaining 1 cup oil to 325 degrees F in a large skillet or fryer. Add the raw peanuts and fry for about 7 minutes, or until they are light golden. Remove with a slotted spoon and place on paper towels to drain. Set aside.

Gradually add all the marinated chicken pieces to the oil. When the chicken turns white, about 2 minutes, turn off the heat. (The chicken will be half-cooked.)

Carefully pour the chicken and the oil through a strainer placed over a large bowl to catch the oil; set aside. The chicken can be cooked to this point up to 4 hours in advance. Cover tightly and refrigerate.

Heat 2 tablespoons of the reserved oil in a large skillet. Add the garlic, ginger-root and bell pepper and cook over high heat for about 2 minutes, or until the garlic is lightly browned.

Add the mushrooms and the scallions. Stir in the Kung Pao Sauce. When it comes to a boil, add the chicken pieces and stir to coat well with the sauce. Cook over high heat for about 5 minutes, or until the flavors are well blended.

Stir in the peanuts. Remove from the heat and place on a serving platter.

*Blanched peanuts can be bought in health food stores and Chinese markets; their outside shells and red papery skins have been removed.

**When fresh artichokes are in season, 2 large artichoke hearts, cut into quarters, can be substituted for the mushrooms.

Low-Fat Variation

Bake the peanuts in 1 tablespoon oil in a preheated 350-degree oven for 15 to 20 minutes, stirring occasionally, until they are light golden. Marinate the chicken as directed, but instead of cooking it in the oil, bring 3 cups of chicken stock (page 79) to a boil in a medium saucepan, reduce the heat to low, add the chicken and simmer, stirring, until it turns white, about 2 minutes. Remove with a slotted spoon, set aside, and continue with the recipe.

Kung Pao Sauce

Makes about 2 cups sauce

I CREATED THIS VERSION OF THE ROBUST SAUCE I remember enjoying as a child. The ancho chiles give it a wonderfully smoky flavor and a lovely red color. This sauce will perk up many beef or meat dishes. It can be used with Aromatic Ginger-Flavored Sweetbreads (page 225) instead of the brown sauce.

2	tablespoons corn oil
½	cup diced onion
2	garlic cloves, sliced
1	teaspoon minced gingerroot
2	star anise
½	teaspoon roasted Sichuan peppercorns (page 111)
2	dried ancho chile peppers, soaked and chopped
1	teaspoon hot red pepper flakes
½	cup dry white wine
2	tablespoons soy sauce
1	teaspoon sugar
4	cups chicken stock (page 79)
1	tablespoon cornstarch, mixed with 1 tablespoon water

Heat the oil in a medium saucepan. Add the onion, garlic, gingerroot, star anise and Sichuan peppercorns. Cook over high heat for about 5 minutes, or until the onion is lightly browned.

Add the ancho chiles and hot pepper flakes and cook for 1 to 2 minutes more.

Add the white wine, soy sauce and sugar, and cook until the mixture starts to boil.

Stir in the chicken stock and the cornstarch mixture. When the liquid returns to a boil, reduce the heat to medium and simmer for 30 minutes, or until the cornstarch loses its raw taste.

Strain the sauce.

The sauce will keep in a covered jar in the refrigerator for up to 1 week or in the freezer for up to 3 months.

CHESTNUTS

ONE OF MY EARLIEST childhood memories of the fall in Shanghai is of watching the street vendors roast chestnuts. Whenever my parents took me out for a walk, the air was permeated with the delicate aroma of those chestnuts, roasting in big woks in rock sugar and coarse sand, as the vendors stir-fried them with big shovels. Sweet and hot, they were a treat.

Chestnuts come from northern China and are usually smaller than those found in this country. Hubei province in central China is famous for its chestnuts, which seem to be sweeter and nuttier than the others. But the best fresh chestnuts I have ever tasted came from Bradford, Pennsylvania.

Chestnuts are considered good luck because they signal lots of children, and a chicken dish stuffed with chestnuts, usually steamed or braised, is served before the New Year holiday.

Fresh Chestnuts

Nothing beats the flavor of fresh chestnuts. To prepare them, cut a crosswise slit in the top of each nut with a sharp paring knife. Arrange the nuts in a ring on a plate and cook in a microwave oven at high power for 4 minutes, or until the shells open. Or bake in a preheated 375-degree oven for about 20 minutes, or until the shells open. Peel while still warm.

Dried Chestnuts

Dried chestnuts, while not pleasant to eat plain, are fine for cooking and convenient be-cause they are already peeled. When they are braised with meat or poultry, they absorb the cooking liquid and deepen in flavor as they sweeten the stock.

Dried chestnuts can be found in most Chinese grocery stores. They are usually packed in 1-pound plastic bags. Choose those that are large and uniform in size; the best are pale yellow. The packages should be free from particles of shell or other debris. Smaller, darker nuts usually have been around too long or are not of the best quality.

To Prepare Dried Chestnuts

Dried chestnuts, much like dried beans, have to be soaked before cooking, so they swell. Soak each cup of dried chestnuts in 3 cups warm water for at least 2 hours. Drain and discard the soaking water. Use a small paring knife to remove any pieces of skin or shell clinging to the nuts. Wash again and drain well.

To enhance the taste of the dried chestnuts and return their original sweetness, I cook them in a sugar-water mixture. For each cup of soaked chestnuts, bring 3 cups water and ¼ cup sugar to a boil, stirring to dissolve the sugar. Add the chestnuts, reduce the heat, and simmer, uncovered, for 15 minutes. If the chestnuts are to be used in stuffing, increase the cooking time from 15 minutes to 30 minutes. Drain and discard the sugar-water. The chestnuts are now ready to use in braised dishes, stuffings, soups or stir-fries. They will need to cook for another 30 minutes, either with meat or in a stock.

ROASTED CHICKEN WITH DRIED CHESTNUT STUFFING

SERVES 4

A WHOLE CHICKEN is slathered with a sweet, salty, spicy mixture of soybean paste and mango chutney, both on and beneath the skin, so it permeates the flesh. Then the bird is stuffed with chestnuts and roasted, with napa cabbage added near the end of the cooking so it becomes sweet and softened in the juices. I prepare this festive dish when both my sons are home for the Thanksgiving or Christmas holidays, serving it with Chinese Risotto with Wild Mushrooms (page 295).

3	tablespoons yellow soybean paste (page 173)
3	tablespoons Madeira
2	tablespoons bottled mango chutney
1	teaspoon freshly ground roasted Sichuan peppercorns (page 111)
1	teaspoon coarse or kosher salt
1	3½-4-pound chicken (preferably fresh kosher)
1	head napa cabbage (2 pounds)
2	tablespoons corn oil
3	shallots, finely chopped
	About 2 cups chicken stock (page 79)
2	cups cooked chestnuts (from 1 cup dried)*
	Coarse or kosher salt
	Freshly ground pepper

Preheat the oven to 375 degrees F.

Mix the soybean paste, Madeira, mango chutney, Sichuan peppercorns and salt in a large bowl; set aside.

Remove the giblets from the chicken and reserve for another use. Wash the chicken and pat dry. Loosen the skin of the chicken by inserting your finger between the skin and the meat. Starting at the neck end, gently loosen the skin from the body of the chicken around the breast and the legs so you can rub the marinade directly on the flesh.

Rub the marinade into the chicken, covering the inside cavity, the outside skin and the meat under the loosened skin. Apply the marinade several times to coat well, then set the bird aside while you prepare the remaining ingredients.

Cut the cabbage lengthwise into quarters. Discard any tough stems. Cut the quarters crosswise into 1-inch strips. Wash well in cold water, drain and set aside.

Heat the oil in a small saucepan. Add the shallots and sauté over high heat, stirring, until they are lightly browned. Add ¼ cup of the chicken stock and the cooked chestnuts and cook for 3 minutes, until the flavors are blended.

Spoon the chestnut stuffing into the cavity of the chicken. Pour in any remaining marinade. Using cotton string, truss the chicken well to secure the stuffing.

Pour ¾ cup of the chicken stock into the bottom of a roasting pan with a rack. Place the chicken on the rack, breast side up. Roast for ½ hour, or until lightly browned.

Add the cabbage to the bottom of the roasting pan and continue to cook for about ½ hour more, or until the chicken and cabbage are tender. Add up to 1 cup more stock, if needed, to keep the cabbage moist as it cooks. At the end of the hour, the cabbage will have absorbed the cooking juices from the chicken.

Remove the chicken from the oven, remove the string and spoon out the stuffing and set aside.

Carve the chicken into serving-sized pieces. Spoon the cabbage onto a serving platter, top with the chicken and the stuffing.

*See page 205 for cooking instructions.

Tea-Smoked Cornish Hens and Sichuan Pickled Vegetables

TEA-SMOKED CORNISH HENS

SERVES 4

A STORE IN T'AIPEI is famous for its Peking smoked chicken. The free-range chickens are first rubbed with a mixture of dry-roasted Sichuan peppercorns and salt. Left overnight to marinate, they are quickly smoked, then broiled to finish the cooking. These chickens are tender and juicy, with a lightly smoked flavor redolent of Sichuan peppercorns. My mother often brings one of them home for the holidays or whenever she has company, and she serves them cold, as a starter, with pickled vegetables and five-spice beef.

Cornish hens make a good substitute for the smaller free-range chickens found in Taiwan. I serve them hot with Sweet Rice, Taro and Pineapple Compote (page 298). I also like them cold with pickled vegetables.

Cornish Hens

4   1-pound Cornish hens*

2   tablespoons Roasted Sichuan Peppercorns and Salt (page 211)

Smoking Mixture

½   cup all-purpose flour

½   cup sugar

½   cup rice (any kind)

½   cup green or black tea leaves

Basting Liquid

1   tablespoon corn or olive oil

2   shallots, chopped

1   tablespoon soy sauce

1   tablespoon balsamic vinegar

1   tablespoon Asian sesame oil

To prepare the hens: Wash the Cornish hens and pat them dry with paper towels. Rub with the peppercorn-and-salt mixture, using about ½ tablespoon for each bird. Place in a bowl, cover tightly with plastic wrap and refrigerate for at least 12 hours or overnight, turning the birds a few times.

To smoke the hens: Mix the smoking ingredients. Line a heavy Dutch oven or cast-iron pot with heavy-duty aluminum foil. Pour the smoking mixture on the foil. (See page 168 for details, particularly if smoking on an electric stove.)

If you are using a gas stove, turn the heat under the Dutch oven or pot to high and place a rack about 3 inches above the smoking mixture so that the hens do not touch it.

Place the hens on the rack. Cover with a heavy lid or a tent made of a double layer of heavy-duty foil.

Cook over high heat for about 5 minutes, or until smoke begins to form. Reduce the heat to medium and continue to smoke for another 10 minutes to allow the flavors to penetrate the meat.

Turn off the heat and let stand, covered, for 10 minutes. To avoid smoking up your house, take the pot outside before uncovering it. Remove the smoked hens; they will be half-cooked.

The hens can be smoked up to 1 week in advance and refrigerated. Or they can be frozen, well wrapped, for up to 2 months. Before broiling, cut the hens in half. The bones can be left in or removed (see page 192).

To make the basting liquid: Heat the oil in a small skillet. Add the shallots and cook over high heat, stirring, until brown, 2 to 3 minutes; turn off the heat. Add the soy sauce, vinegar and sesame oil to the pan. Pour into a medium bowl and set aside.

To broil the hens: Preheat the broiler, with a rack 4 to 6 inches from the heat source. Brush the hens with the basting liquid on both sides. Lay the hen halves on a baking sheet, skin side up. Broil on 1 side for 10 minutes, or until nicely browned. Turn, baste the second side and broil for another 5 minutes, or until the hens are medium to well done. Remove, slice and serve.

*You can substitute poussin (baby chickens), squab or duck breast for the Cornish hens. If smoking duck breast, reduce the smoking time to 7 minutes.

Variation

Instead of broiling the Cornish hens, you can roast them in a preheated 375-degree oven for 20 to 25 minutes, or until done. Brush with the basting liquid before roasting.

ROASTED SICHUAN PEPPERCORNS AND SALT

I LIKE TO KEEP A MIXTURE of roasted Sichuan peppercorns and salt on hand as a spice rub for meat, fowl or fish. Using this dry marinade is an ancient Chinese technique and adds a pleasant, aromatic flavor to smoked, cured and steamed foods.

Mix 2 tablespoons of coarse or kosher salt and 1 tablespoon of Sichuan peppercorns, and roast the mixture over low heat until the salt is lightly browned and the peppercorns just begin to smoke, 20 to 25 minutes. (I roast 1 cup at a time—⅔ cup salt and ⅓ cup peppercorns).

Remove the pan from the heat. Let the mixture cool, then store in a tightly sealed jar. The mixture will keep its strength for about 6 months.

Rub the mixture on chicken, squab, pork or fish and refrigerate for a minimum of 12 hours or even overnight to allow the pungent flavor to penetrate the food.

Soy-Braised Cornish Hens

Serves 4

OY-BRAISED CHICKEN is a common household dish throughout China. It is usually simmered with soy sauce, Shaoxing wine, rock sugar and spices; no water or stock is added. Both my mother and my mother-in-law serve it as a cold starter at the beginning of a meal, much like an antipasto. Or it may be served hot as a main course.

This braising technique works well for chicken, pheasant or Cornish hens. I often serve this dish cold; it makes a great lunch along with a salad. Sliced, the meat makes a wonderful sandwich filler.

The recipe can be completed 1 day in advance. If you want to crisp the skins before serving, preheat the broiler, with a rack 4 to 6 inches from the heat, and brush the birds with a little bit of the sauce. Broil them, turning once, for 15 minutes, or until the skins are crisp and the bird is heated through.

When preparing the hens as a main course for dinner, I reheat them and serve with rice, noodles or Scallion Pancakes (page 305). They are also good with Sweet Rice, Taro and Pineapple Compote (page 298) and Broccoli Rabe with Green Peas (page 151).

4	Cornish hens, about 1 pound each
2	tablespoons corn oil
3	garlic cloves, crushed
2	scallions, cut into 1-inch pieces
1	2-inch piece gingerroot, peeled and sliced
3	star anise
1	teaspoon roasted Sichuan peppercorns (page 111)
1	cup soy sauce*
½	cup water
½	cup sake or brandy
1	tablespoon sugar

Wash the Cornish hens and dry them completely with paper towels, inside and out.

Heat the oil in a large Dutch oven with a tight-fitting lid. Add the garlic, scallions, gingerroot, star anise and Sichuan peppercorns. Cook over high heat, stirring, until the garlic is golden and fragrant, about 2 minutes.

Add the soy sauce, water, sake or brandy and sugar. Cook over high heat, uncovered, for about 10 minutes to develop the flavor.

Reduce the heat to low and add the hens. Cover and simmer for 30 minutes, turning every 7 to 10 minutes to coat the hens with the sauce, until tender.

Turn off the heat and let hens sit for another 10 minutes before removing the lid.

Transfer the Cornish hens to a large serving plate and keep warm. Strain the sauce, skim off the fat and pour the sauce into a serving bowl.

*Preferably Kikkoman soy sauce.

GINGERROOT

DURING MY CHILDHOOD, my mother made a wintertime tonic of gingerroot and brown sugar to give us warmth and energy. In the summer, she steamed gingerroot with pears, which she believed to be good for us.

Fresh gingerroot, the most basic ingredient in Chinese dishes, has gained tremendously in popularity over the past 10 years in this country. In the United States, the best gingerroot comes from Hawaii. It is usually about 6 inches long, but some can be larger than your hand. The skin is smooth and easy to peel and has few small knobs. For dishes where appearance matters, gingerroot should be peeled and julienned.

In the spring and throughout the summer, Chinese markets fill with a real treat: fresh young gingerroot. The skin looks a little like that of a new potato, translucent, with purplish tips. Whereas mature gingerroot is often stringy and pungent and requires peeling, young ginger is tender, with little fiber and a mildly spicy taste.

How to Use Ginger

I use the peel of the gingerroot to flavor stock, the small peeled knobs for braising, sauces or desserts and peeled julienned gingerroot for dressings, sauces, sautés or decoration. The larger pieces are the easiest to handle. To keep gingerroot fresh, I peel and slice it paper-thin and julienne it very fine, rinsing the shreds 2 or 3 times in cold water. I store the julienned gingerroot in the refrigerator in an open glass jar filled with clean water, changing the water occasionally. That way, it keeps for 2 to 3 weeks. Peeled small gingerroot knobs can be refrigerated in clean cold water for 3 weeks to 1 month.

Crispy Duck
with Star Anise Sauce

THIS HAS BEEN OUR MOST POPULAR DISH in the restaurant since we opened, and it's easy to make at home. The duck is first braised, then cut in half, coated with water chestnut flour and deep-fried, producing a crisp skin and a moist bird with no oily taste. Serve with rice.

Double recipe (4 cups) Brown Sauce for Braising
(page 249)
1   5-pound duck, washed, all visible fat removed
¼   cup water chestnut flour*
3   tablespoons warm water
¼   teaspoon freshly ground white pepper
1   tablespoon white vinegar
1   small orange, zest removed and thinly julienned;
     orange sectioned
2   tablespoons balsamic vinegar
2   tablespoons Grand Marnier or other orange
     liqueur, such as Cointreau or Triple Sec
     Corn oil for deep-frying
4   star anise

Bring the brown sauce to a vigorous boil in a large pot. Carefully lower the duck into the sauce.

Return the sauce to a boil, then reduce the heat to low; do not let the liquid boil again.

Simmer the duck, covered, for 1 hour and 15 minutes, turning 3 or 4 times to coat it well with the braising sauce. Remove the duck from the sauce and place it on a platter. Refrigerate the sauce. Cool the duck and store, covered, overnight in the refrigerator. Drain any liquid that accumulates on the platter and add it to the sauce.

The following day, skim the fat from the top and set aside 1 cup of the sauce. Refrigerate or freeze the rest for another use.

Cut the duck in half and remove the backbone, if you wish. With your hand, remove and discard the breast and rib bones. (See page 192 for boning instructions.)

Combine the water chestnut flour, warm water, white pepper and white vinegar on a large shallow plate until the flour is dissolved.

Holding each duck half over the plate, spoon the flour mixture over the duck, making sure to coat both sides. Let stand at room temperature for 5 to 10 minutes, until the coating has dried.

Meanwhile, place the julienned orange zest in a large saucepan with water to cover, and cook until the zest is tender and the bitterness is removed, about 5 minutes; drain. Transfer to a small saucepan, and add the balsamic vinegar and the reserved 1 cup of brown sauce. Bring to a boil, then remove from the heat and stir in the orange liqueur; set aside.

Heat about 6 inches of oil to 325 degrees F in a fryer or large skillet. Carefully lower the duck halves into the hot oil. Spoon the hot oil over the duck as it cooks, turning 2 or 3 times, until the duck has browned, about 5 to 7 minutes. The skin should be very crisp.

Using tongs, remove the duck halves from the oil and drain on paper towels.

Gently heat the sauce while you carve the duck into 2-inch-thick slices.

Place the duck on a serving platter or divide among 4 plates. Garnish with the orange sections and star anise. Serve the sauce on the side.

*Water chestnut flour, also called water chestnut starch, is made from fresh water chestnuts that are ground and then dried. A fine, powdery flour, it is used as a thickening agent and a coating for deep-fried foods. It usually comes in 1-pound boxes. I grind it into an extra-fine powder before mixing it with water to use as a coating. Water chestnut flour gives a crisper coating to foods than does cornstarch.

Eight-Treasure Duck and French Beans and Asparagus with Mushrooms

EIGHT-TREASURE DUCK

SERVES 4 TO 6

BECAUSE THE RICE FINISHES COOKING inside the duck, it absorbs the "eight-treasure" flavors as well as the duck juices. The skin of the duck is crispy and the meat soft and tender. This dish is in a class of its own.

I have tried to stay as close as possible to the original recipe, but I have made enough changes so that the preparation will not take an entire day. I prefer to use Muscovy duck because it is more meaty than regular duck, with much less fat and a larger breast. If you cannot find Muscovy (they are labeled as such and are often twice the price of regular ducks), use whatever kind is available, but more fat will be released.

I like to serve this duck with Sautéed Zucchini with Sun-Dried Tomatoes (page 148) or French Beans and Asparagus with Mushrooms (page 141). If you have any extra stuffing (the size of the cavity will vary), you can steam it and serve alongside the duck. The stuffing can also be used for a 4-pound chicken or a small 10-pound turkey. If you are using the turkey, double the stuffing recipe.

Whenever I roast duck at home, I like to add white or sweet potatoes to the pan. By the time the duck is ready to eat, the potatoes will be infused with the tasty juices in the roasting pan.

1	cup long-grain white sweet (glutinous) rice

Duck and Marinade

1	5-pound duck, preferably Muscovy
¼	cup soy sauce
¼	cup brandy
1	tablespoon Asian sesame oil
1	teaspoon coarse or kosher salt
1	teaspoon crushed roasted Sichuan peppercorns (page 111)

Stuffing

2	tablespoons corn oil
3	shallots, chopped
4	fresh shiitake mushrooms, diced
¼	cup chicken stock (page 79)
½	cup diced fresh water chestnuts or jicama

½   **cup lotus seeds,* lentils** or fresh or dried**
         chestnuts, cooked (page 205)

¼   **cup smoked ham**

1   **teaspoon coarse or kosher salt**
         Freshly ground pepper

Place the rice in a bowl. Cover with 3 cups warm water and soak for 4 hours. Drain and set aside.

To marinate the duck: Remove any visible fat from the duck's cavity. Wash the duck, and dry well. Mix the soy sauce, brandy, sesame oil, salt and Sichuan peppercorns in a large bowl. Turn the duck in the marinade to coat it and spoon some of the marinade inside. Refrigerate for 4 hours or overnight.

Preheat the oven to 400 degrees F.

To make the stuffing: Heat the oil in a large skillet. Add the shallots and cook over high heat, stirring, until lightly browned, about 2 minutes. Add the mushrooms and continue to cook for another 2 minutes. Add the rice and stir until it is well coated with the oil. Pour in the stock and mix well. Turn the heat to low, cover and cook for 5 minutes. Stir. The rice will be almost, but not completely, cooked.

Transfer the rice mixture to a large bowl. Add the water chestnuts or jicama, lotus seeds, lentils or chestnuts and smoked ham and stir until thoroughly combined. Season with salt and pepper to taste and mix well.

Before stuffing the duck, spoon the marinade into the cavity and swirl so that it coats the inside well. Leave the extra marinade inside.

Spoon the rice mixture into the cavity. Truss the duck with a piece of string, tying the legs together so as to secure the stuffing, much as you would a chicken or a turkey.

To cook the duck: Place the duck, breast side down, on a rack set in a roasting pan. Add ½ inch of water to the pan; this will prevent the pan from smoking as the duck fat drips into it. Roast the duck for 45 minutes, until it is half-cooked.

Turn the duck breast side up and continue to roast for 45 minutes to 1 hour more. If the water evaporates from the pan, add another 2 cups to keep the duck fat from smoking. The duck should roast for 1 hour and 15 minutes to 1 hour and 30 minutes total, or until juices run clear when the thigh is pricked with a fork.

Transfer the duck to a serving platter and remove the string.

Scoop out the stuffing before carving the bird. Serve some of the stuffing with each portion of duck.

*To cook the lotus seeds: Soak lotus seeds in 2 cups lukewarm water for 1 hour; the seeds will swell to double their size. Drain, discarding the water.

Bring 2 cups water with 1 tablespoon sugar to a boil in a medium saucepan. Add the lotus seeds. Reduce the heat to medium and cook for about 15 minutes, or until the seeds are tender but not mushy. Drain any remaining water.

**To cook the lentils: Bring 2 quarts water to a boil in a medium saucepan. Add the lentils and cook for 20 to 25 minutes, or until tender; drain.

TREASURED MEMORY

EIGHT-TREASURE DUCK is a great favorite in China. I first tasted this extraordinary dish in my mother-in-law's home, and it made a vivid impression on me—the aroma, the texture, the variety of flavors.

Eight-Treasure Duck was not a dish she prepared often, because it took an entire day. She and the cook went to the market and chose a plump, young duck with healthy-looking, ivory-colored skin. Once the duck had been selected, the butcher killed and cleaned it.

My mother-in-law then spent the rest of the day preparing the stuffing and cooking this dish. First, she washed, dried and boned the bird. Then she marinated it in soy sauce, wine and spices. She and the cook made the stuffing from a mixture of browned shallots, uncooked sweet rice, fresh lotus roots, fresh water chestnuts, smoked ham, dried scallops, shiitake mushrooms and fresh shrimp. They stuffed the duck, trussed it, placed it in a steamer and steamed it for 2 hours. Just before serving, they quickly fried the whole duck in hot oil until its crisp skin was the color of burnished gold.

TSING TAO DUCK

SERVES 4

THIS DISH IS NAMED FOR THE CHINESE BEER with which it is prepared. If you find this beer hard to get, any brand will do. I often make the duck 1 day in advance and serve it cold the next day. It is a popular pot-luck supper dish because it is best served cold or at room temperature. Simple to prepare, the duck is usually marinated overnight, then roasted the next day in its original marinade and served on the third day.

Serve with steamed snow peas, sugar snap peas or green beans. My sons like it made into a sandwich with tomato on toasted bread.

1	4-5-pound duck
1	8-ounce bottle Tsing Tao beer or other beer (not light beer)
1	cup soy sauce*
5	garlic cloves, sliced
1	1-inch piece gingerroot, peeled and sliced
1	tablespoon sugar
4	star anise
1	tablespoon roasted Sichuan peppercorns (page 111)
2	tablespoons corn oil
½	cup chicken stock (page 79)

Trim and discard any excess fat or skin from the duck. Cut off the wing tips and set them aside, along with the heart, gizzard, neck and liver. Wash the duck inside and out and pat dry with paper towels. Place the duck in a large bowl.

Combine the beer, soy sauce, garlic, gingerroot, sugar, star anise and Sichuan peppercorns. Mix well and spoon over the duck. Refrigerate for 8 hours or overnight, turning the duck in the marinade 2 or 3 times.

Preheat the oven to 375 degrees F. Remove the duck from the refrigerator and place it, breast side up, in a roasting pan or Dutch oven.

Heat the oil in a skillet. Add the wing tips, heart, gizzard, neck and liver. Cook, stirring, for 2 minutes. Add them to the roasting pan.

Roast the duck, breast side up, for 45 minutes. Turn and roast for 45 minutes to 1 hour more, or until the skin is crisp and the juices run clear when the thigh is pierced with a fork.

Remove the duck from the pan, place on a large platter and keep warm. Skim off any fat from the roasting pan. Place the pan on the stovetop, add the stock and bring to a boil, scraping the bottom well to loosen all the browned particles. Strain the sauce.

Carve the duck by cutting away the breast and cutting each breast half into thin slices. Place on a platter. Cut the thigh off the drumstick and add these pieces to the platter. Spoon the sauce over the duck. If you wish, refrigerate the duck and serve it cold the following day, with the warmed sauce on the side.

*Preferably Kikkoman soy sauce.

CHAPTER SIX

VEAL, PORK, LAMB AND BEEF

PORK IS THE MEAT OF CHOICE in Chinese cuisine. This is especially true in Taiwan, where the farmers slaughter young pigs before dawn, immediately drain the blood and rush the freshly butchered meat to the morning market. When she did the daily shopping, my mother always stopped at the pork butcher's stall first to select her favorite cuts. She preferred spareribs, the loin and a whole shoulder or fresh bacon. The butchers hung the better cuts from hooks at the top of the open stalls and displayed the lesser cuts on the countertops. Every part of the pig was sold, including the liver, stomach, ears and feet.

Pork is prominently featured in festivals to celebrate the gods' birthdays, which are so much a part of Taiwanese life. One of my most memorable pork meals was at one of these day-long feasts held at a friend's house in Hsin-chu, where my husband and I lived in the 1970s. A pig was butchered and cooked into all kinds of dishes for relatives and friends to share. The whole loin was simmered in fresh water, sliced and served with a pureed garlic sauce. The poaching liquid, made into a creamy white broth, was served with pork balls. The tenderloin was stir-fried with yellow chives; the liver and kidneys were sautéed with mountain celery; and red-braised pork shoulder was served over sun-dried cabbage. This pork was naturally sweet, juicy and fresh—nothing like the meats in this country—and the broth made with it was creamy and flavorful. It was not until I had veal in Tuscany that I tasted anything like it.

Although most Taiwanese did not care for lamb, my parents, because they came from the north of China, loved it. My mother spoke longingly about the clear lamb soup of her childhood, made with garlic, scallions, gingerroot and Sichuan peppercorns, and my father pined for his favorite lamb stew, aromatic and tender and made from a fatty cut. Whenever my mother could find lamb at the market, she bought it and had our cook braise it with lots of garlic, leeks and star anise.

The beef of my early childhood years was tough and tasteless because it came from water buffalo, which were first used for tilling the rice paddies, then slaughtered when they were too old to work. The local "yellow beef," a species named for the color of the fat marbling the flesh, was much more tender, but it was expensive. My mother and mother-in-law liked to stew it to make five-spice beef, which they served cold or cut into julienne strips and stir-fried with mountain celery and chives. Steak of all kinds was a special treat, for it was costly, and filet mignon, a great delicacy, was seen only at banquets.

THE MEAT IN THIS COUNTRY is very different from that in China and Taiwan, and over the years, I have modified many of the traditional preparations to suit the cuts available here. Veal, unknown in China, has a flavor that is close to the pork I remember. In contrast to the strong Mongolian mutton, American lamb is younger and more delicately flavored, lending itself to grilling and more subtle seasonings. Steak—whether flank, sirloin or filet mignon—is all wonderfully tender and reasonably priced, ideal for pan-frying or stir-frying.

Following northern Chinese traditions, I braise larger cuts slowly in a heavy cast-iron pot with little or no water added. Covered tightly and cooked over low heat, the meat becomes more moist and tender than when it is oven-baked. For tender cuts, swift-cooking techniques like stir-frying or grilling are in order. I first marinate beef in a mixture of soy sauce and brandy and then cook it over high heat to sear in the juices; or in the summer, I mix up a less traditional marinade of soy sauce, lemon grass, cilantro and jalapeño peppers and grill the meat outdoors.

VEAL, PORK, LAMB AND BEEF

Aromatic Ginger-Flavored Sweetbreads   225

Twice-Cooked Veal Breast with Mushrooms and Green Pepper   226

Veal Chops with Mushrooms   228

Grilled Pork Loin   230

Mandarin Pork with Brandy-Infused Hoisin Sauce   232

Braised Pork Shoulder with Chestnuts   236

Braised Spareribs   239

Braised Leg of Lamb with Daikon   241

Honey-Grilled Lamb Chops with Jalapeño Pepper Puree   244

Braised Beef Shin with Five Spices   247

Orange Beef with Sun-Dried Tomatoes   251

Sautéed Filet Mignon with Sichuan Peppercorn Sauce   253

AROMATIC GINGER-FLAVORED SWEETBREADS

SERVES 8 AS AN APPETIZER OR 4 AS A MAIN COURSE

SWEETBREADS ARE NOT EATEN IN CHINA. This is too bad, because the Chinese would love this delicate meat, with its luxuriously soft texture and mild, yet rich flavor. Braising gives sweetbreads a particularly smooth texture.

Wrapping the cooked sweetbreads in plastic wrap and twisting them tightly to press out any excess moisture helps firm them so that they can be sliced neatly.

Serve with sautéed vegetables or a salad.

2	pounds sweetbreads
1	recipe Brown Sauce for Braising (page 249)
2	large egg whites, lightly beaten
2	tablespoons cornstarch
¼	cup corn oil

Remove the connective tissue, fat and membranes from the sweetbreads, but be careful to leave the lobes whole.

At least 4 hours ahead of time or the night before, soak the sweetbreads in cold water in the refrigerator, changing the water 2 or 3 times; drain.

Place the brown sauce in a large saucepan and bring to a simmer. Add the sweetbreads and poach in the barely simmering liquid for 20 minutes, turning often. Remove the sweetbreads with a slotted spoon and drain. Reserve the sauce.

Wrap each sweetbread lobe tightly in plastic wrap, forming a log. Secure the ends by twisting the plastic wrap.

Chill the sweetbreads for at least 4 hours or overnight in the refrigerator. Unwrap and cut into ½-inch-thick slices.

Mix the egg whites and the cornstarch in a medium bowl. Dip each slice into this mixture.

Heat the oil in a large nonstick skillet and sauté the sweetbread slices on high heat, turning, for 2 minutes per side, until golden and crisp. Do this in batches, if necessary, so as not to crowd the pan.

Meanwhile, heat the reserved brown sauce.

Serve the sweetbreads immediately, topped with a little of the sauce.

TWICE-COOKED VEAL BREAST WITH MUSHROOMS AND GREEN PEPPER

SERVES 4

IN NORTHERN CHINA, one of the most popular pork dishes is called "twice-cooked pork." I use veal breast to make this dish, as it closely approximates the pork I remember eating in China. Serve with rice.

2	tablespoons corn or olive oil
1	4-5-pound veal breast, with bone
1	small onion, finely chopped
4	garlic cloves, minced
1	teaspoon roasted Sichuan peppercorns (page 111)
1	tablespoon chopped fresh thyme leaves or 1 teaspoon dried
1	cup dry white wine
	Coarse or kosher salt
	Freshly ground pepper
1	quart water
1	jalapeño pepper, thinly sliced (optional)
1	small green bell pepper, cut into 1-inch pieces
3	tablespoons brandy
1	tablespoon yellow soybean paste (page 173) or 2 tablespoons soy sauce
1	tablespoon balsamic vinegar
½	pound wild mushrooms: morels, oysters, shiitakes or chanterelles,* trimmed and cut into quarters, if large

Heat the oil in a Dutch oven or a large casserole.

Place the veal in the pot and cook over medium-high heat, turning to brown on all sides, about 15 minutes.

Add the onion, 1 of the garlic cloves, the Sichuan peppercorns and the thyme and cook for about 5 minutes, or until the onion is lightly browned. Add the wine and season to taste with salt and pepper. Cover and cook over medium heat for 20 minutes.

Add the water to the pot and bring the liquid to a boil. Cover tightly and cook for 30 to 45 minutes, turning 2 or 3 times, until the meat is tender but not so soft that it falls off the bone.

Remove the veal from the pot, place on a cutting board and let cool. Skim the fat from the braising liquid and set aside the fat in a small bowl.

Bring the liquid in the pot to a boil over high heat. Boil until the liquid is reduced by half, ¾ to 1 cup, stirring occasionally. Strain and discard all solids. Set aside.

The recipe can be prepared to this point up to 1 day in advance but will taste better if cooked the same day. Refrigerate the liquid and the meat separately.

When the veal is cool, trim away all the bones and fat. Slice the meat against the grain into ½-inch slices.

Heat 3 tablespoons of the reserved fat in a large skillet. Add the jalapeño pepper (if using), the remaining 3 garlic cloves and the green pepper. Cook over high heat, stirring, for 3 minutes.

Add the sliced veal, brandy, soybean paste or soy sauce and vinegar to the skillet. Cook until the alcohol from the brandy has evaporated, about 5 minutes.

Add the reserved veal liquid and heat through. Add the mushrooms and cook until all the ingredients are heated through and the mushrooms are tender, about 2 minutes. Taste to correct the seasonings.

Transfer the veal slices to a serving platter. Spoon the sauce over the veal and top with the mushroom mixture.

*Or use white button mushrooms, cut into ¼-inch slices

Veal Chops with Mushrooms

Serves 4

Pork chops are the most popular cut of meat in Taiwan. They are usually pounded until thin and marinated in a mixture of soy sauce, ginger and spices. Then they are quickly pan-seared or deep-fried; the outside becomes golden brown and crisp. The chops are often packed in lunchboxes or served on top of a bowl of noodle soup.

In this recipe, I have substituted veal chops, because I find them more delicate than American pork. Serve with steamed or fried rice and a leafy vegetable.

Marinade and Veal

- 3 tablespoons soy sauce
- 2 tablespoons brandy
- 1 tablespoon Asian sesame oil
- 1 tablespoon corn oil
- 3 garlic cloves, minced
- ½ teaspoon freshly ground pepper
- 4 10-12-ounce veal rib chops

- 5 tablespoons olive oil
- 2 scallions, finely chopped
- 3 shallots, finely chopped
- 1 pound mushrooms: chanterelles, shiitakes,
  oysters or white buttons, sliced thin
  (remove the stems if using shiitake
  or button mushrooms)
  Coarse or kosher salt
  Freshly ground pepper

To marinate the veal: Combine all the marinade ingredients, except the veal, in a large shallow bowl. Mix thoroughly and set aside.

Place the veal chops between 2 pieces of wax paper or plastic wrap and pound lightly to tenderize the meat.

Add the meat to the marinade, turning to coat well, and refrigerate for about 20 minutes.

VEAL, PORK, LAMB AND BEEF

Preheat the broiler, with a rack 4 to 6 inches from the heat. Remove the chops from the marinade and drain well; set aside the marinade.

Heat the oil in a large skillet until very hot. Place the chops in the skillet and cook over high heat until they are lightly browned on both sides, about 2 to 3 minutes per side. Do not crowd the meat; cook the chops in 2 batches, if necessary. Do not wash the skillet.

Remove the chops from the skillet and place on the broiler rack. Broil for 3 to 5 minutes, turning once, for medium-rare meat. You can cook the chops for 1 to 2 minutes more if you prefer your meat well done.

Meanwhile, reheat the skillet. Add the scallions and the shallots and cook over high heat, stirring, until they are lightly browned, 2 to 3 minutes.

Add the mushrooms and mix well to coat with the oil. Add the reserved veal marinade and cook, stirring, for 2 to 3 minutes, or until the mushrooms are just cooked. Season to taste with salt and pepper.

When the chops are done, divide them among 4 serving plates and top with the mushrooms and the sauce.

CHINESE LUNCH

WHEN I WAS GROWING UP in Taiwan, my brothers and I brought our lunches to school packed in stainless steel boxes. Every morning, the cook would prepare our lunches, filling each box with a pork chop, a wedge of fish or braised egg halves, rice and a vegetable.

When we arrived at school, our lunchboxes were collected by an attendant who carefully attached a name to each box, then put them away.

Shortly before the lunch hour, the attendant placed the boxes in a steamer. When the bell rang, we collected them and sat down at our desks to enjoy a hot meal.

GRILLED PORK LOIN

SERVES 6 TO 8

WHEN I WAS A COLLEGE STUDENT in T'aipei, barbecues were in fashion. Often, on a Sunday, a group of us would go to the market and buy some fresh pork and pickled vegetables. We then stopped at a nearby bakery for some Western-style bread. Carrying our purchases, we would walk to a nearby stream or take a bus up to the mountains.

Once there, we would begin preparing our barbecue by marinating the thinly sliced pork with soy sauce, garlic and honey. We piled up a circle of small rocks, lit a fire in the middle and covered the whole thing with a piece of steel-wire netting. Once the fire was hot enough, we grilled the pork and made sandwiches with the succulent meat and pickled vegetables.

In the winter of 1987, my husband, sons and I took a vacation to Jamaica and, while there, sampled a robustly flavored jerked pork. Its familiar taste brought back happy memories of my college days and those barbecues.

The combination of these two dishes inspired this creation. The pork is wonderful grilled outside on hot summer days, but it can be cooked under a broiler. Serve with a dense and crusty bread and pickled vegetables such as Spicy Cucumbers with Sichuan Peppercorn Vinaigrette (page 110).

2	tablespoons chopped fresh cilantro leaves
2	garlic cloves, minced
2	tablespoons Jalapeño Pepper Puree (page 243)
1	tablespoon minced fresh lemon grass (page 86)
½	teaspoon freshly ground roasted Sichuan peppercorns (page 111)
¼	cup soy sauce
¼	cup corn oil
2	tablespoons honey
2	pounds boneless pork loin

Combine the cilantro, garlic, jalapeño puree, lemon grass and Sichuan peppercorns in a food processor or a blender and puree.

Add the soy sauce, oil and honey and process until the ingredients form a paste. Transfer to a small bowl and set aside.

Slice the pork loin into ½-inch-thick slices. Place the meat between sheets of wax paper and pound until the slices are about ¼ inch thick.

Spread the herb paste all over each pork slice and refrigerate for 3 hours or overnight.

Meanwhile, preheat an oiled grill or broiler, with a rack 4 to 6 inches from the heat source. Grill the pork slices, turning once, until well browned, about 8 to 10 minutes total.

MANDARIN PORK WITH BRANDY-INFUSED HOISIN SAUCE

SERVES 2 AS A MAIN COURSE WITH RICE OR
4 ROLLED INTO PANCAKES OR FLOUR TORTILLAS

JULIENNED SLICES OF PORK are quickly stir-fried at a high temperature and flavored with hoisin sauce, brandy and slivers of young fresh leeks. The dish is originally from Beijing and is often served in Beijing restaurants in T'aipei as a filler for thin pancakes. I like it with Scallion Pancakes (page 305), Scallion Crêpes (page 315), flour tortillas (allotting 2 per serving) or rice.

½	pound lean boneless pork loin
1	small leek
2	tablespoons brandy
1	tablespoon soy sauce
1	teaspoon cornstarch
3	tablespoons corn oil
1	tablespoon peeled, julienned gingerroot
½	cup thinly sliced red bell pepper
2	jalapeño peppers, cored, seeded and julienned
3	tablespoons Brandy-Infused Hoisin Sauce (page 235)
1	cup finely julienned jicama
¼	cup chicken or pork stock (page 79 or 80)
1	tablespoon chopped fresh tarragon leaves

Cover the pork with plastic wrap and place in the freezer for 15 minutes; the semifrozen meat will be easier to slice and julienne.

Cut off the root end of the leek, and peel off and discard the tough outer green leaves. Cut the leek into 2-inch sections. Cut each section in half lengthwise, then julienne. Wash well in cold water to remove any dirt. Drain and set aside.

Remove the pork from the freezer, cut into ⅛-inch slices, then julienne. Place the julienned pork in a shallow dish.

Combine the brandy and soy sauce in a small bowl. Pour over the pork and mix well. Sprinkle with the cornstarch, and using a fork or chopsticks, mix well to coat. Marinate for 15 minutes.

Heat the oil until it is hot in a large skillet or a wok. Add the pork, along with any marinade, and the gingerroot, and cook over high heat, stirring, for 2 minutes.

Mandarin Pork with Brandy-Infused Hoisin Sauce, Scallion Crêpes and
Spicy Cucumbers with Sichuan Peppercorn Vinaigrette

Add the bell pepper and jalapeño peppers and cook, stirring, for 1 minute. Add the hoisin sauce and cook, stirring, for 2 minutes to coat the meat. Add the leek and the jicama.

Pour the stock into the skillet and cook, stirring, over high heat for 2 to 3 minutes, or until all the ingredients are heated through and the pork is cooked. Mix in the tarragon and serve.

BRANDY-INFUSED HOISIN SAUCE

MAKES ABOUT 2½ CUPS SAUCE

MADE FROM SOYBEANS, SPICES AND GARLIC, hoisin sauce is dark brown and sweet. I think the bottled and canned versions have a somewhat floury taste, as though a thickening agent has changed their true flavor. When I lived in Taiwan, my parents employed a cook from Shanghai who had his own way of improving the flavor of ordinary hoisin sauce by adding Shaoxing rice wine. I have adapted his recipe, using brandy instead of rice wine, producing a sauce with a more intense flavor and a finer texture.

You can use this improved version in any recipe calling for hoisin sauce.

2	tablespoons corn oil
3	garlic cloves, minced
2	cups (16-ounce jar) hoisin sauce
2	tablespoons Asian sesame oil
½	cup brandy
2	tablespoons red wine vinegar or balsamic vinegar
½	cup chicken, pork or beef stock (page 79, 80 or 87)

Heat the oil in a medium saucepan. Add the garlic and cook over high heat, stirring, until it is golden, about 2 minutes. Be careful not to let the garlic brown.

Add the hoisin sauce and the sesame oil and bring to a boil, stirring constantly.

Reduce the heat to medium, add the brandy and vinegar and cook for 5 minutes, stirring constantly to keep the sauce from sticking to the pan.

Add the stock and reduce the heat to low. Cook, stirring occasionally, for 15 minutes, until the sauce is well blended and thickened.

Cool the sauce and pour into a jar with a tight-fitting lid. This sauce will keep well, covered and refrigerated, for up to 1 month.

BRAISED PORK SHOULDER
WITH CHESTNUTS

SERVES 4 TO 6

My MOTHER-IN-LAW BRAISED PORK SHOULDER in a large clay pot on top of the stove along with Shaoxing wine, soy sauce, rock sugar and spices. Sometimes she put in chestnuts. Very little liquid was added to the pot, resulting in a rich, melt-in-your-mouth piece of meat.

This dish can also be made with rabbit or chicken. Substitute a whole rabbit or a 3½-pound chicken for the pork. Cut into small serving pieces, leaving the bones in.

2	tablespoons olive oil
2	garlic cloves, minced
1	1-inch piece gingerroot, peeled and minced
2	pounds pork shoulder, cut into 1-inch cubes
¼	cup brandy
2	tablespoons soy sauce
2	tablespoons balsamic vinegar
2	tablespoons curry paste* or 1 teaspoon curry powder
¼	cup unsweetened coconut milk**
1	small piece rock sugar or 1 tablespoon granulated sugar
1	teaspoon coarse or kosher salt
3-4	cups pork or chicken stock (page 80 or 79)
2	cups fresh chestnuts, cooked and peeled (page 205)***

Heat the oil in a large Dutch oven or casserole with a tight-fitting lid. Add the garlic and the gingerroot and cook over high heat, stirring, for 2 minutes, or until the garlic is golden.

Add the pork and continue to cook, turning the meat so that it browns on all sides.

Add the brandy, soy sauce and vinegar and bring to a boil. Turn the heat to low and simmer for about 10 minutes. Add the curry paste or powder, coconut milk, sugar, salt and 1 cup of the stock. Cover tightly and simmer for about 45 minutes, or until the meat is tender, stirring occasionally. Check from time to time, adding a little more stock, if necessary, to keep the meat from sticking and burning.

Add the remaining 2 cups stock and the chestnuts. Cover and continue cooking for another 30 minutes, or until the chestnuts and the meat are very tender.

*Curry paste, a mixture of curry powder, vinegar, clarified butter and other seasonings, is available in East Indian markets and gourmet shops.

**I prefer the Chaokoh brand, which is carried by most Asian grocery stores.

***Or substitute 1 cup dried chestnuts, which will yield 2 cups of chestnuts when cooked; prepare according to the directions on page 205.

ROCK SUGAR

ROCK SUGAR is a honey-colored crystallized sugar resembling sparkling pieces of amber. Made from raw sugar, it has a subtle sweetness that gives an added dimension to sauces, along with a rich color and a glossy appearance.

I add a lump or two to braised pork and duck dishes and love to watch it slowly melt into the sauce. Unless it has formed into a huge crystal, I do not bother crushing the rock sugar.

Rock sugar is also an excellent sweetener for beverages. I remember my mother's making iced tea sweetened with rock sugar in the summertime. Sometimes she would steam pears with rock sugar and serve them for dessert.

Rock sugar usually comes packaged in 1-pound bags and is easy to find in Chinese food markets. It lasts a long time if sealed and stored in a cool place.

Braised Spareribs and Salad of New Red Potatoes

BRAISED SPARERIBS

SERVES 4 AS A MAIN COURSE OR 8 AS AN APPETIZER

WHEN I WAS GROWING UP, my mother loved to buy meaty spareribs. She would slowly braise them with soy sauce, rice wine, black vinegar and a tiny bit of sugar and serve them with noodles. At home, I often cook a simple one-dish meal; braised spareribs are one of my sons' favorites. I prefer to use baby back ribs, as they are smaller and much meatier than regular spareribs.

By braising the ribs slowly instead of roasting them, you can take advantage of the aromatic sauce that results and serve it over plain white rice or Homemade Noodles (page 263). I serve the dish with lightly sautéed sugarsnap peas for added crunch or with another green vegetable.

2	tablespoons corn oil
2	pounds baby back ribs, cut into individual ribs*
3	garlic cloves, crushed
1	2-inch piece cinnamon stick
2	tablespoons grated orange zest or
	1 piece dried orange peel (page 242)
1	teaspoon anise seed
½	cup Madeira or sherry
2	tablespoons soy sauce
1	tablespoon balsamic vinegar
1	tomato, peeled and cubed
¼	cup fresh chopped thyme leaves or 1 teaspoon dried
	About 1 cup pork or chicken stock (page 80 or 79)
	Coarse or kosher salt
	Freshly ground pepper

Heat the oil in a large Dutch oven. Add the ribs, garlic, cinnamon, orange zest or peel and anise seed. Cook over high heat, turning the ribs in the oil, for about 5 minutes, or until they are lightly seared.

Add the Madeira or sherry, soy sauce, vinegar, tomato and thyme. Cover the pot, reduce the heat to low and cook for 15 minutes. Add ¼ cup of the stock, cover and cook over very low heat for 45 minutes to 1 hour, turning the ribs occasionally to allow the sauce to penetrate the meat, until it is tender and the sauce has almost evaporated. Add more stock as needed to keep the meat from sticking to the pan.

With a slotted spatula, remove the ribs from the pot. Skim any fat off the remaining sauce.

Deglaze the pot by adding ½ cup of the stock and bringing it to a boil, scraping up any particles that have stuck to the bottom. Strain the sauce through a sieve.

Return the ribs to the pot and pour the sauce over them; heat until warm. Season to taste with salt and pepper and serve.

*Ordinary spareribs or country-style ribs may be substituted.

Variation

You can also add pasta to the spareribs. Partially cook 1 pound homemade noodles. After straining the sparerib sauce, add the noodles to the pot with the ribs so they absorb the flavor of the sauce, and cook for 1 to 2 minutes to finish cooking, stirring.

Or you can add a commercial pasta, such as cavatelli or rigatoni: Partially cook the noodles and add them to the sauce, along with the ½ cup stock. Cook, uncovered, stirring occasionally, over medium heat for about 5 minutes, or until the pasta is firm to the bite.

Braised Leg of Lamb with Daikon

Serves 4 to 6

Braising lamb with daikon adds depth of flavor to the dish. This is excellent with Curried Brown Rice with Broccoli Rabe (page 294) or white rice.

2	tablespoons olive or corn oil
1	4-4½-pound leg of lamb (shank end), with bone and skin
1	small onion, cut into large dice
5	garlic cloves, crushed
1	2-inch piece gingerroot, with skin, crushed
3	star anise
2-3	strips dried orange peel (page 242)
1	2-inch cinnamon stick
1	teaspoon cumin seeds
1	teaspoon mustard seeds
½	cup port, red wine or brandy
¼	cup soy sauce
¼	cup balsamic vinegar
3	cups water
1	large daikon (about 2 pounds), peeled and cut into 1-inch cubes

Heat the oil in a large Dutch oven or casserole until hot. Add the lamb and cook over high heat, turning, until all sides are well browned.

Add the onion, garlic, gingerroot and all the spices. Fry, stirring, until the onion is browned and the aroma of the spices has been released, 2 to 3 minutes.

Add the wine or brandy, soy sauce and vinegar. Turn the heat to low, cover the pot with a tight-fitting lid and simmer for 30 minutes, turning the leg 2 or 3 times to allow the flavor of the sauce to penetrate the meat.

Remove the lid and add 2 cups of the water. Cover again and slowly simmer, turning occasionally, for 45 minutes, or until the meat is tender.

Remove the lamb with a slotted spoon and keep warm. Strain the sauce and discard the solids.

Return the sauce to the pot and add the daikon. Add the remaining 1 cup water to cover the daikon. Return the lamb to the pot, cover and continue to cook for 30 minutes, stirring occasionally, until the daikon is tender.

Spoon the daikon onto a serving platter. Carve the lamb into slices and place next to the daikon. Spoon a little of the sauce on top and serve the rest on the side.

DRIED ORANGE PEEL

In SICHUAN PROVINCE before the war, many of the tangerine orchards were open to the public. You could eat as many tangerines as you liked, free of charge, as long as you ate them in the orchard. The peels, however, had to be left there, for the true value of these tangerines was not in the fruit itself but in the peel, which was dried and sold commercially.

Dried citrus peel — either tangerine peel or dried Mandarin orange peel — is treated like a spice in Chinese cookery. Dried citrus peel is also used in many herbal medicine preparations. It yields a tangy flavor to meats, poultry, soups and congee. Sold by weight, it is readily available in Asian markets. The older the peel, the more it is prized. Once dried, it can be stored indefinitely in a cool place.

You can make your own dried peel by air- or sun-drying pieces of skin from tangerines or Mandarin oranges for several days, until completely hard and tan in color.

JALAPEÑO PEPPER PUREE

MAKES ABOUT 1½ CUPS SAUCE

I DEVELOPED THIS PUNGENT MARINADE over the years, using a combination of pureed jalapeño and garlic. In this recipe, the seeds are pureed as well, for they contribute heat and flavor. It's delicious with grilled meat, game and seafood.

I prefer the jalapeño pepper to all other varieties because of its meaty texture, its balanced yet distinct flavor with a subtle hint of sweetness, its consistent level of heat and its year-long availability.

Jalapeño Pepper Puree keeps well — for 1 month in the refrigerator and up to 6 months in the freezer.

1	pound jalapeño peppers, stems removed, with seeds
1	large garlic head, cloves separated and peeled (10-15 cloves)
½	cup olive oil
2	teaspoons coarse or kosher salt

Preheat the oven to 350 degrees F.

Place the jalapeño peppers and garlic cloves in a shallow baking pan in a single layer. Spoon the oil over all and turn to coat the peppers and garlic with the oil.

Roast for 30 minutes. Turn and roast for an additional 30 minutes, or until the peppers and garlic are very soft.

Cool. Transfer to a food processor and puree, adding the salt.

Spoon the puree into a jar with a tight-fitting lid. Cover and refrigerate or freeze.

HONEY-GRILLED LAMB CHOPS WITH JALAPEÑO PEPPER PUREE

SERVES 4

THIS RECIPE IS LOOSELY INSPIRED by a northern Chinese favorite called shashlik. Pieces of lamb tenderloin are marinated in a mixture of egg yolks, Sichuan peppercorns, sesame paste and honey. The meat is then threaded onto long skewers and grilled briefly over a charcoal pit just until the outside is brown and crisp. I found the taste of the original recipe too strong, for the marinade overpowers the lamb, so I have created a more subtle version.

Try to find the youngest lamb rib available. Large chops are often too gamey and lack the delicate flavor this dish requires. Have your butcher remove all fat and sinew from the rib ends.

Serve with Green Apple and Kumquat Relish (page 120), Silver Sprouts with Jicama, Celery and Balsamic Vinaigrette (page 133) or Chinese Risotto with Wild Mushrooms (page 295).

5	tablespoons olive oil
8	rib lamb chops, trimmed (total weight about 2 pounds)
¼	cup soy sauce
1	tablespoon honey
2	tablespoons Dijon mustard
1	tablespoon Asian sesame oil
2	tablespoons Jalapeño Pepper Puree (page 243)
1	tablespoon chopped fresh rosemary leaves or 1 teaspoon crumbled dried
1	tablespoon finely chopped lemon grass (page 86; optional)

Brush a grill with 1 tablespoon of the oil. Preheat the grill, with a rack 4 to 6 inches from the heat source.

Place the lamb chops on a plate large enough to hold them in a single layer.

Combine the remaining ¼ cup oil and the remaining ingredients in a medium bowl and mix thoroughly. Pour this sauce over the lamb chops and marinate at room temperature for 30 minutes, turning once.

Remove the chops from the marinade and grill for 3 to 4 minutes. Turn the chops and continue cooking for 3 to 4 minutes more for medium-rare.

Honey-Grilled Lamb Chops with Jalapeño Pepper Puree and Silver
Sprouts with Jicama, Celery and Balsamic Vinaigrette

GRILLED TO ORDER

FOR A SPECIAL TREAT on nice evenings, my father would take our family to a restaurant specializing in Mongolian barbecue. Some of these dining places were indoors, but I preferred the ones that were outside in a garden. In the center was a flaming pit about 10 feet in diameter, covered with a fine-meshed grill. Three chefs clad in uniforms and hats waited to cook what we brought to them.

On the far side of the garden, a long table was filled with platters of thinly sliced raw beef, chicken, lamb, venison and pork. And a multitude of vegetables: julienned leeks, scallions, spinach, napa cabbage, onions, hot peppers, tomatoes and pickled vegetables. Also on the table were bowls filled with all kinds of sauces, condiments and oils—things such as soy sauce, sesame oil, peanut oil, sugar water, vinegar, sesame paste, rice wine and even hard spirits.

Helping ourselves, we would select the meat of our choice, place it in a large bowl, top it with vegetables and whatever condiments we wanted and present the bowl to one of the waiting chefs. He quickly stir-fried our combinations over the grill and handed it back to us. We ate our custom-made barbecues with a special sesame pocket bread, filling it with the meat and vegetables. My brothers, who had huge appetites, would go back to the table again and again. For dessert, we would have a slice of juicy watermelon, a fitting conclusion to this exciting meal.

BRAISED BEEF SHIN
WITH FIVE SPICES

SERVES 8 TO 12 AS AN APPETIZER

COLD BRAISED BEEF SHIN is one of the most popular dishes at a formal Chinese banquet. It is usually presented on a platter along with honeyed nuts, seafood, duck, chicken and salad. The beef is outstanding not only for its flavor but also for the beautiful pattern that is revealed as it is sliced.

A single beef shin usually weighs 5 to 6 pounds before boning. You can ask your butcher to remove the bone, but have him keep the meat in one piece, if possible. Tie the meat securely with string so that it will hold its round shape while cooking.

> 3-4 pounds boneless beef shin, in 1 piece
> 1 tablespoon Roasted Sichuan Peppercorns
>   and Salt (page 211)
> ¼ cup corn oil
>   Double recipe (4 cups) Brown Sauce
>   for Braising (page 249)

Place the beef shin in a large dish. Rub it all over with the roasted salt-and-pepper combination. Cover with foil or a pot lid and refrigerate for 8 hours or overnight.

Heat the oil in a large heavy pot or Dutch oven. Add the beef and cook over high heat, turning, until the meat is seared on all sides, 5 to 10 minutes.

Add the brown sauce, reduce the heat to low and continue cooking, turning the beef until it is coated on all sides with the sauce.

Cover and simmer, stirring occasionally, for about 2½ hours, or until the beef is tender.

Remove the beef from the sauce. Strain the sauce, cool, and refrigerate if not using immediately.

To serve, warm the sauce. Place the cold beef shin on a board and cut into thin slices. Place the slices on a serving platter and spoon a small amount of the warmed sauce over the meat.

If you plan to reuse the brown sauce, strain it and refrigerate; it will keep for up to 1 week or can be frozen for up to 3 months.

BROWN SAUCE

BRAISING FOODS in a brown sauce, known as red-braising, is a technique used in the preparation of many dishes in the Chinese kitchen. The braising sauce is made with soy sauce, wine and a variety of spices, such as star anise, cloves, cinnamon and Sichuan peppercorns. A large piece of meat—a shoulder of pork, a whole duck or chicken—or eggs are simmered in this sauce for hours until the flavors penetrate the food. Traditionally, this sauce is also used to cook pork stomach, pork liver and feet or ears, pork or beef tongue, tripe, and duck or chicken feet or livers. They can be cooked separately or all together in the same braising liquid. As each new ingredient is added, it contributes to the sauce and enriches it, so the sauce becomes more and more complex. This cooking technique allows a busy cook to start a meal early in the day and pay no attention to the dish for the several hours it takes until the meal is finished.

Before the New Year holidays or the Autumn Moon Festival (a harvest celebration that occurs when the moon is full, similar to the American Thanksgiving), my mother and my mother-in-law would make a huge pot of beef shin, pork, eggs, duck, chicken and pork liver—all braised in a brown sauce. They served them cold as a first course for their guests for the week of the holidays and froze the stock to use again later on.

Their sauces were marvelous, but the same sauce in a restaurant specializing in this style of cooking is even more complex and delicious. Some have 30 different varieties of slow-simmered foods on their menus, and the sauce is used over and over again. Some restaurants claim to have kept the same one for generations, filtering out the impurities and saving the remaining liquid as a base for the next pot.

After being strained and chilled, the braising sauce will gel, much like an aspic, and can be cut into small cubes for decorating the platter on which the meat is served. The braised meat, as well as the meat jelly, can be served cold as a light lunch with salad or fresh fruit. The meat can be sliced thin and used in a sandwich with tomato and lettuce. Or serve it hot as a main course for dinner, using the sauce to braise other vegetables served alongside the meats. Braised dishes have an infinite variety of uses.

If you will not need the sauce for a while, strain it and skim off the fat, then freeze the sauce for the next time.

All large cuts of meat should first be seared in hot oil to seal in the juices before braising. Use a heavy pot with a tight-fitting lid or a Dutch oven in which the meat can be simmered slowly.

BROWN SAUCE FOR BRAISING

MAKES ABOUT 2 CUPS SAUCE

THIS SAUCE can be used to braise beef, pork, lamb, veal, chicken, duck, Cornish hens, sweetbreads, pressed bean curd and eggs. If you want to reuse this sauce for meat, do not braise vegetables in it, since the acid present in them will change the flavor of the sauce.

2 tablespoons corn oil

3 garlic cloves, crushed

2 scallions, cut into 1-inch pieces

1 2-inch piece gingerroot, sliced

1 teaspoon roasted Sichuan peppercorns
   (page 111)

3 star anise

½ cup chicken or beef stock (page 79 or 87)

1 cup soy sauce

½ cup sake or brandy

1 tablespoon sugar

1 teaspoon coarse or kosher salt

Heat the oil in a large Dutch oven. Add the garlic, scallions, gingerroot, peppercorns and star anise and cook over high heat, stirring, until the garlic is golden and you can smell the spices, 2 to 3 minutes.

Stir in the stock, soy sauce, sake or brandy, sugar and salt. Boil the sauce over high heat for about 10 minutes to blend the flavors. Reduce the heat to low and keep the sauce warm, or refrigerate if not using immediately. At this point, the brown sauce is ready to be used for braising.

Orange Beef with Sun-Dried Tomatoes and Lotus Root Salad with Go Chi

ORANGE BEEF
WITH SUN-DRIED TOMATOES

SERVES 2 AS A MAIN COURSE WITH RICE OR 4 IN SANDWICHES

ORANGE BEEF IS A CLASSIC SICHUAN RECIPE in which beef is stir-fried in an infused oil made with dried orange peel and dried hot peppers. I love dried orange peel in braised dishes, but I do not like the burnt flavor it takes on in this preparation. When stir-frying, I prefer to use fresh orange zest, which gives the finished dish a more delicate and refreshing flavor. Sun-dried tomatoes add a slightly smoky note of complexity.

I like to serve this in a sandwich with good bread, over white rice or wrapped in Peking Thin Pancakes (page 313).

Beef and Marinade

- 1 **pound flank steak**
- 2 **tablespoons brandy**
- 2 **tablespoons soy sauce**
- 1 **tablespoon cornstarch**
- 1 **tablespoon corn oil**

Orange Zest

- 8 **cups water**
- 2 **tablespoons sugar**
- ¼ **cup finely julienned orange zest (from 1 large orange)**

- ½ **cup sun-dried tomatoes (not oil-packed)**
- ½ **cup corn oil**
- 4 **scallions, cut on the diagonal into 1-inch pieces**
- 2 **garlic cloves, chopped fine**
- 2 **tablespoons peeled, finely julienned gingerroot**
- 1 **jalapeño pepper, preferably red, chopped, with seeds**
- ¼ **cup chicken or beef stock (page 79 or 87)**
  Coarse or kosher salt
  Freshly ground pepper

To marinate the beef: Place the flank steak on a flat surface and cut in half lengthwise. Cut into ⅛-inch-wide slices on the diagonal, cutting against the grain.

251

Mix the brandy and soy sauce in a bowl. Add the steak; mix. Add the cornstarch and mix well to coat. Add the oil, mixing well to separate the pieces of meat. Let sit at room temperature for 20 minutes or up to 1 hour.

Meanwhile, cook the orange zest: Bring the water and the sugar to a boil over high heat in a saucepan. Add the orange zest and boil for 5 minutes. Drain, rinse under cold water, squeeze dry and set aside.

Soak the sun-dried tomatoes in warm water for about 10 minutes, or until softened. Cut them into julienne.

In a large skillet or a wok, heat the oil until it is very hot, almost smoking (350 degrees F). Add the steak, using chopsticks or a large fork to separate the pieces as they cook. Once the steak has turned golden, about 2 minutes, remove it from the skillet with a slotted spoon and drain well; set aside.

Remove all but 2 tablespoons oil from the skillet. Add the orange zest, sun-dried tomatoes, scallions, garlic, gingerroot and jalapeño. Cook over high heat for 1 to 2 minutes, stirring, until the garlic is golden.

Return the steak to the skillet, add the stock, stir well and cook, stirring, for 3 minutes, until all of the liquid is evaporated. Season to taste with salt and pepper. Transfer to a platter and serve.

STIR-FRY KNOW-HOW

WHEN STIR-FRYING MEAT, I first marinate the slices in a mixture of soy sauce, brandy and cornstarch, then mix in a little oil. Adding some oil at this point and in this order is very important, for when the pieces of meat are later cooked in hot oil, they will separate easily.

The meat should be seared over very high heat to seal in the juices. This quick-cooking technique keeps the outside well browned and crisp, while the inside stays moist.

SAUTÉED FILET MIGNON WITH SICHUAN PEPPERCORN SAUCE

SERVES 6

I N THIS COUNTRY, filet mignon is usually cooked as a steak. In Chinese cuisine, the meat is cut into bite-sized pieces and cooked over high heat. This steak is one of my most popular dishes. The aromatic spices contribute to make an excellent sauce for this expensive cut.

Serve with plain rice, Quick Sauté of Vegetables with Chives (page 150) or Sautéed Green Beans (page 140).

Beef and Marinade

2	tablespoons brandy
1½	pounds filet mignon, trimmed well and cut into ½-inch-thick slices
1	tablespoon cornstarch
1	tablespoon corn oil

½	cup corn oil
2	tablespoons Infused Sichuan Peppercorn Oil (page 112)
¼	cup chopped onion
2	garlic cloves, minced
1	teaspoon peeled, minced gingerroot
1	teaspoon dried green peppercorns
½	cup beef or chicken stock (page 87 or 79), mixed with 1 teaspoon cornstarch
1	tablespoon soy sauce
1	teaspoon coarse or kosher salt
1	red bell pepper, cored, seeded and julienned
¼	cup chopped fresh cilantro leaves

To marinate the beef: Mix the brandy and beef in a large bowl, add the cornstarch, and toss to coat. Add the oil and mix well to separate the pieces of meat; refrigerate for 1 hour.

To cook the beef: In a large skillet or wok, heat the corn oil until it is very hot, almost smoking (350 degrees F). Add half the beef, using chopsticks or a fork to separate the pieces as they cook. Cook quickly on both sides to sear the meat so that it is rare inside and well done on the outside, about 2 minutes. Remove the beef slices with a slotted spoon, drain, set aside and keep warm. Repeat with the remaining beef. Strain the oil and reserve for another use.

Heat the peppercorn oil in a skillet. Add the onion, garlic, gingerroot and green peppercorns and sauté, stirring, over high heat for 1 to 2 minutes, or until the onion is golden.

Add the stock mixture, soy sauce, salt and bell pepper, stir and cook for 2 minutes, or until heated through.

Return the beef to the pan. Add the cilantro and cook, stirring, until the sauce coats the meat, about 3 minutes.

CHAPTER SEVEN

NOODLES

I N PLACE OF THE RICE most Chinese families eat every day, my family ate dumplings, noodles or pancakes made of wheat flour. Shanxi is the only province known for its noodles, and until I enrolled in college and moved away from home, I never realized how different my family was from the majority of Chinese.

My grandmother's homemade noodle dough was prepared from water and a strong hard-wheat flour, which gave tension and elasticity to the dough. The dough was kneaded and stretched and had a firm-to-the-bite, or al dente, texture when cooked—like Italian pasta.

Under my grandmother's guidance, our cook was able to make many shapes of noodles without the aid of modern machinery. I would often go into the kitchen and lean over the table to watch while he prepared them. He would roll out the dough into thin, smooth sheets with a long, slender rolling pin. Folding up the sheets and using a Chinese cleaver, he would cut them into different-sized strips, much like Italian fettuccine or linguine.

Sometimes he shaved the dough into small pieces with his cleaver. At other times, he would cut the dough into inch-wide pieces and, with his fingers, pinch it directly into a pot of boiling water. Occasionally, he would make a much softer dough. Placing it in a bowl, he used his chopsticks to form it into long, narrow rolls, which he pushed off the edge of the bowl into a pot of boiling water.

The most fun of all was when my grandmother took over. My brothers and I would sit beside her as she showed us how to form the dough into cat's ear noodles or fluffy fish noodles, named after their shapes.

My FAMILY ATE PASTA IN A VARIETY OF WAYS. The cook would bring to the table a serving bowl containing a small portion of freshly cooked pasta. Each of us would mix our noodles with some sauce and vegetables. While we were eating, he would keep boiling the noodles and continually bring a fresh supply to the table. Occasionally, he would make up a pot of braised meat and vegetables. He would half-cook the pasta, add it to the braised mixture and finish cooking the noodles in the sauce. We ate this casserole along with a salad as a complete meal.

He would also sauté leftover plain pasta with vegetables, meat, shrimp or chicken, a dish known in this country as lo mein. And he would serve noodle soup with cabbage as a side dish, accompanied by pancakes, steamed buns, pan-fried breads and different kinds of vegetables.

To this day, my parents never eat machine-made noodles. Although my father is 83 and my mother 74, they still make their own fresh noodles daily, since they believe commercial pasta to be inedible.

At home, we also frequently ate mung bean, or cellophane, noodles. My mother tossed them in a salad along with cooked chicken and a mustard-and-horseradish dressing. Wider mung bean noodles became part of a vegetable stir-fry with cabbage, carrots, celery or some julienned pork. My mother cooked the finer threads into soups or chopped them and used them in a cabbage-pork stuffing for steamed buns.

A few years ago, when my husband and I traveled to Italy, I was fascinated to discover how similar Italian pasta is to the noodles of my childhood. The trip inspired me to go back to some of my family's recipes and adapt them. Now, I often serve noodles as a side dish in place of rice.

In this country, most Chinese grocery stores carry a large variety of noodles, both fresh and dried. I prefer to use plain fresh noodles made of flour and water and do not care for those made with eggs, which are much too soft for my taste. But I also like many of the better brands of dried Italian pasta, which have a firm texture and good flavor.

NOODLES

Noodles with Pork from Shanxi   260

Homemade Noodles   263

Mandarin Meat Sauce with Fresh Pasta   264

Sichuan Beef Soup with Rigatoni   266

Cat's Ear Pasta with Chicken and Portobello Mushrooms   269

Pan-Fried Noodles   271

Cold Sesame Noodles   272

Stir-Fried Thin Rice Noodles with Shrimp and Scallions   275

Rice Noodles with Porcini Mushrooms   277

Hot and Spicy Chicken and Cellophane Noodle Salad   281

PASTA PERFECTION

WHEN I COOK PASTA, I never salt the water because there is already enough salt in the sauce. I do, however, like to add a tablespoon of oil to keep the strands of pasta separate.

I never rinse the pasta in cold water after it is cooked, for rinsing causes it to lose much of its flavor. Rather than pouring cooked noodles into a colander to drain them, I scoop them out of the hot water with a Chinese strainer. These strainers are usually made from brass or copper wire and have a bamboo handle. Scooping out the noodles, then pouring them into a colander, drains off the water more quickly and efficiently, leaving the boiling water ready, if needed, to cook another batch. Place the freshly cooked pasta in individual bowls or a large serving bowl.

It is hard to give an exact time for cooking pasta. All a recipe can do is give guidelines, for the time depends on the size of the pot, the heat generated by the stove, the amount of pasta and the thickness and shape of the particular variety. Fresh pasta usually cooks faster than dried.

Follow these basic rules when cooking pasta:

✳ Bring the water to a full boil before the pasta is added.

✳ Don't try to cook too much pasta at one time; cook it in small batches.

✳ Taste frequently to check for doneness; the middle should be cooked through but still have a firm texture.

✳ When the pasta is done, immediately remove it from the water. Overcooked pasta loses not only its texture but its flavor as well.

NOODLES WITH PORK FROM SHANXI

SERVES 4 TO 6

ONE OF MY FATHER'S FAVORITE DISHES was noodles with pork as it is prepared in Shanxi. Made with meat, potatoes, spices and noodles, it was a meal in itself. It was usually served with a lot of small accompaniments, such as fresh hot peppers, julienned leeks, rich black vinegar, fresh cilantro and fresh gingerroot.

My father, who had a taste for hot food, would help himself to the vinegar, peppers and leeks. My mother just added a bit of fresh cilantro to her plate. I liked mine plain.

1	pound boneless lean pork, cut into ¼-inch dice*
3	tablespoons soy sauce
1	tablespoon cornstarch
¼	cup corn oil
¼	cup finely chopped onion
3	garlic cloves, thinly sliced
3	tablespoons brandy
1	large russet potato, peeled and cut into ¼-inch dice
2	cups chicken stock (page 79)
2	large tomatoes, peeled and diced
2	scallions, chopped
	Coarse or kosher salt
	Freshly ground pepper
1	recipe Homemade Noodles (page 263), made as Shanxi noodles, or 1 pound fettuccine or linguine

Place the diced pork in a large bowl and mix in the soy sauce and the cornstarch. Add 2 tablespoons of the oil, mix well and marinate for a few minutes at room temperature while preparing the rest of the ingredients.

Heat 1 tablespoon of the oil in a large, heavy saucepan or Dutch oven. Add the onion and the garlic and cook over high heat, stirring, until the onion is lightly browned, 2 to 3 minutes.

Add the pork, along with any marinade, and continue to cook, stirring, until the pork is no longer pink.

Add the brandy. Cover the pot, turn the heat to medium and cook for about 10 minutes. Add the potato and mix well. Pour in the stock, cover and cook for 30

Noodles with Pork from Shanxi

minutes, or until the pork and potatoes are completely cooked.

Add the tomatoes and the scallions. Continue to cook, stirring often, for 3 minutes more, or until the sauce is thickened. Season with salt and pepper to taste.

While the sauce is cooking, bring a large pot of water to a boil. Add the remaining 1 tablespoon oil and the pasta. When the water returns to a boil, add ¼ cup of cold water. Cook for 3 to 5 minutes for fresh pasta or 8 to 10 minutes for dried, until tender but firm to the bite. Scoop the noodles out of the pot with a Chinese strainer or slotted spoon and place in a large bowl.

Spoon the cooked pork into a large bowl and serve, along with a bowl of the freshly cooked pasta. Allow people to help themselves to the pasta and the sauce.

Optional Garnishes

Present the pork and pasta along with small bowls filled with any or all of the following: balsamic vinegar, chopped fresh jalapeño peppers, julienned cucumber, chopped fresh basil, chopped fresh cilantro and julienned leeks.

*I chop the pork by hand, using a cleaver or a chef's knife rather than grinding it in a meat grinder or a food processor. These larger pieces help the meat retain moisture when it is cooked.

If you do not want to chop it yourself, ask your butcher to grind the meat coarsely. Do not use finely ground (prepackaged) meat. Meat that has been forced through a commercial grinder loses its natural moisture when cooked, and the flavor of the finished dish suffers.

HOMEMADE NOODLES

SERVES 6

W E ATE THESE NOODLES at least twice a week during my childhood. Our cook would boil them in small batches, and we'd mix them with sauce and different vegetables and condiments.

This pasta has a firm, chewy texture. Eggs, which would make a softer dough, are not used. The dough can be shaped into long Shanxi noodles, for the preceding recipe, or into cat's ear pasta (page 270).

3 cups all-purpose flour

1 cup cold water

1 tablespoon corn oil

To mix by hand: Place the flour in a large bowl and make a well in the middle. Pour the water into the well, stirring to incorporate into the flour. Turn out onto a lightly floured work surface and knead by hand until smooth, about 5 minutes.

To mix in a food processor: Place the flour in the food processor and, with the motor running, add the water. Process until smooth, about 3 to 5 minutes.

Place the dough in a large bowl and cover with a damp towel, then loosely cover with a piece of plastic wrap and set aside at room temperature for 1 to 2 hours so the gluten in the dough relaxes.

To make Shanxi noodles: Lightly flour the work surface and roll out the dough into a ¼-inch-thick rectangle. Sprinkle the surface of the dough lightly with flour and fold the rectangle in half to form another smaller rectangle. With a sharp knife, cut the dough into ¼-inch-wide strips. Place the noodles on a baking sheet. Sprinkle them lightly with flour and separate them with your hands. Cover with a towel.

To make cat's ear pasta: Divide the dough into 4 equal pieces. Roll each piece out on a lightly floured surface to a 6-inch circle, ½ inch thick. Cut into ½-inch-wide strips. Break off a ¼-inch-long piece from each strip with your fingers and flatten it with your thumb, pushing your thumb along the edge to curl up the end slightly. Repeat with the remaining strips. Lightly sprinkle the noodles with flour to keep them from sticking together.

Bring a large pot of water to a boil over high heat. Add the oil and half the pasta. Cook for 3 to 5 minutes, tasting 1 noodle to make sure the center is cooked but still firm to the bite. When the noodles are cooked, scoop them out of the water with a Chinese strainer or slotted spoon and place in a colander to finish draining. Repeat with the remaining noodles. Serve immediately.

MANDARIN MEAT SAUCE WITH FRESH PASTA

SERVES 4 TO 6

THIS IS A POPULAR DISH in northern China, developed in the days when the Mandarins ruled the country. Chopped marinated pork is cooked in a combination of sauces. As it cooks, the meat absorbs all the surrounding flavors, and the result is spicy and pungent. The meat sauce is then spooned over freshly cooked noodles and served with an array of cold and crunchy vegetables.

I prefer this sauce with hot noodles, but it will work with cold ones as well. If serving the dish hot, cook the sauce first. If serving cold, you can make both the sauce and noodles as much as 1 day ahead; just heat the sauce at the last minute before adding it to the noodles.

1	pound boneless pork butt or pork loin*
3	tablespoons brandy
2	tablespoons soy sauce
2	teaspoons cornstarch
5	tablespoons corn or olive oil
1	cup chicken stock (page 79)
6	scallions, chopped
3	garlic cloves, minced
2	shallots, minced
1	tablespoon Brandy-Infused Hoisin Sauce (page 235)
2	tablespoons yellow soybean paste (page 173)
1	jalapeño pepper, cored, seeded and minced
1	teaspoon sugar
	Coarse or kosher salt
	Freshly ground pepper
1	pound fresh Chinese plain noodles or fresh linguine
¼	cup julienned fresh basil leaves or chopped cilantro leaves
1	small cucumber, peeled, seeded and julienned
2	Belgian endives, julienned, soaked in ice water (page 175) and drained

Coarsely chop the pork by hand into ¼-inch dice and place it in a bowl. Do not grind the pork finely: you need the coarse texture for this dish, or it will not taste right (see page 262).

Combine the brandy, soy sauce and 1 teaspoon of the cornstarch in a small bowl; pour over the pork and mix well. Add 1 tablespoon of the oil. Stir to combine and marinate the pork for 30 minutes at room temperature.

Meanwhile, combine the stock with the remaining 1 teaspoon cornstarch; set aside.

Heat 3 tablespoons of the oil in a large skillet. Add the scallions, garlic and shallots and cook over high heat, stirring, for about 2 minutes, or until the garlic and shallots have become aromatic and golden brown.

Add the pork, along with the marinade, and cook, stirring, until the meat is lightly browned, about 5 minutes.

Add the hoisin sauce and soybean paste, and cook over medium heat, stirring occasionally, until the meat is well coated with the sauce, about 10 minutes.

Add the jalapeño pepper, sugar and the stock mixture and stir to combine. Cover and cook over medium-low heat until the sauce is reduced, about 30 minutes. Season with salt and pepper to taste and remove from the heat.

Bring a large pot of water to a boil over high heat, add the remaining 1 tablespoon oil and cook the pasta until it is tender but firm to the bite, 3 to 5 minutes. Lift out the noodles with a Chinese strainer or slotted spoon and drain well in a colander; stir to separate the noodles.

Spoon the cooked pasta into a large serving bowl. Serve the sauce on the side. Garnish with the basil or cilantro, cucumber and endive.

*Veal shoulder may be substituted.

SICHUAN BEEF SOUP WITH RIGATONI

SERVES 6

SICHUAN BEEF NOODLE SOUP is served by many street vendors in T'aipei. Each one jealously guards his or her own recipe, claiming its uniqueness in the thousands of years of family tradition that have gone into its creation. More a noodle dish than a soup, this is a favorite lunch of college students and office clerks alike. It makes a perfect family supper, especially in winter.

I have substituted the shorter Italian rigatoni for the traditional Chinese long noodles, which can be difficult to eat. For this recipe, I use beef chuck, which has a marbled pattern and becomes especially tender and juicy when braised.

2	pounds beef chuck, preferably chuck eye roast
3	tablespoons corn oil
2	garlic cloves, crushed
1	1-inch piece gingerroot, peeled and chopped
3	star anise
¼	cup brandy, Scotch or bourbon
3	tablespoons soy sauce
1	tablespoon sugar
1	teaspoon coarse or kosher salt
2	jalapeño peppers, cored, seeded and chopped
1	tablespoon freshly ground roasted Sichuan peppercorns (page 111)
2	quarts chicken or beef stock (page 79 or 87)
1	large tomato, peeled, cut in half and thinly sliced
2	scallions, chopped
1	pound rigatoni
1	tablespoon Asian sesame oil
1	cup julienned peeled daikon, soaked in ice water (page 175) and drained (optional)

Cut the beef into 1½-inch chunks.

Heat 2 tablespoons of the oil in a large Dutch oven or heavy stock pot. Add the beef and sear over high heat on all sides, about 5 minutes.

Add the garlic, gingerroot and star anise and cook, stirring, for 2 to 3 minutes, until fragrant.

Add the spirits, soy sauce, sugar, salt, jalapeño peppers and Sichuan peppercorns. Cover, bring to a boil, reduce the heat to medium and cook for 15 minutes, stirring occasionally, to coat the meat with the seasonings.

Add the stock, cover and simmer over low heat, stirring occasionally, for about 1 hour, until the meat is tender. Add the tomato and scallions and simmer for about 10 minutes.

Bring a large pot of water to a boil, add the remaining 1 tablespoon oil and the rigatoni and cook for 7 to 10 minutes, or until it is half-cooked. Scoop out the noodles with a Chinese strainer or a slotted spoon and place in a large bowl. Mix in the sesame oil.

Just before serving, add the half-cooked noodles to the soup, bring to a boil, stir and cook just until the noodles are firm to the bite, another 5 minutes.

Divide the soup and noodles among 6 soup bowls. Garnish with the daikon, if using.

RAINY DAY SOUP

WHEN I ATTENDED TAIWAN UNIVERSITY, majoring in Chinese and American history, I would meet my friends around noon and we would walk over to a street lined with food vendors. These small pushcarts sold a variety of foods: hot sweet potato pancakes, dim sum, noodles and wonton or rice noodle soups.

My favorite was Sichuan beef noodle soup. For a few pennies, I bought a large bowl of spicy, hot soup brimming with wide, chewy homemade noodles, topped with slices of braised beef shin, scallions and pickled mustard greens.

The stove on which the dish was prepared was covered with a small tin roof. There were a few tiny stools set up outside next to the stove, and we were each given a pair of chopsticks and plastic spoons.

No rain could dilute that fragrant soup, though we often got wet as we ran with it to shelter in a doorway when the weather was inclement.

Cat's Ear Pasta with Chicken and Portobello Mushrooms

CAT'S EAR PASTA WITH CHICKEN AND PORTOBELLO MUSHROOMS

SERVES 4

THIS IS A MEMORABLE ONE-DISH MEAL of noodles, chicken, cabbage and mushrooms stir-fried together. It is simple to prepare, but there are a few preliminary steps. Place the chicken breast in the freezer for about 20 minutes. It is much easier to slice and julienne raw chicken if it is partially frozen. It will then be ready for marinating.

Separate the noodles with chopsticks or a large fork as they cook to prevent them from sticking together.

½	pound boneless, skinless chicken breast
3	tablespoons gin
2	tablespoons soy sauce
1	large egg white, lightly beaten
1	teaspoon cornstarch
5	tablespoons corn oil
1	recipe Homemade Noodles (page 263),* made as cat's ear pasta, or ¾ pound cavatelli
1	pound green cabbage, shredded (about ½ head)
3	shallots, thinly sliced
1	large Portobello mushroom, stem removed, cap halved and thinly sliced
1	cup chicken stock (page 79)
1	large tomato, peeled and diced (about 1 cup)
3	scallions, halved lengthwise, cut into 1-inch pieces
	Coarse or kosher salt
	Freshly ground pepper

Cover the chicken with plastic wrap and freeze for 20 minutes.

Thinly slice the chicken, then cut into ⅛-inch julienne; transfer to a medium bowl. Add the gin, soy sauce, egg white and cornstarch and mix thoroughly. Add 1 tablespoon of the oil to allow the chicken to separate easily. Set aside to marinate until needed.

Bring a large pot of water to a boil and add 1 tablespoon of the oil. If using the homemade pasta, cook for 3 to 5 minutes, until it is half-done. If using the cavatelli, cook for about 15 minutes, until firm to the bite; the pasta should still be raw in the middle. Remove with a Chinese strainer or a slotted spoon, place in a colander and set aside; keep the water at a boil.

Add the cabbage to the boiling water and cook for about 5 minutes to soften. Drain in a colander; set aside.

Heat the remaining 3 tablespoons oil in a large, heavy pot. Add the shallots and cook over high heat until brown, about 2 minutes. Add the chicken, along with the marinade. Cook over high heat, stirring, for 3 to 5 minutes, or until the chicken is no longer raw.

Add the Portobello mushroom. Cook, stirring, until soft, about 3 minutes. Stir the pasta to separate it and add it to the pot with the stock. Cook until the liquid is absorbed, about 5 minutes. Add the cabbage, tomato and scallions and sprinkle with salt and pepper to taste. Continue to cook, stirring, for about 2 minutes, or until the pasta is fully cooked. Serve immediately.

*Orecchiette can be substituted.

CAT'S EARS AND GOSSIP

Cat's EAR PASTA was one of our favorite dishes. As a child, I would sit beside my grandmother and mother in our kitchen as they prepared a dough made of flour and water. My grandmother would work the dough into a rope about ½ inch in diameter. She would pinch off a tiny piece and press her thumb into the dough to create a shape much like a cat's ear.

She tried, with much patience, to teach me this technique. I finally did manage to learn it, but she could turn out 10 or 20 cat's ears in the time it took me to make one. I enjoyed those hours spent in the kitchen, enlivened as they were by much gossip of their memories of China, their relatives and friends, their land and their houses and gardens.

We topped the cat's ear pasta with my father's favorite Shanxi pork sauce. Or we made a braised meat sauce with tomatoes and mushrooms, added half-cooked cat's ears to it and simmered it until the pasta was done. This was home cooking at its best. Sometimes our cook would use up any leftover plain pasta by sautéing it along with some julienned pork and shredded cabbage and serving it for our lunch the next day.

Homemade pasta is best, but I find that Italian cavatelli comes very close to the cat's ear pasta of my childhood and is more convenient.

PAN-FRIED NOODLES

MAKES ONE 8-INCH ROUND NOODLE CAKE; SERVES 2 AS A SIDE DISH

T HIS IS ONE OF THE MOST POPULAR family-style noodle dishes in all of China. The noodles are also called "two-sides brown," which means that both sides of the noodles are pan-fried until they are crispy on the outside. My family usually made this dish from leftover noodles. Topped with all kinds of seafood, meat or vegetable combinations, it makes a quick lunch.

I like to use fresh, thick and chewy plain Chinese noodles that are at least ⅛ inch thick or linguine cooked al dente. Dried linguine can be substituted, but the cooking time will be longer. Thinner noodles, such as capellini, or very soft, thin egg noodles do not work well; they do not have enough body. Never rinse the cooked noodles in water before frying them.

Serve hot, topped with Soy-Braised Chinese Eggplant with Zucchini and Mushrooms (page 144), Kung Pao Chicken (page 202) or Sautéed Shrimp with Corn in Spicy Wine Sauce (page 183).

¼   cup corn oil
½   pound fresh Chinese plain noodles or fresh linguine
½   cup chopped red onion
½   cup chopped scallions
½   teaspoon coarse or kosher salt
¼   cup chicken stock (page 79)

Bring a large pot of water to a boil, add 1 tablespoon of the oil and cook the noodles until they are firm to the bite, 3 to 5 minutes. Drain well and immediately add 1 tablespoon of the oil. Mix well to coat all the noodles and spread them out on a baking sheet so they remain separate. The noodles may be cooked up to 1 day in advance; when cold, place in a bowl, cover with plastic wrap or seal in a plastic bag and refrigerate.

In a large bowl, mix the noodles with the onion and scallions. Sprinkle with the salt and toss.

In a heavy 8-inch nonstick skillet, heat 1 tablespoon of the oil. Add the noodles and press down in an even layer. Add the stock, cover and cook over medium heat for 10 minutes, or until the bottom is crisp and brown.

Turn the noodle cake, add the remaining 1 tablespoon oil to the side of the skillet and continue cooking, over medium heat, for another 5 minutes, or until the second side is nicely browned. Remove from the pan, cut into quarters and serve.

Cold Sesame Noodles

Serves 4 as a main course or 8 as part of a multicourse dinner

I N TAIWAN, the summers are extremely hot and humid, making it just about impossible even to consider consuming anything hot. These cold noodles were one of my family's favorite lunches during those long summers.

The cook always made this dish out of fresh pasta, much like Italian linguine, which he cooked ahead and kept in the refrigerator. He served the cold noodles with sesame sauce, poached julienned chicken, steamed eggplant salad, julienned egg crêpes, cucumbers, bean sprouts, cilantro and hot peppers. He placed everything on the table, and we mixed whatever we wanted into our noodles.

I prefer to use fresh rather than dried pasta for cold noodle dishes because it has a sweeter flavor and a firmer texture.

Pasta

2 tablespoons corn or olive oil

1 pound fresh Chinese plain noodles or fresh linguine

Sesame Dressing

2 tablespoons corn or olive oil

2 garlic cloves, minced

½ cup sesame paste*

⅓ cup soy sauce

1 tablespoon balsamic vinegar

1 teaspoon Tabasco sauce

1 tablespoon sugar

⅓ cup chicken stock (page 79)

¼ cup finely chopped unsalted fried peanuts
   (page 324)

Garnish

½ cup julienned Belgian endive, soaked in ice water
   (page 175)

½ cup peeled, julienned seeded cucumber

¼ cup julienned red bell pepper

¼ minced fresh cilantro leaves

¼ cup toasted sesame seeds**

To cook the pasta: Bring a large pot of water to a boil and add 1 tablespoon of the oil. Add the pasta and cook for 3 to 5 minutes, or until tender but firm to the bite; do not overcook. Lift out the noodles with a Chinese strainer or a slotted spoon. Place in a large bowl and toss with the remaining 1 tablespoon oil. Spread out the pasta on a large baking sheet; when cool, cover with plastic wrap or place in a sealed plastic bag and refrigerate. The dish may be prepared up to 1 day in advance.

To make the dressing: Heat the oil in a large skillet. Add the garlic and cook over high heat, stirring, for 2 minutes, or until golden. Remove from the heat.

Add the sesame paste, soy sauce, vinegar, Tabasco and sugar and stir until the mixture forms a thick paste.

Meanwhile, bring the chicken stock to a boil in a small saucepan. Add it to the sesame paste mixture and mix well. Stir in the peanuts. You will have about 1½ cups dressing.

To assemble and garnish: Before serving, toss the noodles together with ½ to ¾ cup of the dressing. (The leftover dressing will keep for up to 1 week, covered and refrigerated, or can be frozen for up to 3 months.) Mound the noodles onto individual plates and garnish with the endive, cucumber, bell pepper, cilantro and sesame seeds.

*I prefer Lan Chi Sesame Paste from Taiwan. It has been manufactured by the same company for over 50 years, and the quality of the ingredients has never changed. It can be found in many Chinese grocery stores.

**To toast sesame seeds: Place on a dry baking sheet in a 350-degree oven, and toast, stirring occasionally, until lightly browned and fragrant, about 10 minutes.

Stir-Fried Thin Rice Noodles with Shrimp and Scallions

STIR-FRIED THIN RICE NOODLES WITH SHRIMP AND SCALLIONS

SERVES 2 AS A MAIN COURSE OR 6 TO 8 AS A SIDE DISH

RICE NOODLES are one of the most popular street foods in Taiwan. You can buy a large plate of them stir-fried with shrimp, squid or pork or a bowl of soup brimming with them for just a few pennies. I love to cook these noodles with seafood, chives and wild celery or cabbage. They make an excellent lunch.

½	pound thin rice stick noodles (rice vermicelli)
½	pound medium shrimp, peeled, deveined and cleaned with salt (page 182)
1	tablespoon vodka
3	tablespoons olive oil
4	shallots, chopped
1	teaspoon peeled, finely chopped or grated gingerroot
4	fresh shiitake mushrooms, stems removed, caps thinly sliced
½	pound shredded napa or green cabbage or chopped broccoli rabe
2	scallions, finely chopped
1	tablespoon soy sauce
1	cup chicken stock (page 79)
1	teaspoon coarse or kosher salt
	Freshly ground pepper
¼	cup chopped fresh basil or cilantro leaves or any other fresh herb, such as tarragon or chives

Cover the rice stick noodles with cold water and soak for 15 to 20 minutes, until softened. Do not soak any longer, as they will become too soft and the texture of the dish will be ruined. Drain well. Cut the noodles in half; set aside.

Dry the shrimp with paper towels and cut into small pieces. Marinate them in the vodka while you prepare the rest of the ingredients.

Heat the oil over high heat in a heavy skillet. Add the shallots and the gingerroot and cook over high heat for 2 minutes, or until the shallots are lightly browned. Add the shrimp and mushrooms and cook, stirring, until the shrimp turn pink and the mushrooms are soft.

Add the cabbage or broccoli rabe, scallions, rice noodles, soy sauce, stock and salt. Cook until the liquid is completely absorbed, about 5 minutes. Season with pepper to taste. Mix in the fresh herbs and serve.

RICE FLOUR NOODLES

NOODLES MADE FROM RICE FLOUR are commonly eaten in southern China, where most rice is grown. Called "rice sticks," they come in different thicknesses. In this country, it is hard to find them fresh.

I prefer thin rice noodles, since they are the kind I grew up with. Called "rice vermicelli," they come in 12-to-16-ounce plastic packages and are usually divided into skeins. They must be soaked in cold water for about 15 to 20 minutes, until they become soft. Drain and discard the soaking water. Cut the noodles in half. They are then ready to use.

I stir-fry them with meat, seafood or vegetables. They will absorb the flavors of the other ingredients with which they are cooked, and they have a light texture. They are excellent alone or with grilled meat or game.

Use a large skillet or wok when stir-frying these noodles; if you fry them in a pot that is too small, you will make a mess of your stove.

RICE NOODLES
WITH PORCINI MUSHROOMS

SERVES 4 AS A MAIN COURSE OR 8 AS A SIDE DISH

THIS WAS ONE OF MY FAVORITE NOODLE DISHES when I was a child. Rice noodles do not have a lot of flavor themselves and therefore should be cooked with lots of aromatic vegetables, such as shallots, onions and garlic. The vermicelli should never be cooked with big chunks of vegetables or meats: all ingredients should be thinly sliced, julienned or chopped. Because they do not absorb oil, the dish will taste greasy if too much fat is used.

½   **pound thin rice stick noodles (rice vermicelli)**

1   **ounce dried porcini mushrooms***

1   **cup warm water**

½   **pound napa or green cabbage**

1   **leek, white part only**

¼   **pound fresh wild mushrooms, such as shiitakes, chanterelles or oyster mushrooms,** ** **stems removed; thinly sliced**

3   **tablespoons olive or corn oil**

2   **garlic cloves, minced**

¼   **cup minced shallots**

2   **tablespoons minced soaked dried shrimp (page 134; optional)**

     Coarse or kosher salt

     Freshly ground pepper

Soak the rice stick noodles in cold water to cover for 15 to 20 minutes, or until softened. Do not soak any longer, as they will become too soft. Drain well, cut the noodles in half and set aside.

Meanwhile, soak the dried mushrooms in the warm water for 30 minutes. Drain, strain the liquid through a piece of cheesecloth and set aside.*** Rinse the mushrooms well to remove any grit or sand. Squeeze dry, slice thinly and set aside.

Wash the cabbage well and shred.

Cut the white part of the leek into 2-inch lengths. Discard any coarse outer leaves. Cut the sections in half lengthwise, then into julienne. Wash well, drain and set aside.

Wipe the fresh mushrooms with a damp paper towel to remove any grit. If using shiitakes, remove and discard the tough stems.

Heat the oil over high heat in a large skillet or pot. When hot, add the garlic and shallots and cook, stirring, for about 2 minutes, or until they are lightly browned. Add the dried and fresh mushrooms and the dried shrimp, if using, and cook for 3 minutes, or until the mushrooms are soft.

Add the cabbage, leek, rice noodles and reserved mushroom-soaking liquid to the skillet. Cook over medium heat, stirring often, for 5 minutes, or just until everything is hot. Season with salt and pepper to taste. Serve hot or at room temperature.

*Dried shiitake mushrooms can be substituted. Use ½ cup chicken stock in place of the mushroom liquid.

**If you cannot get fresh wild mushrooms, substitute fresh white button mushrooms.

***Although I usually discard the soaking liquid from dried shiitakes because it is sandy and not worth using, I save the porcini liquid, as these mushrooms do not have much grit, and the liquid has a pleasing color and flavor.

CELLOPHANE NOODLES

IN THE NORTHERN PART OF CHINA, where soybeans and mung beans are important crops, cellophane noodles are a staple. Made from ground mung beans, the same plant that yields bean sprouts, cellophane noodles are popular in Mandarin and Sichuan provinces and in Shanghai.

Cellophane noodles are known by many different names: bean thread noodles, glass noodles, shining noodles, silver noodles, transparent noodles or Chinese vermicelli. They come in a variety of thicknesses: some are very thin (like rice vermicelli noodles), some are quite wide (like fettuccine), and some are formed into sheets.

I grew up with this noodle, and we treated it like a vegetable, cooking the wide ones with pork and napa cabbage and using the cooked sheets in a salad with chicken and cucumbers in a pungent mustard dressing.

Cellophane noodles have little flavor of their own and will readily absorb the juices of the other ingredients with which they are cooked. They lend a delightfully slippery texture to stir-fried vegetables and can be added to soups and stuffings.

Soak cellophane noodles in cold water for about 20 minutes, or until they are softened. Cut the noodles in half or into smaller lengths. Dip them into a pot of boiling water for 1 minute, drain and rinse well under cold running water.

Most cellophane noodles sold in the United States are imported from Taiwan and are usually sold in skeins in 7-to-8-ounce packages. They are readily available in Chinese grocery stores. I use the Long Kon brand.

Hot and Spicy Chicken and Cellophane Noodle Salad

HOT AND SPICY CHICKEN AND CELLOPHANE NOODLE SALAD

SERVES 4 AS A SALAD COURSE OR 2 AS A MAIN COURSE

THIS COLD NOODLE SALAD is a specialty in most northern Chinese restaurants, where it is served as a first course. It has a marvelous blend of textures: the crispness of the cucumber, the chewiness of the mung bean noodles and the softness of the chicken breast all complement each other.

The pungent dressing is an unusual combination of flavors with its blend of horseradish, mustard, hot peppers and sesame paste. When I ate this dish as a child, the dressing always made me sneeze.

Chicken and Noodles

2   skeins (about 2 ounces) cellophane noodles
1   cup chicken stock (page 79)
1   ½-pound chicken breast, with skin and bones
    (1 breast half)

Sauce

2   tablespoons olive oil
2   garlic cloves, minced
2   tablespoons sesame paste*
2   tablespoons soy sauce
1   teaspoon Asian sesame oil

1   small seedless cucumber, julienned (about 2 cups)
1   Belgian endive, julienned, soaked in ice water
    and drained (page 175)
1   cup julienned radicchio, soaked in ice water
    and drained (page 175)
¼   cup fresh cilantro leaves
1   tablespoon horseradish, preferably freshly grated
1   tablespoon minced jalapeño pepper
1   tablespoon hot mustard**
    Coarse or kosher salt
    Freshly ground pepper

To prepare the chicken and noodles: Soak the noodles in cold water to cover for 20 minutes, until softened. Meanwhile, bring the stock to a boil in a medium saucepan. Reduce the heat to low and add the chicken breast and slowly simmer over low heat, covered, for 10 minutes, turning occasionally, until the meat is cooked. Remove the chicken and let it cool; reserve the stock. Remove and discard the skin and bones and shred the meat; set aside.

Drain the noodles and cut into 2-inch lengths. Bring the stock to a boil, add the noodles and cook for 1 minute. Drain well; separate the noodles. Set aside.

To make the sauce: Heat the oil in a small saucepan. Add the garlic and cook over high heat, stirring, for 1 to 2 minutes, until golden. Stir in the sesame paste, soy sauce and sesame oil and remove from the heat. Set aside to cool.

The salad can be prepared up to 1 day in advance to this point.

To assemble: Just before you are ready to serve the salad, place the chicken, noodles, cucumber, endive, radicchio and cilantro in a large bowl. Add the horse-radish, jalapeño pepper and mustard to the sauce, mix well, pour over the salad and toss. Season to taste with salt and pepper and serve.

*I prefer Lan Chi Sesame Paste from Taiwan. It has been manufactured by the same company for over 50 years and the quality of the ingredients has never changed. It can be found in Chinese grocery stores.

**Or use 1 tablespoon dry mustard powder, mixed with 1 teaspoon water and 1 teaspoon white wine vinegar or red wine vinegar. Stir well and let sit for 10 minutes before using.

CHAPTER EIGHT

RICE

I N THE CHINESE LANGUAGE, "cooked rice" and "meal" are the same word. In most families, particularly in the south of China, boiled or steamed rice is served throughout every meal: no lunch or dinner would be considered complete without it. Freshly cooked plain white rice has an importance — and a taste — that is hard to explain to anyone who has grown up in the West. Those who find it bland have probably never tasted rice that has been cooked correctly.

My mother-in-law is very particular about her rice and always buys the best long-grain brand available. Like most Chinese cooks, she is careful to add just the right amount of water, for the subtle flavor of the rice is absorbed into the liquid in which it is cooked. If too much is added, the natural, delicate sweetness will be lost, and the rice will lose its firm texture and become mushy.

If cooked rice sits for too long, its flavor deteriorates. At my mother-in-law's table, no one dares to open the lid of the rice pot until the dinner is completely ready. When they were young, each of my brothers-in-law would eat three or four bowls of plain rice along with all the other dishes served.

My mother, on the other hand, served rice only when my father was not at home, for he did not like it. She preferred medium-grain for savory dishes. I do, too, because medium- and short-grain varieties readily absorb flavor from surrounding ingredients. When the lid is first removed from the pot, the wonderful aroma never fails to give me pleasure.

For sweet dishes, my mother used sweet rice, which she especially loved. For holidays, she made eight-treasure rice pudding, or she would cook the rice, layer it with sweet red bean paste and serve it cold. For New Year's, she ground the sweet rice into a paste, mixed it with sugar and vanilla-scented flowers, formed it into cakes and steamed it for hours. These hot rice cakes were my breakfast of choice during the holidays. My cousin made the best rice cakes, stuffing them with red bean paste and deep-frying them until they were crisp.

IN RECENT YEARS, to accommodate Western tastes, I have begun to serve flavored rice, instead of plain. My sons, who grew up in this country, prefer fried rice, so I make that often at home. Rather than using leftover rice for it, though, I always cook a fresh pot because the taste is infinitely better.

I don't limit sweet rice to dessert, as my mother did. One of the most memorable sweet-rice dishes I have ever tasted—now one of my own specialties—was taught to me by a local woman in Taiwan. Mrs. Wong's family had lived in the city for at least three generations, and she had learned the dish from her grandmother. She stir-fried soaked sweet rice in a wok with browned shallots, dried shrimp and wild mushrooms, slowly adding stock until the rice was completely cooked—the same technique that Italians use for risotto. I have made the dish ever since, calling it "Chinese risotto." I also combine sweet rice with vegetables or fruit to make a kind of compote to accompany game or lamb dishes.

I've introduced untraditional varieties into my repertoire. Although I don't particularly care for brown rice on its own, I love it with curry. Two years ago, I began using black sweet rice, popular in Thailand and other countries in Southeast Asia, whose taste combines the nuttiness of wild rice with the delicate stickiness of white sweet rice. The result of all these influences: a score of dishes whose variety would amaze my mother.

RICE

My Favorite Fried Rice   288

Jade Green Fried Rice with Crabmeat   291

Vegetable Rice   292

Curried Brown Rice with Broccoli Rabe   294

Chinese Risotto with Wild Mushrooms   295

Sweet Rice, Taro and Pineapple Compote   298

Black Rice, Lentil and Corn Compote   300

RULES OF RICE

WHEN YOU CHOOSE RICE, look for uniformly sized grains with few or no broken pieces. White rice should have a gloss or sheen.

Be careful not to use too much liquid when cooking plain rice, or its natural sweetness will be lost. The worst thing you can do is to boil rice in lots of water, as you would pasta. Even if properly tender, it will be tasteless and not worth eating. I never add salt to my rice.

In today's modern Chinese kitchen, the rice cooker has become a necessity, for it is the easiest way to cook perfect rice with the least amount of attention. It also has the advantage of keeping the rice warm until it is ready to be served. If you cook a lot of rice, I recommend that you invest in one. If you don't own one, the following standard directions will give you good results:

To cook medium-grain and short-grain white rice, first wash the rice 2 or 3 times, or until the water is clear; drain well. Use a heavy medium pot with a tight-fitting lid. For every 2 cups rice, measure out 2 cups cold water into the pot. Bring the water to a boil over high heat. Add the rice, turn the heat very low and stir once to loosen any grains sticking to the bottom. Cook for 5 minutes. Cover. Simmer for 15 minutes, without lifting the lid. Remove the pot from the heat and let stand, covered, for another 10 minutes, until all the water is absorbed. When you finally remove the lid, a wonderfully delicate aroma will be released. Separate the grains with a fork while the rice is still hot: they should be tender, with just a trace of stickiness.

Cooking Rice

Rice (1 cup raw)	Water	Cooking Time
medium- or short-grain white	1 cup	20 minutes
long-grain white	1¼ cups	20 minutes
short-grain brown	2½ cups	30 minutes
short- or medium-grain white sweet (glutinous)*	½ cup	15 minutes
long-grain white sweet (glutinous)*	½ cup	15 minutes
black sweet*	1 cup	25 minutes

*Both white sweet and black sweet rice must be soaked before cooking; see page 297 and 301. The best method for cooking them is steaming.

MY FAVORITE FRIED RICE

SERVES 4 AS A MAIN COURSE OR 8 AS A SIDE DISH

I LOVE THE FLAVOR that the fresh tomato and basil give this rice. Most fried rice recipes call for long-grain, but I prefer to use the medium- or short-grain varieties, as they have a richer, sweeter taste.

Since I always use a rice cooker, I assemble the whole dish right in it. I stir the bacon-vegetable mixture and the cooked eggs directly into the freshly cooked rice and mix well.

Serve with Breast of Chicken Sautéed with Mushrooms (page 194), grilled steak or on its own for lunch.

2	cups medium- or short-grain white rice, washed and drained
5	tablespoons corn or olive oil
4	large eggs, lightly beaten
½	cup diced red onion
1	cup diced Canadian bacon*
½	cup cooked fresh or frozen, thawed, peas
½	cup fresh or frozen, thawed, white or yellow corn kernels
4	scallions, finely chopped
1	cup diced, seeded tomato (1 large)
2	teaspoons coarse or kosher salt
	Freshly ground pepper
½	cup chopped fresh basil leaves

Cook the rice in a rice cooker, following the manufacturer's instructions, or cook according to the directions on page 287. Set aside.

Heat 4 tablespoons of the oil in a large nonstick skillet until hot. Add the eggs and cook over medium heat until lightly set. Stir with chopsticks or a wooden spoon to break the eggs into tiny pieces. Continue to cook, stirring, until the eggs are lightly browned and their aroma is released, 4 to 5 minutes. Remove to a small bowl with a slotted spoon and set aside.

Heat the remaining 1 tablespoon oil in the same skillet, add the onion and cook over high heat until soft and lightly golden, about 2 minutes. Add the bacon, peas, corn and scallions and stir-fry until heated through, about 3 minutes.

Add the tomato and sprinkle with the salt. Stir in the cooked rice and the egg, breaking up any lumps. Mix well and heat through, 1 to 2 minutes. Season to taste with pepper and stir in the basil.

*Chicken, shrimp or ham can be substituted.

PROPER FRIED RICE

FRIED RICE IS IN A CLASS BY ITSELF. When I was a child, this was my favorite kind of rice, and I often ate it for lunch as a full meal. The traditional version calls for leftover cold rice, which is stir-fried with scrambled eggs, scallions and ham. Because rice loses some of its sweetness when kept in the refrigerator, I use freshly cooked.

There are hundreds of recipes for fried rice. You can start with fresh ingredients or use up bits and pieces of cooked leftovers: grilled or roasted meat or fish, seafood, carrots or peas. Whatever your ingredients, the basic technique is much the same.

The egg must be fried until it is lightly golden and aromatic and the scallions cooked until soft, or you will not achieve the flavor and aroma associated with classical fried rice.

Never add soy sauce to the rice; it will spoil the delicacy of this dish. Use plain salt to add flavor, if needed.

Jade Green Fried Rice with Crabmeat

JADE GREEN FRIED RICE
WITH CRABMEAT

SERVES 4 AS A MAIN COURSE FOR LUNCH

I LIKE TO SERVE this as a luncheon dish accompanied by Water Chestnut, Arugula and Endive Salad (page 129) or a baby arugula salad.

2 cups medium- or short-grain white rice,
washed and drained

½ pound fresh spinach

¼ cup corn or olive oil

3 garlic cloves, thinly sliced

4 large eggs, lightly beaten

3 scallions, finely chopped

6 ounces jumbo lump crabmeat

½ cup peeled, diced tomato

2 teaspoons coarse or kosher salt
Freshly ground pepper

Cook the rice in a rice cooker, following the manufacturer's instructions, or cook according to the directions on page 287. Set aside.

Wash the spinach, remove the stems and dry on paper towels. Julienne the spinach finely, then dice into small pieces.

Heat the oil in a large nonstick skillet until hot and add the garlic. Cook over high heat, stirring, for 30 seconds.

Add the eggs and cook over medium heat until lightly set. Cook for about 3 minutes, stirring with chopsticks or a wooden spoon to separate the eggs into small pieces, until they are golden brown and you can smell their aroma. Add the scallions. Stir-fry for 2 minutes.

Add the cooked rice and the spinach and mix well; the spinach should coat the rice and give it a green color.

When the rice is hot, add the crabmeat, tomato, salt and pepper to taste. Fold together carefully with a wooden spoon so as not to break up the lumps of crabmeat. Serve as soon as the mixture is heated through.

Vegetable Rice

Serves 4 to 6 as a side dish

IN THIS FAMOUS BUT SIMPLE SHANGHAI DISH, the vegetables are cooked together with the rice. Serve as a side dish with meat or other main dishes. Bok choy, a leafy member of the cabbage family, is available in supermarkets year-round in this country. It tastes best from October through March, when the ivory-colored stalks are sweeter and the green leaves are more tender. Shanghai bok choy is one-third to one-quarter the size of regular bok choy and comes bundled in packs of five to six plants. Readily available all year in Asian grocery stores, it is much sweeter and more tender than the larger variety and is one of my favorite vegetables.

½	pound Shanghai bok choy* (about 3 plants)
2	tablespoons corn oil
1	cup finely chopped celery
½	cup chopped scallions
2	cups long-grain white rice, washed and drained
2¼	cups chicken stock (page 79)
2	teaspoons coarse or kosher salt
	Freshly ground pepper

Wash the bok choy well. Cut off the bottoms of the stems and remove any tough outer leaves. Cut each bok choy in half lengthwise and thinly slice, then chop.

In a medium saucepan with a tight-fitting lid, heat the oil and add the celery and the scallions. Cook over high heat, stirring, until lightly browned, about 3 minutes.

Add the rice and the stock. Bring to a boil, reduce the heat to low and stir to loosen any grains sticking to the bottom. Cook for 5 minutes.

Mix in the bok choy and salt. Cover and cook, without lifting the lid, for 15 minutes. Remove from the heat and let the pan sit for 10 minutes without removing the lid. Stir with a fork to separate the grains of rice.

Season to taste with pepper.

*You can substitute about ½ pound of regular bok choy, Swiss chard or green cabbage, chopped. You will need 3 cups.

BROWN RICE

Brown rice has gained in popularity because of its nutritional value, and I have been serving it for the past eight years. Now 90 percent of my customers ask for it instead of white.

Brown rice does not have the richness and sweetness of white, but it possesses a nutty flavor and a slightly chewier texture. And unlike white rice, it remains toothsome rather than becoming mushy or sticky if cooked too long and is just about impossible to ruin.

Brown rice comes in short-, medium- and long-grain varieties. I prefer short-grain because it seems to have a better flavor than long-grain. Instead of using water, I always cook brown rice in a good chicken stock to give it more body and add sautéed onion and shallots to give it a better flavor.

CURRIED BROWN RICE
WITH BROCCOLI RABE

SERVES 4 TO 6 AS A SIDE DISH

WHEN MIXED WITH LOTS OF SEASONINGS and vegetables, as in this recipe, brown rice makes a delicious dish. Do not overcook or the greens will lose their fresh taste.

½	pound broccoli rabe or Swiss chard
3	tablespoons olive oil
1	cup diced onion
½	cup diced red bell pepper
½	cup chopped celery heart (center yellow-white stalks only)
1	teaspoon curry powder
½	teaspoon freshly ground pepper, plus more to taste
5	cups chicken stock (page 79)
3	tablespoons unsweetened coconut milk*
2	teaspoons coarse or kosher salt
2	cups short-grain brown rice, washed and drained
½	cup peeled, diced tomato

Wash the broccoli rabe or chard and cut off the tough leaves. If using chard, remove the stems and use only the leaves. Chop into small pieces; you should have about 2 cups. Set aside.

Heat the oil in a medium saucepan, add the onion and cook over high heat, stirring, until soft and lightly golden, 2 to 3 minutes.

Add the bell pepper, celery, curry powder and pepper and mix well.

Add 4½ cups of the stock, the coconut milk and the salt. Bring to a boil, add the rice and stir well to loosen any grains sticking to the bottom. Cook for 5 minutes, reduce the heat to low and cover with a tight-fitting lid. Simmer for 25 minutes; the rice should be soft. Stir with a fork to separate the grains.

Meanwhile, place the remaining ½ cup stock in a small saucepan, add the broccoli rabe or chard and bring to a boil over high heat. Add the tomato and cook for 2 minutes more, or until the greens are barely soft. Pour over the rice and stir in well. Season with more pepper and serve.

*I prefer the Chaokoh brand, which is carried by most Asian grocery stores.

CHINESE RISOTTO WITH WILD MUSHROOMS

SERVES 6

THIS DISH, POPULAR IN TAIWAN, is prepared in the same fashion as Italian risotto but with sweet rice instead of the Arborio variety used in Italy. In both countries, stock is slowly added to the rice until it is cooked. Chinese Risotto makes a good one-dish lunch, or it can be served as a side dish to accompany meat or seafood.

2	cups short- or medium-grain white sweet (glutinous) rice
¼	cup corn or olive oil
6	shallots, chopped
4	large fresh shiitake mushrooms, stems removed; caps cut into small dice (1½ cups)
1	medium Portobello mushroom, stem removed; cut into small dice (1½ cups)
2	tablespoons minced soaked dried shrimp (page 134) or ½ cup diced fresh shrimp (optional)
½	cup finely diced smoked ham, preferably Virginia or Smithfield (optional, but the rice will taste better if it is included)
1-1¼	cups chicken stock (page 79)
2	teaspoons coarse or kosher salt
	Freshly ground pepper
2	scallions, finely chopped
2	tablespoons chopped fresh chervil or cilantro leaves or another fresh herb

Place the rice in a large bowl and cover with 6 cups warm water. Soak for 4 hours, or refrigerate overnight. Drain well. Set aside.

Heat the oil in a large nonstick saucepan. Add the shallots and cook over high heat, stirring, for 2 or 3 minutes, or until they are soft and golden. Add the mushrooms and the shrimp and ham, if using, and cook for 3 to 4 minutes more.

Add the rice to the saucepan, reduce the heat to low and stir until the grains are well coated with the oil, about 5 minutes.

Add ½ cup of the stock and the salt and cook, stirring constantly, until the liquid is absorbed, about 5 minutes.

Gradually add ½ cup more stock, stirring constantly and allowing the rice to absorb the liquid before adding more. This should take about 15 minutes; the rice should be tender but not soft or sticky, and all the liquid should be absorbed. If the rice is not done, continue cooking, gradually adding the remaining ¼ cup stock as needed. Season with pepper to taste.

Stir in the chopped scallions and herbs and serve.

WHITE SWEET RICE

SWEET RICE is also known as sticky rice, or glutinous rice. It is opaque when raw and becomes transparent when cooked. Softer than most other types, it cooks quickly and has a delicate texture and sweet flavor. However, it becomes sticky, heavy and unpleasantly glutinous if overcooked.

Sweet rice can be short-, medium- or long-grain and is grown in many Asian countries, such as Japan, Korea, China and Thailand. All of the varieties of the different countries vary slightly. The Chinese and Japanese prefer short-grain sweet rice, which has a richer, sweeter flavor. In Thailand, long-grain is preferred, as it is less sticky. For soups and congee, I prefer long-grain.

To control its texture, I steam sweet rice without adding any liquid. Or I cook it in a risotto, slowly adding stock little by little until it reaches the right consistency.

Cooking Sweet Rice

Using 3 cups water for each 1 cup rice, soak the rice in a large bowl for 4 hours or refrigerate overnight. Drain and discard the soaking water; the rice will have swelled to about 1½ cups.

Steaming is the best method for cooking sweet rice, eliminating any extra moisture and making the rice less glutinous. Prepare the steamer by placing a layer of cheesecloth in the bottom of the rack. Spread the rice thinly over the cheesecloth in an even layer. Fill the bottom of the steamer with water close to, but not touching, the rack and bring to a boil. Place the rack on top, cover and steam the rice for 25 minutes, replenishing the water if necessary, until tender.

To cook sweet rice without a steamer, place ½ cup water in a medium saucepan and bring to a boil over high heat. Add the drained soaked rice and reduce the heat to low. Keep stirring the rice with a wooden spoon for 5 minutes; it will gradually become translucent. Cover the pan and continue to simmer for 10 minutes more. Turn off the heat and let sit for 10 minutes more without disturbing. Remove the lid and add 1 tablespoon butter, stirring it into the hot rice with a fork. The rice is now ready to serve.

Sweet Rice, Taro and Pineapple Compote

Makes about 3 cups rice; serves 6 as a side dish

RICE WITH TARO AND PINEAPPLE is often eaten in Canton and Southeast Asia as a dessert. I have reduced the amount of sugar and coconut milk in the traditional version so that it is less sweet. It makes a good accompaniment to smoked or braised game or lamb. Make a double portion; it tastes even better the next day.

  2   cups short- or medium-grain white sweet
      (glutinous) rice*
  1   cup taro root, cut into ⅛-inch dice**
  ½   cup fresh pineapple, peeled,
      cored and chopped
  ½   cup unsweetened coconut milk***
  1   tablespoon butter
  1   tablespoon sugar
  ½   teaspoon coarse or kosher salt

Place the rice in a large bowl and cover with 6 cups warm water. Soak for 4 hours, or refrigerate overnight. Drain.

Prepare a steamer by placing a layer of cheesecloth in the bottom of a rack. Spread the rice and taro in an even layer over the cheesecloth. Fill the bottom of the steamer with water close to, but not touching, the rack and bring to a boil. Place the rack on top, cover and steam for about 30 minutes, until the rice is cooked and the taro tender. (To cook the rice without a steamer, see page 297. If you are not using a steamer, cook the taro separately. Place it in a small saucepan with ¼ cup water. Bring to a boil over high heat. Cover, reduce the heat to low and simmer for about 10 minutes, or until tender. Stir the taro into the cooked rice.) Transfer the rice mixture to a large bowl.

Combine the pineapple, coconut milk, butter, sugar and salt in a small saucepan. Heat over high heat until the sugar melts, about 2 minutes. Bring to a boil and remove from the heat. Stir into the rice mixture and serve.

The leftover rice can be stored, covered, in the refrigerator for up to 2 days. Do not freeze.

Warm by either steaming or heating in a microwave.

*Do not try to substitute another rice. Sweet rice has a completely different texture and flavor than regular rice and is the only one that can be handled in this manner.

**If you cannot find taro root, substitute butternut squash. Steam it separately for 5 minutes, then add the rice and steam as directed.

***I prefer the Chaokoh brand, which is carried by most Asian grocery stores.

BLACK RICE, LENTIL AND CORN COMPOTE

SERVES 8 TO 10 AS A SIDE DISH

BLACK SWEET RICE combines perfectly with cooked lentils and mushrooms. This dish is beautiful to look at, subtle yet full of flavor and good with game, duck or chicken.

2	cups black sweet rice
½	cup lentils
3	tablespoons corn or olive oil
4	shallots, chopped
2	cups diced white button mushrooms or fresh shiitake mushrooms (½ pound)
1	cup fresh corn kernels
2	scallions, finely chopped
¼	cup chicken stock (page 79)
2	teaspoons coarse or kosher salt
1	teaspoon freshly ground pepper

Place the rice in a large bowl and cover with 6 cups warm water. Soak for 4 hours, or refrigerate overnight. Rinse well and drain.

This rice is best steamed,* but it can also be cooked in a saucepan. Bring 2½ cups water to a boil in a heavy medium saucepan. Add the rice and stir to loosen any grains sticking to the bottom. Cook over high heat for 5 minutes. Reduce the heat to low, cover with a tight-fitting lid and simmer for 25 minutes without lifting the lid. Turn off the heat and let sit for 10 minutes before removing the lid. Using a fork or chopsticks, separate the grains before they become cold. If you wait, the rice will form clumps and become too sticky to handle. The rice may be cooked up to 1 day in advance and refrigerated.

Meanwhile, bring 3 cups water to a boil in a medium saucepan. Add the lentils and cook for 20 to 25 minutes, or until they are tender but not mushy; set aside.

Heat the oil in a large skillet. Add the shallots and cook over high heat, stirring, until soft and lightly browned. Add the mushrooms and cook for 3 minutes more.

Add the corn, lentils, scallions, stock, salt and pepper and cook, stirring, for 2 minutes. Cover and cook over medium heat for 5 minutes to cook the corn and heat the lentils.

Stir in the black rice with a fork or chopsticks. Cook over medium heat until the rice is heated through and soft, stirring occasionally, about 3 minutes. Remove from the heat and spoon into a serving bowl.

*To steam the rice, follow the instructions on page 297 but increase the cooking time to 35 minutes.

BLACK SWEET RICE

BLACK SWEET RICE, also known as wild sweet rice, or red sweet rice, is a favorite throughout Southeast Asia. It has a nutty flavor and a firm texture, similar to that of wild rice, but with some of the sweet stickiness of white sweet rice. When cooked, it is a little firmer than white sweet rice and goes well with meat and game dishes.

Black sweet rice must be soaked in warm water for 4 hours; 1 cup will swell to 1½ cups. Best if steamed, it can, however, be simmered in water, using 1 cup water for every 1 cup rice, for about 25 minutes. Black rice should be cooked by itself, as it will turn any other ingredients an unappetizing reddish purple.

The variety I like to use is reddish black with white spots and comes from Thailand. Priced at about $1 per pound, it is much less expensive than American wild rice.

CHAPTER NINE

BREADS, PANCAKES AND CRÊPES

S HANDONG PROVINCE, in the north of China, is famous for its breads. After the Communist takeover, the naval academy that was located in Tsing Tao, a seaport in that province, moved its headquarters to Kao-hsiung, Taiwan, where my family lived. I was often invited to my Shandong classmates' homes for meals, and I remember the wonderful steamed yeast buns their mothers made. Sometimes the buns were plain, and sometimes they were made with layers of chopped scallions or stuffed with various meats and vegetables. These buns were made with hard wheat flour with a high gluten content, sourdough starter and water. They were glimmering white, dense and full of flavor — nothing like the ones in many Chinatown restaurants in this country, which tend to be too sticky and soft.

To earn extra money, the wives and relatives of the soldiers from Shandong opened stalls or small restaurants in the neighborhood, where they sold their homemade pancakes, baked breads and steamed buns, together with braised meats and pickled vegetables. These entrepreneurs made their specialties with primitive baking equipment, often in a charcoal or wood-burning stove fashioned from a steel barrel whose walls were lined with baked clay—much like an Indian tandoori oven. The breads, which were cooked on the walls of the ovens, were either chewy, with a taste and texture similar to that of a bagel, or soft and puffy so they could be pulled open, stuffed with meat and eaten as a sandwich. My mother would sometimes buy them and serve them along with our favorite Mongolian hot pot, or she would braise some pork and stuff it into sesame bread.

At home, my family often made steamed buns, either plain or stuffed with pork and napa cabbage. I loved them all, but especially the plain breads that our cook would slice and pan-fry until they were golden and crispy, sprinkle with sugar and serve for breakfast. He always saved a small piece of the yeast dough for the next batch, and my grandmother inspected it to make sure that the dough was firm and had risen properly. Sometimes, my family ate scallion pancakes, aromatic scallion crêpes or pan-fried scallion bread with just a few side dishes.

THE CAPITAL OF CHINA is famous for its variety of delicate pancakes, and it was always a treat when my father took us to a Beijing-style restaurant. Thin pancakes were made from a dough using boiling water and wrapped around Peking duck or mu-shu pork. The thousand-layer pancakes, with inner layers of soft, moist dough and crispy outsides, were incomparable, as were the pocket breads stuffed with delicious meats or chives.

Many of these breads were made with a roux—oil and flour cooked together until very thick, similar to the mixture that the French use to thicken soups and sauces. In Chinese breads, however, the roux functions differently, playing the same role that butter does in puff pastry, keeping the layers of dough separate so that the bread remains tender.

I still make the traditional northern breads of my childhood for my family, including several varieties of pancakes. But when I moved to Valparaiso, Indiana, a friend of my mother's showed me a time-saving innovation I have relied on ever since, which she called "lazy scallion pancakes." Rather than making the pancakes from scratch, she layered ready-made flour tortillas with chopped scallions and bacon and sealed them with beaten egg yolk. Ever since, whenever I am rushed or tired, I do the same. (For the recipe, see page 306.) The breads in this chapter can be eaten with the main course, like French bread, or alone, with a few well-chosen side dishes.

BREADS, PANCAKES
AND CRÊPES

Scallion Pancakes   305

One-Thousand-Layer Pancakes   308

Stuffed Chive Pockets   310

Peking Thin Pancakes   313

Scallion Crêpes   315

Pan-Fried Scallion Bread   316

SCALLION PANCAKES

MAKES 8 PANCAKES

M Y COUSIN FROM SHANXI PROVINCE makes the best scallion pancakes I have ever tasted. At least once a month when I was in college, she would call me to come over to make a meal of them. First, she made a very soft dough, which she allowed to rest for 1 hour. She rolled the dough flat into very thin sheets, topped them with the chopped scallions, chopped pork fat and salt, rolled them up and cut them into small pieces. Then she rolled them out again and pan-fried them. I would eat them as fast as she could make them.

I use more hot water than in the traditional recipe, because I want the dough to have a softer consistency. The filling is traditional, made with a little bit of pork fat, which gives it a wonderful flavor.

Boiling-Water Dough

1¼   **cups water**

2-2½   **cups all-purpose flour**

Scallion Filling

½   **bunch scallions, trimmed and minced (about ½ cup)**

¼   **cup minced pork fat**

1   **tablespoon olive or corn oil**

1   **teaspoon coarse or kosher salt**

About ½ cup corn oil for frying

To make the boiling-water dough: Bring the water to a boil in a medium saucepan. Turn off the heat and let sit for 2 minutes. Sift 2 cups of the flour into a large bowl. Add the boiling water in a slow, steady stream, mixing well with a wooden spoon to form a dough. Keep mixing until you can form it into a smooth ball. This can also be done in a food processor: Place the flour in the food processor fitted with the metal blade, and with the motor running, add the water through the feed tube; process until the dough forms a ball, 3 to 5 minutes.

Let stand, covered with a damp cloth or towel, for 30 minutes so the gluten relaxes.

To make the scallion filling: In a small bowl, combine the scallions, pork fat, oil and salt; mix well.

Place the dough on a lightly floured surface. Shape it into a log, cut the dough into 8 portions and sprinkle lightly with flour; it should be very soft and easy to handle.

Roll out 1 piece of the dough on a floured surface into a ⅛-inch-thick oval (**opposite page, A**). Spread 1 tablespoon of the scallion filling in a thin layer over the dough, leaving a ½-inch margin all around (**B**). Roll up the dough jelly-roll fashion (**C**).

Seal the ends of each piece by pinching them closed (**D**). Twirl both the ends; the piece will bend a little in the middle (**E**). A little of the scallion filling may come out, but that is all right. Spiral the dough around itself, making a concentric circle (**F and G**). Flatten it with your palm and press it out gently with a rolling pin into a 5-inch round (**H**). Repeat, making 8 rounds in all.

To cook the pancakes: Heat a heavy skillet over medium heat. Add 1 tablespoon of the oil to the pan, and fry the pancakes, 1 at a time, for 2 to 3 minutes on each side, or until golden in color, adding more oil as needed. Drain on paper towels and serve hot.

"LAZY" SCALLION PANCAKES

INSTEAD OF MAKING THE DOUGH from scratch, you can substitute 12 six-inch flour tortillas; you will also need 2 large egg yolks, lightly beaten, for sealing the tortillas. Place 1 tortilla on a flat surface and spread 1 tablespoon of the scallion filling over the top, leaving a ½-inch margin all around. Moisten the edge of the tortilla with a little bit of the egg yolk. Place a second tortilla on top and press to seal the edges. Spread with another tablespoon of the filling and place a third tortilla on top; press to seal. Repeat, using the remaining tortillas, making 4 Scallion Pancakes in all. Cook as directed.

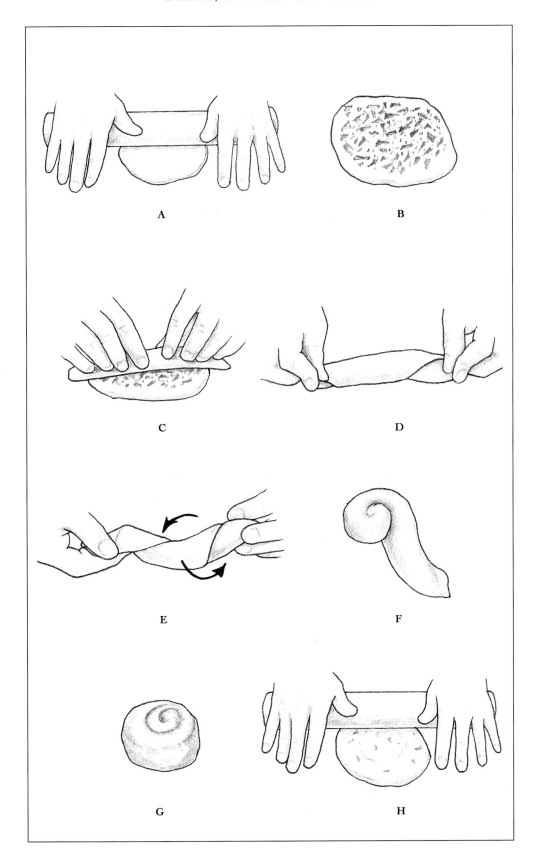

A

B

C

D

E

F

G

H

ONE-THOUSAND-LAYER PANCAKES

MAKES 4 PANCAKES

FAMOUS IN PEKING, these pancakes are often served along with stir-fries, but they are also good with salad, soup or meat courses. Similar to French puff pastry dough, they are a great favorite of mine.

The roux, a mixture of flour and oil cooked together until thick, keeps the layers of dough separate, producing a tender, crunchy pastry. I prefer the taste of peanut oil here, but corn oil can be substituted.

> About 6 tablespoons all-purpose flour
> 1 teaspoon coarse or kosher salt
> ½ teaspoon five-spice powder
> 6 tablespoons peanut oil
> 1 recipe boiling-water dough
> (see Scallion Pancakes, page 305)
> ¼ cup sesame seeds
> About ¼ cup corn oil for frying

Sift the 6 tablespoons flour, salt and five-spice powder together; set aside.

Heat the peanut oil over medium heat in a heavy skillet. Gradually add the flour mixture, stirring well to incorporate it into the oil.

Keep stirring the roux while it cooks, for about 5 minutes, or until it is lightly browned and you can smell the five-spice powder. Remove from the heat; cool.

Make the boiling-water dough and place it on a lightly floured surface. Using your hand and a floured rolling pin, roll out the dough and pat into an 8-x-12-inch rectangle.

With a knife, spread the cooled roux evenly over the top of the dough. Roll up the dough into a log. Wrap well in a piece of plastic wrap and refrigerate for 1 hour.

Using a rolling pin and additional flour as needed, roll out the filled dough into a 4-x-12-inch rectangle.

The dough now needs to be turned and rolled. With the short end of the rectangle facing you, fold the top one-third of the dough down toward the middle, as you would a business letter. Fold the bottom third up to meet the top edge. You should now have a small square, about 4 inches square.

Turn the dough a quarter turn to the right. Roll out into a 4-x-12-inch rectangle. Repeat the same folding process. The dough has now made 2 turns.

Cut the square of dough into 4 pieces. Roll and turn each piece once more.

Form each piece of the dough into a ball and flatten with the palm of your hand. Sprinkle both sides of the dough with 1 tablespoon of the sesame seeds. Roll, using a rolling pin, into a ⅛-inch-thick circle. Repeat with the remaining 3 pieces of dough. Let the dough rest at room temperature for ½ hour, covered with a damp towel.

Heat 2 tablespoons corn oil over medium-low heat in a large skillet. Pan-fry each bread circle, one at a time, for 3 minutes, then turn and cook on the other side for 3 to 5 minutes. When cooked, the breads should be lightly browned and crisp on the outside and flaky. Repeat with the remaining dough rounds, adding oil to the skillet as needed to keep the dough from sticking.

Serve hot.

UNIQUE BREADS

IN THE NORTHERN PART OF CHINA, especially in Shandong, Shanxi and Beijing, wheat flour is the primary grain, for rice is scarce. Doughs there are much firmer and have a different flavor from those in the south, for they are made with hard wheat flours, and eggs are rarely added.

Northerners also employ a unique method I have never seen anywhere else. They slowly pour boiling water into the flour to partially cook it, creating a dough with a soft texture and a naturally sweet flavor. No yeast is added. This dough is the basis for steamed dumplings, pan-fried scallion pancakes, stuffed pancakes and pocket bread. It is also traditionally used to make thin pancakes for Peking duck or mu-shu pork.

For yeasted breads — either steamed, pan-fried or baked — cold-water dough is used. It has a firmer texture than boiling-water dough, can be handled more without becoming tough and will stand up to longer cooking.

Stuffed Chive Pockets

Makes 8 stuffed pancakes; serves 8

O F ALL THE FAMOUS PEKING PANCAKES, I love chive pockets most of all. Small, round pancakes, they are stuffed with mushrooms, chives, cabbage and cellophane noodles. To save time, I often make them with tortillas.

You can vary this recipe by adding 1 cup of ground beef or ground pork. Sauté the meat in the oil first and then add the mushrooms and continue with the recipe. Serve the pancakes warm as an appetizer, as a side dish with soup or with meat. They also make a nice lunch with a green salad.

1	cup soaked cellophane noodles* (from 1 small skein uncooked)
1	cup finely chopped napa cabbage or Shanghai bok choy (page 292)
1	tablespoon coarse or kosher salt
	About ½ cup corn oil
2	cups finely chopped white button mushrooms (about 1 pound)
5	medium shrimp (¼ pound), peeled, deveined and cleaned with salt (page 182), chopped; or 2 tablespoons minced soaked dried shrimp (page 134)
1	cup finely chopped garlic chives**
1	tablespoon chopped fresh cilantro leaves
	Freshly ground pepper
1	recipe Peking Thin Pancakes (page 313) or 16 six-inch flour tortillas
2	large egg yolks, lightly beaten

While the noodles are soaking, place the chopped cabbage in a bowl. Sprinkle with 1 teaspoon of the salt and set aside for 20 minutes.

Lightly squeeze out the liquid from the cabbage.

Heat 2 tablespoons of the oil in a large skillet and add the mushrooms. Cook over high heat, stirring, for 5 minutes, or until dry. Add the fresh or dried shrimp and cook for another 2 minutes, or until the fresh shrimp are no longer translucent.

Stuffed Chive Pockets

Add the chives and cook for about 1 minute. Turn off the heat and add the noodles, cabbage or bok choy and the cilantro and stir until all the ingredients are blended. Season with the remaining 2 teaspoons salt and pepper.

Place 1 pancake or tortilla on a work surface and brush the edges with some of the beaten egg yolk. Place ⅓ cup of the shrimp mixture in the center and spread the mixture to within 1 inch of the edge. Cover with another pancake or tortilla and press the edges together to seal.

Repeat with the remaining pancakes or tortillas and the shrimp mixture; you will have 8 pancakes.

Heat 2 tablespoons of the oil in a large skillet. Place the pancake or tortilla in the skillet and cook over medium heat, until golden and crisp, about 3 minutes. Turn the pancake and cook on the second side, 3 to 4 minutes more.

Remove from the skillet and keep warm. Repeat with the remaining pancakes, using more oil as needed.

Before serving, cut each pancake or tortilla into 4 wedges. Serve hot.

*Soak the noodles in cold water to cover for 20 minutes; drain. Dip them in boiling water for 1 minute, rinse in cold water, drain and cut into ½-inch lengths.

**Leeks or onions can be substituted.

KING OF CHIVES

In China, three kinds of chives are available in spring and summer:

Chinese chives have wider leaves than the varieties grown in the West. They are known in this country as "garlic chives." They are most often used for stuffing, sautés and soups. Half the quantity of scallions may be substituted.

Chive flower buds are stems with flower buds attached at the top. Used before they begin to open or flower, they are tender and their flavor is prized.

Yellow chives are considered a delicacy, and their price is about three times that of regular Chinese chives. They are, in fact, the same variety, but they are covered with a blanket of rice hay to keep them from being exposed to sunlight as they grow, as are white asparagus and Belgian endive. Yellow chives are milder, sweeter in flavor and more tender than green chives. They are considered the "king of chives."

PEKING THIN PANCAKES

MAKES 16 PANCAKES

W HEN I WAS A CHILD, a stack of these pancakes was served all the time, along with a steaming platter of mu-shu pork and other accompaniments. The pancakes are light and faintly sweet. They make good wrappers for all kinds of julienned meat and vegetable dishes. Be sure to put enough sesame oil between the two pancakes before pan-frying; if there is too little, they will stick together and will not taste as good. (Cooking them sandwiched together makes each pancake much softer than if it were cooked separately.)

If I don't have the time to make my own pancakes, I substitute 6-inch flour tortillas, wrap them in plastic wrap to keep out any extra moisture and steam for 10 minutes before serving.

Serve with Mandarin Pork with Brandy-Infused Hoisin Sauce (page 232) or Orange Beef with Sun-Dried Tomatoes (page 251).

1   cup water
    About 2 cups all-purpose flour
3   tablespoons Asian sesame oil
    About ⅓ cup corn oil for frying

Bring the water to a boil in a small saucepan. Turn off the heat and let sit for 2 minutes.

Sift the 2 cups flour into a large mixing bowl. Add the boiling water in a slow, steady stream, mixing well with a wooden spoon to form a dough. Keep mixing until you can form it into a smooth ball. This can also be done in a food processor: Place the flour in the food processor fitted with the metal blade, and with the motor running, add the water through the feed tube; process until the dough forms a ball, 3 to 5 minutes.

Let stand, covered with a damp cloth or towel, for 30 minutes so the gluten relaxes. Place the dough on a lightly floured surface and knead until it is smooth, about 3 minutes.

Shape the dough into a log 1 to 2 inches in diameter. Cut into 16 pieces.

Flatten each piece of dough on a floured surface with the palm of your hand into a 2-to-3-inch round.

Brush each piece all the way to the edges with a little of the sesame oil. Sandwich 2 rounds of dough together, sesame-oiled sides on the inside. Roll out each double pancake on a lightly floured surface until it is about 6 inches in diameter, keeping it as round as possible. You will have 8 rounds.

Heat a large nonstick skillet over medium heat. Lightly oil the skillet, using 1 scant tablespoon corn oil and cook 1 pancake at a time for about 1 to 2 minutes per side, or until lightly browned. Remove from the pan and immediately separate the sandwiched-together pancakes. Stack them on a plate and cover with a damp cloth while you cook the remaining pancakes, using more oil as needed.

Serve immediately.

The pancakes can be wrapped in plastic wrap and frozen. Remove from the freezer and steam on high heat, still tightly wrapped in plastic, for 10 minutes.

SCALLION CRÊPES

MAKES 10 TO 12 CRÊPES

SCALLION CRÊPES were served often at our house while I was growing up. They were brought to the table hot, fragrant and soft with crispy edges, along with julienned pork prepared with leeks and potatoes or julienned pressed tofu tossed with bean sprouts and emerald green spring chives.

We helped ourselves, spooning a favorite filling onto a crêpe and rolling it into a fat cylinder, which we ate with a large bowl of steaming hot and sour soup.

Scallion Crêpes are a versatile addition to a home cook's repertoire. Easy to prepare, they can be offered as an appetizer, as part of a buffet supper or for brunch. I like them with such dishes as Mandarin Pork with Brandy-Infused Hoisin Sauce (page 232), Sun-Dried Tomatoes, Black Bean and Eggplant Salsa (page 118), Silver Sprouts with Jicama, Celery and Balsamic Vinaigrette (page 133), Quick Sauté of Vegetables with Chives (page 150) or with almost any soup.

To release the lovely aroma of the scallions, these pancakes must cook until they are golden and crisp. Similar to a French crêpe, they are softer than Scallion Pancakes (page 305) because of the eggs in the batter.

1½	**cups all-purpose flour**
1½	**cups water**
4	**large eggs**
1	**tablespoon coarse or kosher salt**
1	**cup finely chopped scallions**
	About ½ cup corn oil for frying

Combine the flour, water, eggs and salt in a food processor and process until all the ingredients are thoroughly combined. Pour the batter into a medium bowl. Or to mix by hand, whisk the water and eggs together in a large bowl, add the flour and the salt and mix well.

Add the scallions and mix thoroughly.

Heat 1 tablespoon of the oil over medium heat in an 8-inch nonstick skillet. When the oil is medium-hot, ladle ¼ cup of the batter into the skillet. Tilt the pan so that the batter spreads evenly. Cook until the crêpe is golden brown, 2 to 3 minutes, then turn and brown on the second side, about 2 minutes. Transfer to a platter and repeat, using the remaining batter and oil as needed.

Serve warm; the crêpes are best when freshly made.

Pan-Fried Scallion Bread

Makes 4 breads

M Y FAMILY MAKES THIS BREAD OFTEN. It is layered with scallions, sugar and lard and shaped into a large round loaf. The loaf is pan-fried with a little water so that it partially steams, then is cut into pie-shaped wedges. It remains moist inside from the filling and has a marvelous crust. Serve with meats, vegetables and soups, as you would French bread.

Bread

⅔   cup warm water

¼   cup sugar

1   package active, dry yeast

2   large eggs

    About 3½ cups all-purpose flour

Filling

3   tablespoons corn or olive oil

½   cup finely chopped scallions

1   teaspoon coarse or kosher salt

    About ¼ cup oil for frying

To make the bread: Place the water and the sugar in a small bowl. Add the yeast and let stand until bubbly, 5 to 10 minutes. Place this mixture in a food processor.

With the motor running, add the eggs, one at a time. Gradually add the 3½ cups flour and work it into the dough until it forms a smooth ball.

Remove the dough from the food processor and place in a lightly oiled bowl. Cover with a towel and let rise in a warm place for 4 hours, or until doubled in bulk.

Punch down the dough and shape into an 8-inch log. Cut into 4 pieces. Sprinkle with a little flour and with a rolling pin, flatten each piece into an 8-inch round on a lightly floured surface.

To make the filling: Mix the oil, scallions and salt in a small bowl. Spoon some of the mixture on top of each round and spread evenly over the surface, leaving a ½-inch margin all around. Roll up each piece jelly-roll fashion.

Pan-Fried Scallion Bread

To cook the bread: Sprinkle with a little flour and roll each piece into a 6-inch round. Cover the rounds with a towel and let rise in a warm place for about 2 hours, or until nearly doubled.

Heat 1 tablespoon oil with 2 tablespoons water in a large skillet. Add 1 round of dough and cover the pan tightly. Cook over medium heat for 7 to 8 minutes, then turn and fry on the second side for 7 to 8 minutes more; the dough will rise as it fries.

Remove with tongs or a spatula and drain on paper towels. Cook the remaining rounds of dough, using more oil and water as needed. Serve warm or at room temperature.

Variation

If you don't want to fry the dough, you can brush the tops of the rounds with a mixture of oil and egg yolk beaten together and bake in a 350-degree oven until they are nicely browned, about 30 to 35 minutes.

CHAPTER TEN

DESSERTS

I WENT TO AN ELEMENTARY SCHOOL on a naval base that had been
converted from an old orchid farm. It was filled with tropical fruit
trees of all kinds: mango, dragon-eye (similar to lychee), lychee,
papaya and star fruit. After school, we would sit outside the classrooms under the trees, pretending to study, but really waiting for the wind
to blow a mango into our laps. The mangos in Taiwan are small, about
the size of an extra-large egg, with very little meat on them. But their
flavor and fragrance are intense, much more so than those found here.

The star fruit grew on trees that were more like bushes, and we used
to play hide-and-seek among them. There were two types, one sweet and
succulent, the other as sour as a lemon. I knew which was which. The
boys would often tease us by threatening to turn us in for stealing the
fruit, and being caught meant certain punishment. Sadly, as the school expanded, many of the trees were felled to make way for more classrooms
and offices.

At home, we had three or four papaya trees in our backyard and mango and dragon-eye trees in front. I miss these fruits, for there is no comparison to the taste of a piece of fruit eaten just minutes after it is picked.

During the past 15 years, however, many of the exotic tropical fruits I grew up loving have become available in this country. Star fruit, persimmons, pomegranates, mangos, kumquats, lychees and loquats are now relatively easy to get. In this chapter, I have included many Chinese recipes featuring these tropical fruits.

How to Select Tropical Fruits

WHEN SELECTING PINEAPPLE, choose those with a faintly yellow hue, not green ones, which are unripe. Let the pineapple ripen at room temperature.

Carambola, commonly known as star fruit, should be thick and large, bright yellow, with no black spots. To prepare them for eating, trim the outer five edges by cutting a very thin slice from each edge to remove the brownish rim. Remove the ends and slice across the star. There may be a few seeds inside, but they are edible.

Most of the papayas available in this country are small, hard and green. Let them sit out until they are ripe. The color of the outer skin will turn yellowish red. The top of the fruit should give a little when gently pressed, and it should have a sweet smell.

When buying mangos, select those that are orange-red and still firm; soft fruit will be rotten inside. Avoid green mangos, which are unripe. Don't buy the ones that are greenish yellow; they have been ripened off the tree and will have little flavor.

Desserts

Lychee Ice Cream   323

Peanut Ice Cream   325

Frozen Mango Soufflé   326

Persimmon Sorbet   328

Chilled Mango Soup   329

Pears with Ginger   330

Honey-Fried Bananas with Caramelized Ginger Sauce   332

Fresh Pineapple with Berry Sauce   335

Caramelized Kumquat Sauce   336

Mixed Tropical Fruit Salad with Rum Sauce   337

Warm Rice Pudding with Coconut Cream Sauce   339

Lychee Ice Cream

Makes 1 quart ice cream

ICE CREAM IS A POPULAR TREAT IN TAIWAN. My mother often made an egg-cream mixture and sent it to a local shop that had an ice-cream maker so they could freeze it for her. My brothers and I usually ate every bit within a few days. The most popular ice creams, flavored to appeal to Chinese tastes, are red bean, peanut, vanilla, artificial strawberry (when I was small, Taiwan did not grow its own strawberries) and lychee.

We usually ate lychee ice cream from June to August, when the fruit was in season and abundant everywhere. Lychees are best when fresh, but you can use canned if fresh are not available.

8	large egg yolks
⅔	cup sugar
2	cups milk
2	cups heavy cream
1	vanilla bean, split, or 1 teaspoon pure vanilla extract
3	pounds fresh lychees, peeled and pitted*
2	tablespoons rum

Beat the egg yolks and sugar together with an electric mixer or whisk in a large mixing bowl until they are thickened and light in color, 3 to 5 minutes.

In a medium saucepan, bring the milk, cream and vanilla bean, if using, to a boil. Slowly whisk one-third of the cream mixture into the egg mixture, then stir in the remaining liquid.

Return the mixture to the saucepan. Cook gently over low heat, stirring constantly, until the mixture coats the back of a spoon. Strain through a sieve into a large chilled bowl.

Puree the lychees in a food processor. Strain through a fine sieve; discard the fiber. Add the rum. Stir the lychee mixture into the cream mixture. Stir in the vanilla extract, if using. Chill until very cold, at least 1 hour.

Place the mixture in an ice-cream maker and freeze according to the manufacturer's instructions.

*Or substitute 3 one-pound cans of lychees. Drain well and dry with paper towels.

RAW PEANUTS

I CAN STILL REMEMBER the satisfaction I felt digging peanuts out of the ground during a second-grade class in which each group was assigned a small plot of land to farm. That class developed my love for gardening and for peanuts.

Peanuts figure prominently in Chinese cooking. They are slowly simmered until they are soft, much the way dried beans are in the West. They are added to braised dishes or sautéed with other vegetables and meats. Fried and ground, peanuts are used as a garnish for dim sum or are sprinkled into dipping sauces. They are also commonly used in making soups and sweet desserts.

Shelled raw peanuts, labeled "blanched shelled," are sold in some supermarkets and health food stores. They usually come packaged in plastic bags and are sold by the pound.

Freshly harvested peanuts in the shell are available at the end of summer and are very popular in the southern United States. When I lived in Florida, I was able to buy them in many markets. Chinese grocery stores often carry them in the summertime.

Frying Shelled Raw Peanuts

I prefer to fry raw peanuts rather than use packaged roasted nuts, because salted roasted peanuts taste stale and are too dry; fried nuts are moister and crunchier.

Frying raw peanuts is simple to do and well worth the little bit of effort. Heat some oil in a fryer or large skillet to 325 degrees F. Place the raw peanuts (I usually fry 1 pound at a time) in a fryer basket and lower them into the oil. Fry for about 7 minutes, or until the peanuts are light golden in color. Lift out the basket and test to see if the nuts are done. If they are still raw, continue to cook for 1 to 2 minutes more. Place the basket over a plate lined with paper towels to absorb any excess oil. The peanuts will continue to cook for a few minutes from their internal heat and will darken a little as they cool.

Boiling Shelled Raw Peanuts

Soak blanched raw peanuts in warm water for 2 to 4 hours, or overnight. The peanuts will swell and turn white. Drain and discard the soaking water.

Place the nuts in a large heavy pot. Cover each cup of nuts with 4 cups of water plus 1 teaspoon baking soda. Bring the water to a boil. Reduce the heat to medium-low, cover the pot and simmer the nuts for 1½ to 2 hours, or until they are soft. Drain.

The nuts are then ready for braising, stuffing or pureeing. They can be frozen in an airtight container.

Boiling Newly Harvested Peanuts in the Shell

Wash the freshly dug peanuts well to remove any dirt clinging to the shells. Cook in lightly salted boiling water for 10 minutes to soften. Drain well. These peanuts can be shelled and eaten as a snack or used in cooking. They will shrink somewhat after being boiled but will be very tender and sweet.

Peanut Ice Cream

Makes about 1 quart ice cream

USING THE FRESH MILK and cream from its dairy farm, Taiwan University made its own ice cream and popsicles. One of the most popular flavors—and my own favorite—was peanut. The nuts had been boiled until they were very soft—almost, but not quite, a puree.

2 cups heavy cream
1 cup whole milk
¾ cup sugar
2 vanilla beans, split, or 2 teaspoons pure
   vanilla extract
4 large egg yolks
1 cup boiled, pureed peanuts (previous page)

Heat the cream, milk, sugar and vanilla beans, if using, in a medium heavy saucepan. Cook over medium heat, stirring occasionally, until the sugar is dissolved and the mixture is hot.

Place the egg yolks in a medium bowl and whisk them together. Slowly whisk in 1 cup of the hot liquid. Return this mixture to the saucepan, whisking constantly.

Cook over low heat, stirring constantly, until the mixture thickens a little and coats the back of a spoon, 7 to 8 minutes. Do not allow the mixture to boil, or it will curdle.

Strain through a fine sieve into a clean bowl, stir in the vanilla extract, if using, and mix in the pureed nuts.

Chill until cold, then pour into an ice-cream maker and freeze according to the manufacturer's directions.

FROZEN MANGO SOUFFLÉ

SERVES 8

T HIS IS A LIGHT, refreshing and easy summer dessert. It can be frozen in individual soufflé cups, glasses or dishes that have been sprinkled with toasted almonds, then topped with slices of fresh mango, with a little mango puree alongside. Or it can be frozen in a single container, scooped out and topped with the almonds and the mangos.

3	cups diced ripe mango, plus more mango slices for garnish (about 3 large mangos)
3	tablespoons kirsch
⅔	cup sugar
2½	tablespoons water
¼	teaspoon fresh lemon juice
3	large egg whites
1¼	cups heavy cream
½	cup blanched almond slices, toasted*

If using individual soufflé cups, make "collars" for them by cutting pieces of wax paper or parchment paper into 8 rectangles large enough to wrap around the inside of each cup so the paper extends about 1 inch over the top. Lightly oil the bottoms of the cups to prevent the soufflés from sticking. Wrap 1 piece of the paper around each cup.

Blend the diced mango in a food processor for 1 to 2 minutes. Strain through a fine sieve to remove the fiber. Add the kirsch.

Bring the sugar, water and lemon juice to a boil in a small saucepan, stirring, until the sugar is completely melted and the liquid is clear. Meanwhile, beat the egg whites in a large bowl with an electric mixer until soft peaks form. Pour the hot syrup slowly into the egg whites, beating constantly. Continue to beat the mixture until the whites are stiff and glossy, 3 to 5 minutes.

Whip the cream until soft peaks form.

Fold 2½ cups of the mango mixture into the egg white mixture. Fold in the whipped cream.

Sprinkle the toasted almond slices into the prepared soufflé dishes, if using, and spoon the mango mixture over the nuts, or spoon the mixture into a large container. Cover with plastic wrap and freeze for 4 hours or longer.

Before serving, remove the soufflé cups from the freezer and let sit at room temperature for 5 minutes. Divide the remaining ½ cup mango puree among 8 individual serving plates and invert the frozen soufflé onto the plate so that the almonds are on top or scoop out the soufflé, allotting 3 to 4 scoops per serving. Sprinkle with some of the almonds. Garnish with the fresh mango slices.

*To toast almonds: Place on a dry baking sheet in a 350-degree oven and toast, stirring occasionally, until lightly browned and fragrant, about 10 minutes.

PERSIMMON SORBET

SERVES 6

THIS SORBET CAN BE SERVED FOR DESSERT or between courses as a palate cleanser. The persimmons must be totally ripe and very soft. I let them sit out until they are absolutely ripe, then place them in plastic bags and freeze them for 20 minutes. Freezing loosens the skin and makes peeling much easier. Let the persimmons thaw halfway, peel, remove the stem end, cut them in half and remove and discard the seeds. Puree the flesh in a blender or a food processor.

> About 4 large, fully ripe persimmons
> ¼ cup cold water
> 1   tablespoon unflavored gelatin
> ½   cup boiling water
> ¼   cup sugar
> 1   cup fresh grapefruit juice

Peel, seed and puree the persimmons; you should have 2 cups. Set aside.

Pour the cold water into a medium heatproof bowl. Sprinkle the gelatin on top and let stand for 5 minutes to soften. Pour in the boiling water and stir well to dissolve.

Stir in the sugar and the grapefruit juice and refrigerate until cool, about 1 hour. Mix in the persimmon puree.

Pour into an ice-cream maker and freeze, following the manufacturer's directions, or pour into a flat container, such as an ice-cube tray, cover with plastic wrap and freeze until solid.

CHILLED MANGO SOUP

SERVES 8 TO 10

THIS COLD FRUIT SOUP can be served at the beginning of a summer meal or for dessert. If I am preparing a banquet, I like to offer it in place of the sorbet, usually between the fish and meat courses.

4   very ripe medium mangos

2   cups water

1   cup sugar

4   whole cloves

4   star anise

1   tablespoon cornstarch, mixed with 2 tablespoons water,
      or 1 tablespoon small-grain tapioca

1   cup unsweetened coconut milk*

3   tablespoons dark rum

1   cup chilled white wine
      Mint sprigs for garnish

Peel and pit the mangos. Reserve the pulp of half a mango for garnish. Puree the remaining mango pulp in a food processor; set aside.

In a heavy medium saucepan, combine the water, sugar, cloves, star anise and cornstarch mixture or tapioca. Bring to a boil. Reduce the heat to medium-low, and simmer gently for about 15 minutes, uncovered, stirring often, until the liquid is thick and syrupy.

Add the pureed mango, coconut milk and rum to the syrup and stir to combine. Cook until the soup just returns to a boil; remove from the heat.

Strain the soup through a fine sieve, pressing the mango pulp through the sieve. Discard all the solids.

Cool the soup. Stir in the wine and refrigerate until chilled.

Dice the reserved mango for the garnish.

Pour the soup into 8 to 10 large red wine glasses and garnish with diced mango and mint sprigs.

*I prefer the Chaokoh brand, which is carried by most Asian grocery stores.

Pears with Ginger

Serves 6

COLD POACHED PEARS make a light dessert any time of the year. I add star anise and some fresh gingerroot to the poaching liquid along with the usual cinnamon stick and lemon for a Chinese flavor. A good company dessert, the pears can be prepared a few days ahead.

Leftover cooked pears can be served with Berry Sauce (page 335), plain or with a scoop of ice cream.

1	cup sugar
3	cups water
1	cup white wine
	Juice of 1 lemon
2	2-inch pieces of lemon zest
1	4-inch cinnamon stick
1	2-inch piece gingerroot, sliced
2	star anise
6	firm pears, preferably Anjou or Comice

Place the sugar, water, wine, lemon juice, lemon zest, cinnamon stick, gingerroot and star anise in a saucepan just large enough to hold all of the pears in a single layer.

Bring the liquid to a boil, stirring occasionally to dissolve the sugar, and cook for about 5 minutes to allow the spices to flavor the liquid.

Peel and core the pears. You can either leave them whole or cut them into halves. Carefully place the pears in the boiling liquid, adding more water, if necessary, to cover them.

Return the liquid to a boil. Cover the pan and reduce the heat to low. Simmer the pears gently until they are just tender, 10 to 20 minutes, depending on the ripeness of the pears.

Using a slotted spoon, remove the pears from the liquid and set aside. Increase the heat to high and boil to reduce the liquid to about 2 cups. Strain the sauce, discarding the solids.

If serving hot, place the pears in individual serving dishes and spoon some sauce over each.

If serving cold, place the pears in a bowl, pour the sauce over them and refrigerate, covered. The pears will keep for 2 to 3 days in the refrigerator.

Pears with Ginger

Honey-Fried Bananas with Caramelized Ginger Sauce

Serves 6

H ONEY-FRIED BANANAS are a classic Chinese dessert. Hot fried bananas are first dipped into caramelized sugar, then quickly plunged into ice water to harden the caramel coating. The presentation is dramatic — cold, crunchy caramel on the outside and hot, soft banana inside.

This rendition is much easier: the hot bananas are simply placed in a cold sauce, which can be made ahead of time.

Ripe bananas in Taiwan are always called "sesame" bananas, because the small black dots on the skin resemble sesame seeds. If you buy larger bananas that are not quite ripe enough, leave them out at room temperature for a few days — just until the skin develops the black spots. Then use them immediately. Never store bananas in the refrigerator, as the skins will turn completely black, and they will not taste good.

Fritter Batter

1	cup all-purpose flour
¼	teaspoon salt
1	cup beer
2	teaspoons corn oil
2	large egg whites

Bananas

6	medium bananas, firm but ripe
	Corn oil for deep-frying
2	tablespoons honey
2	tablespoons Grand Marnier or other orange liqueur, such as Cointreau or Triple Sec
½	cup Caramelized Ginger Sauce (page 334)
½	cup Caramelized Ginger (page 334; optional)

To make the fritter batter: Sift the flour and the salt into a large bowl. Pour in the beer and the oil and mix until smooth.

Cover and let stand at room temperature for 1 hour.

Beat the egg whites until they hold stiff peaks; fold into the batter.

To prepare the bananas: Cut each banana crosswise into 6 sections, about 1 inch thick.

Pour the oil into a fryer or large skillet to a depth of 6 inches and heat until it is hot (about 350 degrees F).

Mix the honey and the orange liqueur in a large bowl. Add the bananas and mix well to coat each piece.

Dip each piece of banana into the fritter batter, then place in the hot oil and fry for about 3 minutes, until golden, turning often. Remove with a slotted spoon and drain on paper towels.

Spoon the ginger sauce into the center of each of 6 dessert plates.

If you like, pour some of the Caramelized Ginger into a small bowl and dip the fried banana pieces into the ginger to coat them. Place 6 banana pieces on each plate and serve immediately.

FOREIGN FRUIT

WHEN I WAS A SMALL CHILD, my grandmother lived with us in Taiwan. She often reminisced about the apples she used to eat when she lived in Shanxi. According to her, they were wondrous fruits—large, fragrant, sweet and crunchy. They were probably the same species as the Japanese Fuji apples.

Because Taiwan has a tropical climate, apples do not grow well there. In the 1950s, they were finally imported from the United States, but they remained scarce and expensive. My parents, however, always managed to locate some to give to my grandmother as a present for the holidays. She would hoard them, keeping them until they were well past their prime. Whenever we walked into her room, it smelled of apples.

Once in a great while, she would peel and slice one for us to eat. Usually, they had become soft and mushy. Even so, these apples seemed to us a very special treat.

CARAMELIZED GINGER

MAKES ABOUT 2½ TO 3 CUPS

2   cups sugar

2   cups water

½   cup peeled, finely grated gingerroot

¼   cup brandy

In a heavy nonaluminum saucepan, bring the sugar and ⅓ cup of the water to a boil, stirring to dissolve the sugar. Boil over medium-high heat until the mixture turns light brown and is caramelized, about 5 minutes.

Remove from the heat and carefully add the gingerroot; mix thoroughly. Add the remaining 1⅔ cups water and bring to a boil.

Simmer, covered, over low heat for about 45 minutes, or until the gingerroot is cooked in the syrup. Stir occasionally to prevent the sugar from sticking to the sides of the pan.

Stir in the brandy. Remove from the heat and set aside until cooled. Pour into a glass jar and refrigerate until needed. The Caramelized Ginger will keep for about 2 months, refrigerated.

CARAMELIZED GINGER SAUCE

MAKES ABOUT 1½ CUPS SAUCE

THIS FLAVORFUL SAUCE is excellent hot or cold, spooned over vanilla ice cream or fresh fruit. It is also great with chocolate cake. Or serve the sauce cold with Honey-Fried Bananas (page 332).

½   cup Caramelized Ginger (see above)

1   cup heavy cream

1   teaspoon pure vanilla extract

Place the Caramelized Ginger and the heavy cream in a medium saucepan. Cook over medium heat until very hot and well blended. Stir in the vanilla extract.

FRESH PINEAPPLE
WITH BERRY SAUCE

SERVES 4

FRESH BERRIES MAKE A MARVELOUS SAUCE, but when they are pureed, as in this recipe, frozen can be substituted. This light, refreshing dessert is the perfect finale to a heavy meal or a barbecue.

Berry Sauce

1   10-ounce package frozen raspberries, thawed, or 1 pint fresh
1   10-ounce package frozen strawberries, thawed, or 1 pint fresh
½   cup sugar, or more to taste
1-2 tablespoons kirsch

Pineapple

½   large pineapple
Fresh mint for garnish (optional)

To make the berry sauce: Puree the berries along with their juice in a food mill, a food processor or a blender. If using a processor or blender, strain the sauce to remove the seeds.

Stir the sugar and the kirsch into the puree.

The sauce keeps well refrigerated, stored in a covered container, for 2 to 3 days. It can be frozen for up to 3 months.

To prepare the pineapple: Cut the pineapple into very thin slices. Spoon some of the sauce onto each of 4 dessert plates. Overlap one-quarter of the pineapple slices on each plate. Garnish each with a sprig of fresh mint, if desired, and serve.

Caramelized Kumquat Sauce

Makes about 1½ cups sauce

I LIKE TO CANDY KUMQUATS and use them for all kinds of desserts. The following sauce is excellent served over ice cream or fresh fruit.

1	cup fresh kumquats
½	cup sugar
½	cup water
2	tablespoons fresh lime juice
1	tablespoon brandy

Wash the kumquats well. With a sharp knife, slice them into rounds about ¼ inch thick. Pick out the seeds with the tip of a paring knife. Set the slices aside.

In a heavy medium saucepan or a skillet, heat the sugar with 2 tablespoons of the water over medium heat. Cook, stirring often, until the sugar has melted, turns light brown and is caramelized (220 degrees F on a candy thermometer).

Carefully but quickly add the kumquat slices to the pan, stirring to coat them with the caramel. Add the remaining 6 tablespoons water and continue to cook, stirring, until all the sugar is dissolved, 2 to 3 minutes.

Add the lime juice and cook, stirring often, until the mixture comes to a boil. Remove from the heat. When the sauce is cooled, stir in the brandy.

The sauce can be refrigerated in a sealed glass jar for up to 2 weeks.

KUMQUATS

THE SWEET YET SHARP FLAVOR of this small oval citrus fruit combines well with both desserts and savory dishes, and its bright orange skin and flesh add a splash of color. The skin of the kumquat does not need to be removed before eating; it has a delicious flavor.

MIXED TROPICAL FRUIT SALAD WITH RUM SAUCE

SERVES 4

EVERY HOUSE IN KAO-HSIUNG had at least one or two papaya trees in the yard. Whenever we ate the fruit, we would throw the black seeds on the ground. Pretty soon, little papaya plants would appear, and within two years, the plant had produced fruit, ready to be harvested.

1	small papaya
2	star fruit (carambola)
1	small mango
1	cup diced fresh pineapple
2-3	tablespoons sugar, depending on the sweetness of the fruit
3	tablespoons rum
½	cup fresh raspberries
½	cup Caramelized Kumquat Sauce (page 336; optional)
¼	cup blanched almond slices, toasted (page 327)

Peel the papaya, cut it in half and scoop out and discard the seeds. Cut each half on the diagonal into 6 slices. Divide and arrange the slices on each of 4 dessert plates.

Cut off a thin slice from the top and bottom ends of the star fruit, then trim ⅛ inch from each edge of the stars. (The skin at the edges is darker and the fruit will look prettier if it is removed.) Slice each fruit into 8 pieces. Place 4 pieces of star fruit on each plate.

Peel, pit and dice the mango and place in a medium bowl. Add the pineapple. Stir in the sugar, the rum and the raspberries. Spoon some of this mixture over each plate of fruit. Top with 2 tablespoons of the kumquat sauce, if using.

Sprinkle with the almonds and serve chilled or at room temperature.

Warm Rice Pudding with Coconut Cream Sauce

Warm Rice Pudding
with Coconut Cream Sauce

Serves 6

IN TAIWAN, the most popular dessert at holiday time, whether it be the New Year or the Moon or Dragon Festival, is called eight-treasure rice pudding. Usually served warm, it is traditionally made with steamed sweet rice and mixed with such things as red bean paste, lotus seeds, jujubes (red dates), dried candied orange peel and other dried and candied fruits.

My family loved this dessert, and when I was small, we ate it often. But I never liked the taste of the candied fruits. I have adapted this traditional dish by eliminating many of the filling ingredients and using regular long-grain rice. I serve it hot, topped with a creamy coconut sauce.

You can substitute "Honeyed" Pine Nuts for the cooked split mung beans, but the mung beans are more traditional.

½	cup long-grain white sweet (glutinous) rice or long-grain white rice
½	cup split yellow mung beans or "Honeyed" Pine Nuts (page 58)
1½	cups water
1	cup milk
¼	cup sugar
½	vanilla bean or 1 teaspoon pure vanilla extract
	Pinch of salt
2	tablespoons butter
¾	cup Red Bean Paste (page 342)
1	recipe Coconut Cream Sauce (page 341), warmed
½	mango, cut into small dice

Wash the rice and drain well. Bring a large saucepan filled with water to a boil over high heat. Add the rice, stir and continue to boil for 10 minutes; the rice will be half-cooked. Drain and set aside.

If using the mung beans, place them in a medium saucepan with the water. Bring to a boil over high heat. Reduce the heat to medium-low and simmer for 15 to 20 minutes, or until tender. Drain; set aside.

Meanwhile, in a heavy medium saucepan over medium heat, heat the milk, sugar, vanilla bean, if using, and salt. Simmer for 10 minutes, stirring occasionally, then add the rice. Stir, cover and cook over low heat for 10 minutes, or until the rice is completely cooked.

Stir in the butter and remove from the heat. Mix in the mung beans or pine nuts and let cool; remove the vanilla bean or add the vanilla extract.

Generously butter 6 timbale molds or ½-cup ramekins.

Once the rice is cool, remove from the pan and divide into 12 portions. Fill the bottoms of each mold with 1 rice portion and pack firmly.

Spread a layer of the bean paste over the rice; top with another portion of rice and pat down firmly.

This dish can be made to this point up to 1 day in advance and refrigerated, covered.

Place the timbales or ramekins on the rack of a steamer. Fill the bottom of the steamer with water close to, but not touching, the rack and bring to a boil. Place the rack on top. Cover and steam for 15 minutes, replenishing the water, if necessary, until the rice is heated through.

Remove the timbales or ramekins and carefully unmold each by placing a dessert plate on top and inverting, rapping the bottom gently.

Spoon some of the warm coconut sauce over each of the puddings. Sprinkle with a little of the diced mango and serve immediately.

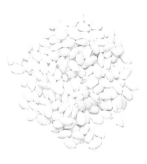

Coconut Cream Sauce

Makes about 1¼ cups sauce

THIS SAUCE is also delicious served over fried bananas. It is great with almost any kind of chocolate dessert and spectacular over warm rice pudding.

½ cup unsweetened coconut milk*

½ cup half-and-half

½ vanilla bean or 1 teaspoon pure vanilla extract

2 large egg yolks

¼ cup sugar

1 tablespoon kirsch

In a heavy medium saucepan or in the top of a double boiler, over medium-low heat, heat the coconut milk, half-and-half and the vanilla bean, if using, to a simmer. Be careful not to boil.

Meanwhile, beat the egg yolks with the sugar in a medium bowl with a whisk or an electric mixer until the mixture is thick and light in color, 3 to 5 minutes.

Remove the vanilla bean from the milk or add the vanilla extract. Gradually whisk the egg mixture into the milk. Continue to simmer, beating constantly, until the mixture thickens just slightly and coats the back of a spoon. Do not overcook, or the eggs will curdle.

The sauce can be made to this point and refrigerated for up to 2 days.

Just before you are ready to serve, reheat the sauce in a double boiler until very warm. Remove from the heat, stir in the kirsch and serve.

*I prefer the Chaokoh brand, which is carried by most Asian grocery stores.

RED BEAN PASTE

MAKES ABOUT 6 CUPS PASTE

OR USE IN DELICATE DISHES, this paste is usually pureed by pushing cooked red beans through a fine sieve to remove the coarse outer skin. But I prefer the chunky texture of coarsely pureed red beans, as it is more natural.

Traditionally, lard is added to the paste to give it smoothness and richness, but I find the paste too greasy and the flavor much too strong and prefer a mixture of butter, vanilla extract and brandy.

5	cups cooked red beans (opposite page)
½	pound pitted dates, chopped fine
1	cup boiling water
½	cup (1 stick) butter
1	cup sugar
	About 1 cup water
1	teaspoon coarse or kosher salt
1	tablespoon pure vanilla extract
2	tablespoons brandy

Place the cooked red beans in a food processor and pulse until they form a thick paste; remove and set aside.

Soak the chopped dates in the boiling water for about 30 minutes, or until they are softened. Drain well and finely chop.

Heat the butter and the sugar over medium heat in a large saucepan. Add the 1 cup water and the chopped dates. Mix well and cook for a few minutes, stirring to dissolve the sugar. Stir in the salt and the red beans.

Reduce the heat to low and cook, stirring frequently, for about ½ hour, or until a thick paste forms. Add the vanilla extract and the brandy.

This paste can be refrigerated in a covered container for 1 week. Or freeze, tightly sealed, for up to 3 months.

RED BEANS

RED BEANS ARE A FAVORITE OF MINE, and it is impossible not to mention them in connection with Chinese desserts. But when I talk about how good they are, my Western friends make a wry face and say, "How can beans be a dessert?"

When cooked with butter, sugar, brandy and dates, these tiny red beans, which are only slightly larger than rice grains, take on a delicious flavor. Properly cooked and pureed, they taste similar to good chocolate. They are often served as a stuffing for sweet pastries for birthdays, weddings and for the New Year. They are never cooked in savory dishes. Their red color may be why we have always associated them with festivals and happy times, for the color red is said to bring good luck.

You can buy canned or jarred red bean paste in Chinese markets, but these pastes are usually cooked with flour and lard and are much too sweet and too rich for my taste. I prefer to make my own. It is not hard to do, but it does take time, so I like to cook a whole bag's worth at once.

The beans, which are known as adzuki beans in Japan, where they are also popular, are usually sold in 14-ounce plastic bags. The best variety comes from Tientsin.

To Cook Red Beans

To make red bean paste, soak 1 package of red beans in water for 4 hours, or overnight. Bring 6 cups of water and a dash of salt to a boil in a large saucepan. Drain the red beans and add them to the boiling water. When the water returns to the boil, lower the heat to medium, cover and cook for 1½ hours, or until the beans are soft but not mushy. You should have about 5 cups of cooked beans. The water should be completely evaporated by the time the beans are finished cooking.

The paste will keep in the refrigerator for a short while, and it freezes beautifully.

MAIL-ORDER SOURCES

House of Rice
4112 University Way NE
Seattle, WA 98105
(206) 545-6956

Kim Man Food
200 Canal Street
New York, NY 10013
(212) 571-0330

Oriental Food Market
2801 West Howard Street
Chicago, IL 60645
(312) 274-2826

Oriental Pantry
423 Great Road
Acton, MA 01720
(800) 828-0368

INDEX

Numbers in boldface refer to photographs.

Ancho Chile Sauce, 33

Apple, Green, and Kumquat Relish, 120

Aromatic Ginger-Flavored Sweetbreads, 225

Artichoke Hearts, Oil-Braised, 149

Arugula, Water Chestnut and Endive Salad, 129, **128**

Asparagus
with Dried Shrimp Vinaigrette, 135
and French Beans with Mushrooms, 141, **216**
Mango and Ginger, Chicken with, 199, **198**

Auntie Wu's Braised Red Snapper with Garlic and Ginger, 160

Balsamic Vinaigrette, 69

Bananas, Honey-Fried, with Caramelized Ginger Sauce, 332

Banquet, Five-Course, 23; Four-Course, 22

barbecue, Mongolian, 246

bean curd (tofu), about, 153; fresh, 153; Japanese, 153

Bean Sprouts, 132
Silver Sprouts with Jicama, Celery and Balsamic Vinaigrette, 133, **245**

beans. *See* black beans; red beans

Beef, 247-53, about, 223
Broth with Pea Shoots, Tomato and Gingerroot, 88
Filet Mignon with Sichuan Peppercorn Sauce, Sautéed, 253
Orange, with Sun-Dried Tomatoes, 251, **250**
Shin, Braised, with Five Spices, 247
Soup, Sichuan, with Rigatoni, 266
Stock, 87

Beer Shrimp, Cold, 71

Bell Pepper, Red, Sauce, 45

Berry Sauce, Fresh Pineapple with, 335

Black Bean(s)
fermented, 119
Sauce, 159; Salmon with, 157, **158**

Black Rice, Lentil and Corn Compote, 300

black sweet rice, about, 301

bok choy, 292; Shanghai dish, 292

braised foods. *See* Beef; Lamb; Pork

braising foods (in brown sauce), 248

Brandied Go Chi, 126

Brandy-Infused Hoisin Sauce, 235

Bread(s)
Scallion, Pan-Fried, 316, **317**; variation, 318
unique, 309

Breast of Chicken Sautéed with Mushrooms, 194

Broccoli Rabe
Curried Brown Rice with, 294
with Green Peas, 151, **158**

Broth. *See also* Stock
Beef, with Pea Shoots, Tomato and Gingerroot, 88

Brown Rice, about, 293
with Broccoli Rabe, Curried, 294

Brown Sauce, 248; for Braising, 249

Brunch Menu, 22

Cabbage
bok choy, 292; Shanghai, 292
Green, with Sichuan Peppercorn Vinaigrette, 113
Napa, Baked Creamy, 143
Napa, Daikon and Carrots, Pickled, 117
Savoy, Oxtail Soup with, and Tomato, 90

Cantonese open-faced dumplings, Crab Sui Mei with Red Bell Pepper Sauce, 40, **41**, **42**

Caramelized
Ginger, 334; Sauce, 334
Kumquat Sauce, 336
Sweet-and-Sour Ginger Sauce, 165

Cat's Ear Pasta, 263
with Chicken and Portobello Mushrooms, 269, **268**
and gossip, 270

Celery Salad with Wasabi Vinaigrette, 131

Cellophane Noodle, 279
Salad, Hot and Spicy Chicken and, 281, **280**

Chestnuts
Braised Pork Shoulder with, 236
dried, fresh, preparing, 205

Chicken, 194-206. *See also* Cornish Hens; Duck
about cubing breast of, 200
about preparation for cooking, 192

Breast of, Sautéed with Mushrooms, 194
and Cellophane Noodle Salad, Hot and
    Spicy, 281, **280**
cutting and boning, 192
Dumplings, Curried, 38
Kung Pao, 202; legend about, 201; low-fat
    variation, 203
with Mango, Asparagus and Ginger, 199;
    198
and Portobello Mushrooms, Cat's Ear
    Pasta with, 269, **268**
Roast, with Black Bean Sauce, 196;
    variations, 197
Roasted, with Dried Chestnut Stuffing,
    206
Stock, Rich, 79
Chile Peppers. *See* Ancho Chile
China, map of, 10-11
Chinese
    lunch, 229
    technique of smoking (food), 168
Chive(s)
    Chinese, about, 312; flower buds, 312;
        yellow, 312
    Pockets, Stuffed, 310, **311**
Chutney, Spicy Persimmon, 125
Classic Hot and Sour Soup, 82
Coconut
    Cream Sauce, 341
    milk, about, 180
Coho Salmon Shanghai-Style, 176;
    variations, 177
Cold Sesame Noodles, 272
Compote
    Black Rice, Lentil and Corn, 300
    Sweet Rice, Taro and Pineapple, 298
Congee (rice soup), 99
    Salmon, 97, **96**
Corn, Black Rice and Lentil Compote, 300
Cornish Hens
    Soy-Braised, 212
    Tea-Smoked, 209, **208**; variation, 210
cornstarch, about using, 83
Crab(meat)
    Cakes, One-Hundred-Corner, 49, **48**
    Jade Green Fried Rice with, 291, **290**
    Soufflé, Steamed, 186, **187**; variations,
        188
    Spicy Soft-Shell, 185
    Sui Mei with Red Bell Pepper Sauce, 40,
        41, **42**
Crêpes, Scallion, 315, **233**. *See also* Pancakes
Crispy Duck with Star Anise Sauce, 214

Cucumbers, Spicy, with Sichuan Peppercorn
    Vinaigrette, 110, **233**
Curried (Curry)
    Brown Rice with Broccoli Rabe, 294
    Chicken Dumplings, 38
    Sauce, 181

Daikon (Oriental radish), 116
    Braised Leg of Lamb with, 241
    Fish Soup, 95
    Pickled Napa Cabbage, Carrots and, 117
Dessert, 322-43
    Bananas, Honey-Fried, with Caramelized
        Ginger Sauce, 332
    Caramelized Kumquat Sauce, 336
    Frozen Mango Soufflé, 326
    Lychee Ice Cream, 323
    Mango Soup, Chilled, 329
    Peanut Ice Cream, 325
    Pears with Ginger, 330, **331**
    Persimmon Sorbet, 328
    Pineapple, Fresh, with Berry Sauce, 335
    Red Bean Paste, 342
    Rice Pudding, Warm, with Coconut
        Cream Sauce, 339, **338**
    Tropical Fruit Salad, Mixed, with Rum
        Sauce, 337
Dim Sum (and other small delights), 24-74.
    See also Dumplings
    about, 24
    Crab Cakes, One-Hundred-Corner, 49,
        48
    Dumplings, 27-29; 31, 35, **41**. *See also*
        Dumplings
    Eggplant, Chinese Grilled, with Balsamic
        Vinaigrette, 68
    Eggplant Salsa, Chinese, 57, **55**
    "Honeyed" Pine Nuts, 58
    "Honeyed" Walnuts, 59, **128**
    Jalapeño Peppers with Pork Stuffing, 67
    Rice Cakes, Sizzling, 54, **55**
    Scallops, Cold Marinated, 70
    Shiitake Mushrooms, Spiced, 66
    Shiitake Mushrooms Stuffed with Lamb,
        60
    Shrimp, Cold Beer, 71
    Shrimp Toast, Baked, 51
    Spring Rolls, 45
    Squid Salad with Five-Flavor Vinaigrette,
        73, **72**
    Taro Pancakes, 64
    Tea Eggs, Marbled, 62, **63**

Dried
　　orange peel, about, 242
　　Scallops, Braised Vegetables with, 146
　　shrimp and dried scallops, about, 134
Duck
　　Crispy, with Star Anise Sauce, 214
　　Eight-Treasure, 217, **216**
　　Tsing Tao, 220
dumpling contests, 37
Dumplings
　　about cooking (boiling, pan-frying),
　　　freezing, stuffing, wrappers for, 27-29;
　　　31, 35, **41**
　　Crab Sui Mei with Red Bell Pepper
　　　Sauce, 40, **41**, **42**
　　Curried Chicken, 38
　　Pork, with Soy-Ginger Sauce, 34
　　Veal, in Ancho Chile Sauce, 30, **32**

Eggplant, Chinese, 145
　　Grilled, with Balsamic Vinaigrette, 68
　　Salsa, 57, **55**
　　Soy-Braised with Zucchini and
　　　Mushrooms, 144
　　Sun-Dried Tomatoes and Black Bean
　　　Salsa, 118
Eggs, Marbled Tea, 62, **63**
Eight-Treasure Duck, 217, **216**
　　about stuffing, 219
Endive, Water Chestnut and Arugula Salad,
　　129, **128**

Family memories, anecdotes about
　　apples, 333
　　bread, pancakes and crêpes, 302-3
　　cat's ears and gossip, 270
　　cellophane noodles, 279
　　dim sum, 24-25
　　dried orange peel, 242
　　dumpling contests, 37
　　early years, 12-20
　　Eight-Treasure Duck, 219
　　fish and seafood, 154-55
　　fowl, 190-93
　　gingerroot, 213
　　lotus flowers, 137
　　meats (beef, lamb, pork), 222-23
　　Mongolian barbecue, 246
　　noodles, 256-57
　　pea shoots, 89
　　picnics with father, 177
　　rainy day soup (Sichuan Beef Noodle),
　　　267

　　raw peanuts, 324
　　rice, 284-85
　　soup, 76-77
　　spring rolls, 44
　　tropical fruit trees, 320-31
　　vegetables and salads, 106
　　wedding banquets, 21
fermented black beans, 119
Filet Mignon with Sichuan Peppercorn
　　Sauce, Sautéed, 253
Fish, 157-76. *See also* Seafood
　　Mahimahi with Pineapple-Coconut Sauce,
　　　166
　　Monkfish Fillets, Red-Braised, 171
　　Pompano, Pan-Sautéed, with Sun-Dried
　　　Tomatoes, Black Bean and Eggplant
　　　Salsa, 174
　　Pompano, Tea-Smoked, 169
　　Red Snapper with Garlic and Ginger,
　　　Braised, Aunti Wu's, 160
　　Salmon with Black Bean Sauce, 157, **158**
　　Salmon, Coho, Shanghai-Style, 176;
　　　variations, 177
　　Salmon Congee, 97, **96**
　　Sea Bass, "Squirrel" with Caramelized
　　　Sweet-and-Sour Ginger Sauce, 162, **164**
　　Soup, Daikon, 95
　　Stock, 94
　　Tuna, Grilled, with Jalapeño Pepper
　　　Puree, 172; variation, 173
A Five-Course Banquet, 23
A Four-Course Banquet, 22
Four-Treasure Relish, 122
Fowl, 192-220. *See also* Chicken; Cornish
　　Hens; Duck
　　about, 190-92; preparing (chicken) for
　　　cooking, 192
French Beans and Asparagus with
　　Mushrooms, 141, **216**
Fried Rice, 289
　　Jade Green, with Crabmeat, 291, **290**
　　My Favorite, 288
Frozen Mango Soufflé, 326
Fruit. *See also* Dessert
　　Salad, Mixed Tropical, with Rum Sauce,
　　　337
　　tropical, about selecting, 321
Fuyu persimmons (Sharon fruit), 124

Garnishes, Vegetable, 175
Ginger
　　Caramelized, 334
　　-Soy Sauce, 36

Sweet-and-Sour Sauce, Caramelized, 165
gingerroot, how to use, 213
Go Chi, 126
    Brandied, 126
    Lotus Root Salad with, and Chinese
        Vinaigrette, 139, **250**
Green Apple and Kumquat Relish, 120
Green Beans
    (French) and Asparagus with
        Mushrooms, 141, **216**
    Sautéed, 140
Green Cabbage with Sichuan Peppercorn
    Vinaigrette, 113
Green Peas, Broccoli Rabe with, 151, **158**
Grilled
    Chinese Eggplant with Balsamic
        Vinaigrette, 68
    Pork Loin, 230
    Tuna with Jalapeño Pepper Puree, 172;
        variation, 173

Hoisin Sauce, Brandy-Infused, 235
Homemade Noodles, 263; Shanxi noodles,
    263; cat's ear pasta, 263
Honey
    -Fried Bananas with Caramelized Ginger
        Sauce, 332
    -Grilled Lamb Chops with Jalapeño
        Pepper Puree, 244, **245**
"Honeyed"
    Pine Nuts, 58
    Walnuts, 59, **128**
Hot and Sour Soup, Classic, 82
Hot and Spicy Chicken and Cellophane
    Noodles Salad, 281, **280**

Ice Cream. *See also* Sorbet
    Frozen Mango Soufflé, 326
    Lychee, 323
    Peanut, 325
Infused Sichuan Peppercorn Oil, 112

Jade Green Fried Rice with Crabmeat, 291,
    290
Jalapeño
    Pepper Puree, 243
    Peppers with Pork Stuffing, 67
Jicama, 130
    Mango and Cucumber Salad, 130
    Silver Sprouts and Celery, and Balsamic
        Vinaigrette, 133, **245**

Kumquat(s), 336
    and Green Apple Relish, 120
    Sauce, Caramelized, 336
Kung Pao
    Chicken, 202; legend about, 201; low-fat
        variation, 203
    Sauce, 204

Lamb, 223
    Chops, Honey-Grilled, with Jalapeño
        Pepper Puree, 244, **245**
    Leg of, with Daikon, Braised, 241
    Shiitake Mushrooms Stuffed with, 60
    Soup, Turkestan, with Mung Beans, 92
lemon grass, 86
Lentil, Black Rice and Corn Compote, 300
lotus
    plants (roots, seeds), about, 137-38
    Root Salad with Go Chi and Chinese
        Vinaigrette, 139, **250**
    seeds, about cooking, 219
lunch, Chinese, 229
A Luncheon Menu, 22
Lychee Ice Cream, 323

Mahimahi with Pineapple-Coconut Sauce,
    166
Mandarin
    Meat Sauce with Fresh Pasta, 264
    Pork with Brandy-Infused Hoisin Sauce,
        232, **233**
Mango
    Asparagus and Ginger, Chicken with, 199,
        198
    Jicama and Cucumber Salad, 130
    Soufflé, Frozen, 326
    Soup, Chilled, 329
Marbled Tea Eggs, 62, **63**
Marinated Scallops, Cold, 70
Meat Dishes, 222-23. *See also* Beef; Lamb;
    Pork; Veal
    Sauce, Mandarin, with Fresh Pasta, 264
Menus and Wines, 22-23
Mongolian barbecue, about, 246
Monkfish Fillets, Red-Braised, 171
mung beans, about, 93
Mushroom(s). *See also* Porcini; Portobello;
    Shiitake; Wild Mushrooms
    Breast of Chicken Sautéed with, 194
    French Beans and Asparagus with, 141,
        216
    and Green Pepper, Twice-Cooked Veal
        Breast with, 226

Spicy, with Garlic and Black Bean Sauce, 147

Veal Chops with, 228

and Zucchini, Soy-Braised Chinese Eggplant with, 144

My Favorite Fried Rice, 288

Napa Cabbage, 142

Baked Creamy, 143

Daikon and Carrots, Pickled, 117

Noodle(s), 260-81

about cooking, 259

Cat's Ear Pasta with Chicken and Portobello Mushrooms, 269, **268**

Cellophane, Hot and Spicy Chicken and, Salad, 281, **280**

Cold Sesame, 272

Homemade, 256-57, 263; Shanxi noodles, 263; cat's ear pasta, 263

Mandarin Meat Sauce with Fresh Pasta, 264

Pan-Fried, 271

with Pork from Shanxi, 260, **261**

rice flour, 276

Rice, with Porcini Mushrooms, 277

Sichuan Beef Soup with Rigatoni, 266

Thin Rice, Stir-Fried, with Shrimp and Scallions, 275, **274**

Oil-Braised Artichoke Hearts, 149

One-Hundred-Corner Crab Cakes, 49, **48**

One-Thousand-Layer Pancakes, 308

Orange Beef with Sun-Dried Tomatoes, 251, **250**

orange peel, dried, 242

Oriental radish (daikon), 116

Oxtail Soup with Savoy Cabbage and Tomato, 90; first-class, 91

Pan-Fried

Noodles, 271

Scallion Bread, 316, **317**; variation, 318

Pan-Sautéed Pompano with Sun-Dried Tomatoes, Black Bean and Eggplant Salsa, 174

Pan-Seared Tofu with Scallions and Ginger, 152

Pancakes, 305-15. See also Bread

Taro, 64

One-Thousand Layer, 308

Peking Thin, 313

Scallion, 305, **307**; "Lazy," 306

Stuffed Chive Pockets (Peking), 310, **311**

Pasta. See also Noodles

about cooking, 259

cat's ear, 263

Cat's Ear, with Chicken and Portobello Mushrooms, 269, **268**

Peanut Ice Cream, 325

peanuts, raw, 324; about boiling, 324; using, 324

pea shoots, 89. See also snow peas

Pears with Ginger, 330, **331**

Peking

Stuffed Chive Pockets, 310, **311**

Thin Pancakes, 313

peppercorns, Sichuan, 111; roasting, 111; roasted Sichuan and salt, 211

Peppers. See Chile Peppers; Jalapeño Peppers; Red Bell Peppers

Persimmon(s)

Chutney, Spicy, 125

Fuyu (Sharon fruit), 124

Sorbet, 328

Pickles and Relish, 110-26. See also Salsa

Brandied Go Chi, 126

Cucumbers, Spicy, with Sichuan Peppercorn Vinaigrette, 110, **233**

Four-Treasure Relish, 122

Green Apple and Kumquat Relish, 120

Green Cabbage with Sichuan Peppercorn Vinaigrette, 113

Pickled Napa Cabbage, Daikon and Carrots, 117

Sichuan Pickled Vegetables, 114, **208**

Spicy Persimmon Chutney, 125

picnic, Chinese, 177

Pine Nuts, "Honeyed," 58

Pineapple

Fresh, with Berry Sauce, 335

Salsa, 121

Pompano

Pan-Sautéed, with Sun-Dried Tomatoes, Black Bean and Eggplant Salsa, 174

Tea-Smoked, 169

Porcini Mushrooms, Rice Noodles with, 277

Pork, 230-39

about, 222-23

Dumplings with Soy-Ginger Sauce, 34

Loin, Grilled, 230

Mandarin, with Brandy-Infused Hoisin Sauce, 232, **233**

Mandarin Meat Sauce with Fresh Pasta, 264

Noodles with, from Shanxi, 260, **261**

Shoulder, Braised, with Chestnuts, 236

Spareribs, 239; variation, 240, **238**
Stock, Rich, 80
Stuffing, Jalapeño Peppers with, 67
Portobello Mushrooms
   and Chicken, Cat's Ear Pasta with, 269,
     268
   French Beans and Asparagus with, 141,
     216
Potatoes, New Red, Salad of, 136, **238**
Poultry Dishes. *See* Fowl
Prawns with Poached Pears and Curry
   Sauce, 179, **178**

Red-Braised Monkfish Fillets, 171
red-braising, 248
Red Bean Paste, 342
red beans, about, 343; cooking, 343
Red Bell Pepper Sauce, 45
Red Snapper with Garlic and Ginger,
   Braised, Aunti Wu's, 160
Relish. *See also* Pickles and Relish
   Four-Treasure, 122
   Green Apple and Kumquat, 120
Rice, 284-301
   about, 284-85; rules for cooking, 287
   Black, Lentil and Corn Compote, 300
   black sweet, 301
   brown, 293
   Cakes, Sizzling, 54; Chinese Eggplant
     Salsa for, 57, **55**
   Chinese Risotto with Wild Mushrooms,
     295
   Curried Brown, with Broccoli Rabe, 294
   flour noodles, 276
   Fried, Jade Green with Crabmeat, 291,
     290
   Fried, My Favorite, 288; about preparing,
     289
   Noodles with Porcini Mushrooms, 277
   Noodles, Stir-Fried Thin, with Shrimp
     and Scallions, 275, **274**
   Pudding, Warm, with Coconut Cream
     Sauce, 339, **338**
   soup (congee), 99; Salmon, 97, **96**
   Sweet, Taro and Pineapple Compote, 298
   Vegetable, 292
   white sweet, 297
Rigatoni, Sichuan Beef Soup with, 266
Roast Chicken with Black Bean Sauce, 196;
   variations, 197
Roasted Chicken with Dried Chestnut
   Stuffing, 206
roasted Sichuan peppercorns and salt, 211

rock sugar, about, 237

Salad, 129-39. *See also* Vegetables
   Asparagus with Dried Shrimp
     Vinaigrette, 135
   Celery, with Wasabi Vinaigrette, 131
   Chicken and Cellophane Noodle, Hot and
     Spicy, 281, **280**
   Cucumbers, Spicy, with Sichuan
     Peppercorn Vinaigrette, 110, **233**
   Fruit, Mixed Tropical, with Rum Sauce,
     337
   Green Cabbage with Sichuan Peppercorn
     Vinaigrette, 113
   Lotus Root, with Go Chi and Chinese
     Vinaigrette, 139, **250**
   Mango, Jicama and Cucumber, 130
   Napa Cabbage, Daikon and Carrots,
     Pickled, 117
   of New Red Potatoes, 136, **238**
   Sichuan Pickled Vegetables, 114, **208**
   Silver Sprouts (bean) with Jicama,
     Celery and Balsamic Vinaigrette, 133,
     245
   Squid, with Five-Flavor Vinaigrette, 73,
     72
   Water Chestnut, Arugula and Endive,
     129, **128**
Salmon
   with Black Bean Sauce, 157, **158**
   Coho, Shanghai-Style, 176; variations,
     177
   Congee, 97, **96**
Salsa. *See also* Sauce
   Eggplant, Chinese, 57, **55**
   Pineapple, 121
   Sun-Dried Tomatoes, Black Bean and
     Eggplant, 118
Sauce. *See also* Salsa
   Ancho Chile, 33
   Black Bean, 159
   Brown, for Braising, 249
   Caramelized Ginger, 334
   Caramelized Kumquat, 336
   Coconut Cream, 341
   Curry, 181
   Hoisin, Brandy-Infused, 235
   Kung Pao, 204
   Red Bell Pepper, 45
   Soy-Ginger, 36
   Sweet-and-Sour Ginger, Caramelized, 165
Scallion
   Bread, Pan-Fried, 316, **317**; variation, 318

Crêpes, 315, **233**
Pancakes, 305, **307**; "Lazy," 306
Scallops
    Cold Marinated, 70
    dried, about, 134
    Dried, Braised Vegetables with, 146
Sea Bass, "Squirrel" with Caramelized
    Sweet-and-Sour Ginger Sauce, 162, **164**
Seafood, 179-86. *See also* Crab(meat);
  Fish; Shrimp
    Crab Sui Mei with Red Bell Pepper
        Sauce, 40, **41, 42**
    Crabmeat Soufflé, Steamed, 186, **187**;
        variations, 188
    Crabs, Spicy Soft-Shell, 185
    One-Hundred-Corner Crab Cakes, 49, **48**
    Prawns with Poached Pears and Curry
        Sauce, 179, **178**
    Scallops, Cold Marinated, 70
    Squid Salad with Five-Flavor Vinaigrette,
        73, **72**
    Wonton Soup, 103, **102**
Sesame Noodles, Cold, 272
Shanxi noodles, 263
Shiitake Mushrooms
    about fresh, dried, 61
    Spiced, 66
    Stuffed with Lamb, 60
Shrimp
    about cleaning, fresh, frozen, 182
    Ball Soup, 100
    Cold Beer, 71
    dried, about, 134
    improving flavor of, 182
    One-Hundred-Corner Crab Cakes, 49, **48**
    Prawns with Poached Pears and Curry
        Sauce, 179, **178**
    Sautéed with Corn in Spicy Wine Sauce,
        183
    and Scallions, Stir-Fried Thin Rice
        Noodles with, 275, **274**
    Stock, 105
    Toast, Baked, 51
Sichuan
    Beef Soup with Rigatoni, 266
    Peppercorn Vinaigrette, 112; Infused Oil
        for, 112
    peppercorns, 111; roasting, 111; and salt,
        roasted, 211
    Pickled Vegetables, 114, **208**
Silver Sprouts (bean) with Jicama, Celery
    and Balsamic Vinaigrette, 133, **245**

Sizzling Rice Cakes, 54; Chinese Eggplant
    Salsa for, 57, **55**
Smoked. *See* Tea-Smoked
smoking food, The Chinese technique of, 168
snow peas. *See* pea shoots
Soft-Shell Crabs, Spicy, 185
Sorbet, Persimmon, 328
Soufflé
    Crabmeat, Steamed, 186, **187**; variations,
        188
    Frozen Mango, 326
Soup, 76-105
    about, 76-77
    Beef Broth with Pea Shoots, Tomato and
        Gingerroot, 88
    Beef Stock, 87
    Chicken Stock, Rich, 79
    congee or rice, 99
    Fish, Daikon, 95
    Fish Stock, 94
    Hot and Sour, Classic, 82
    Lamb, with Mung Beans, Turkestan, 92
    Mango, Chilled (dessert), 329
    Oxtail, with Savoy Cabbage and Tomato,
        90; first-class, 91
    Pork Stock, Rich, 80
    Salmon Congee, 97, **96**
    Seafood Wonton, 103, **102**
    Shrimp Ball, 100
    Shrimp Stock, 105
    Wild Mushroom, 85; **84**
Soy-Braised
    Chinese Eggplant with Zucchini and
        Mushrooms, 144
    Cornish Hens, 212
Soy-Ginger Sauce, 36
soybean(s)
    fresh, 123
    paste, yellow, 173
Spareribs, Braised, 239, **238**
Spiced Shiitake Mushrooms, 66
Spicy Dishes. *See* Chutney; Crabs;
    Cucumbers; Mushrooms
Spring Rolls, 45; about, 44; wrappers, 47, **46**
Squid, Salad with Five-Flavor Vinaigrette,
    73, **72**
"Squirrel" Sea Bass with Caramelized Sweet-
    and-Sour Ginger Sauce, 162, **164**
Starters. *See* Dim Sum; Fish; Salad
Steamed Crabmeat Soufflé, 186, **187**;
    variations, 188
steaming, about, 53

Stir-Fried Thin Rice Noodles with Shrimp and Scallions, 275, **274**
Stir-Fry know how, 252
Stock. *See also* Broth
    Beef, 87
    Chicken, Rich, 79
    Fish, 94
    Pork, Rich, 80
    Shrimp, 105
Stuffed Chive Pockets, 310, **311**
Sun-Dried Tomatoes
    Black Bean and Eggplant Salsa, 118
    Orange Beef with, 251, **250**
    Sautéed Zucchini with, 148
Sweet-and-Sour Ginger Sauce, Caramelized, 165
Sweet Rice
    black, about, 301; sweet white, 297
    Taro and Pineapple Compote, 298
Sweetbreads, Aromatic Ginger-Flavored, 225

Taro
    Pancakes, 64
    and Pineapple, Sweet Rice Compote, 298
    root, about, 65
Tea Eggs, Marbled, 62, **63**
Tea-Smoked
    Cornish Hens, 209, **208**; variation, 210
    Pompano, 169
Tofu
    (bean curd), about, 153; fresh, 153; Japanese, 153
    Pan-Seared, with Scallions and Ginger, 152
Tomatoes. *See* Sun-Dried Tomatoes
Tropical Fruit Salad, Mixed, with Rum Sauce, 337
Tsing Tao Duck, 220
Tuna, Grilled, with Jalapeño Pepper Puree, 172; variation, 173
Turkestan Lamb Soup with Mung Beans, 92
Twice-Cooked Veal Breast with Mushrooms and Green Pepper, 226

Veal
    Breast, Twice-Cooked, with Mushrooms and Green Pepper, 226
    Chops with Mushrooms, 228
    Dumplings in Ancho Chile Sauce, 30, **32**
    Mandarin Meat Sauce with Fresh Pasta, 264
    Sweetbreads, Aromatic Ginger-Flavored, 225
Vegetable(s). *See also* Name of Vegetable
    Braised, with Dried Scallops, 146
    with Chives, Quick Sauté of, 150
    Garnishes, 175
    Rice, 292
    Sichuan Pickled, 114, **208**
Vinaigrette
    Balsamic, 69
    Chinese, 139
    Five-Flavor, 73
    Sichuan Peppercorn, 112

Walnuts, "Honeyed," 59, **128**
Wasabi Vinaigrette, Celery Salad with, 131
Water Chestnut
    Arugula and Endive Salad, 129
    flour (starch), 215
wedding banquet, about, 21
white sweet rice, about cooking, 297
Wild Mushrooms
    Chinese Risotto with, 295
    and Green Pepper, Twice-Cooked Veal Breast with, 226
    Soup, 85, **84**
    Veal Chops with, 228
Wines and Menus, 22-23
Wonton(s)
    about making, 104
    Seafood Soup, 103, **102**

yellow soybean paste, about, 173

Zucchini
    and Mushrooms, Soy-Braised Chinese Eggplant with, 144
    Sautéed, with Sun-Dried Tomatoes, 148